SOCIAL WORK AND THE MAKING OF SOCIAL POLICY

Edited by
Ute Klammer, Simone Leiber and Sigrid Leitner

This paperback edition first published in Great Britain in 2021 by

Policy Press, an imprint of
Bristol University Press
University of Bristol
1-9 Old Park Hill
Bristol
BS2 8BB
UK
t: +44 (0)117 954 5940
e: bup-info@bristol.ac.uk

Details of international sales and distribution partners are available at
policy.bristoluniversitypress.co.uk

© Policy Press 2021

British Library Cataloguing in Publication Data
A catalogue record for this book is available from the British Library

978-1-4473-4915-0 hardback
978-1-4473-4916-7 paperback
978-1-4473-4917-4 ePdf
978-1-4473-4918-1 ePub
978-1-4473-4919-8 Mobi

The rights of Ute Klammer, Simone Leiber and Sigrid Leitner to be identified as editors of this work has been asserted by them in accordance with the Copyright, Designs and Patents Act 1988.

All rights reserved: no part of this publication may be reproduced, stored in a retrieval system, or transmitted in any form or by any means, electronic, mechanical, photocopying, recording, or otherwise without the prior permission of Policy Press.

The statements and opinions contained within this publication are solely those of the authors and not of the University of Bristol or Policy Press. The University of Bristol and Policy Press disclaim responsibility for any injury to persons or property resulting from any material published in this publication.

Bristol University Press and Policy Press works to counter discrimination on grounds of gender, race, disability, age and sexuality.

Cover design by Bristol University Press
Front cover image: iStock

Research in social work

Series editors:
Ian Shaw, National University of Singapore, Singapore and John Gal, Hebrew University of Jerusalem, Israel

The *Research in Social Work* series, published with the European Social Work Research Association, examines current, progressive and innovative research on social work in Europe. A leading collection for social work academics, researchers and practitioners, it makes a unique contribution to this international field.

The series editors invite proposals for books drawing on original and cutting-edge research and which aim to influence social work academia and practice. They can be contacted through either the office of the European Social Work (info@eswra.org) or Policy Press (pp-info@bristol.ac.uk).

Forthcoming titles in the series:

Jobling, H. (2019) *Power and control in social work: An ethnographic account of mental health practice*

Devlieghere, J. (2019) *Digital technologies and social work: Opportunities and illusions*

Nygren, L., Oltedal, S. and White, S. (2019) *International social work with families: Comparing contexts and complexities in Europe, Latin America and Australia*

Contents

List of figures and tables		vii
Notes on contributors		ix
Acknowledgements		xvii

1	Introduction: social work and the making of social policy Ute Klammer, Simone Leiber and Sigrid Leitner	1

Part I: Social work, problem definition and agenda setting

2	Social work as policy innovator: challenges and possibilities in the UK Roger Smith	21
3	Social work, problem definition and policy change in the US: the case of sex-trafficked youth Lisa Werkmeister Rozas, Megan Feely and Jason Ostrander	37
4	The voices of Italian social workers: from a pilot anti-poverty intervention to a national policy Matteo D'Emilione, Giovannina Assunta Giuliano, Paolo Raciti and Paloma Vivaldi Vera	53

Part II: Social work interests in policy formulation and decision making

5	Social reform in the US: lessons from the Progressive Era Francisco Branco	71
6	Social work academia and social policy in Israel: on the role of social work academics in the policy process Idit Weiss-Gal and John Gal	89
7	Social workers' collective policy practice in times of austerity: Italy and Spain compared Riccardo Guidi	105
8	Social policy and welfare movements 'from below': the Social Work Action Network (SWAN) in the UK Rich Moth and Michael Lavalette	121

Part III: Social work and implementation

9	Policy work and the ethics of obedience and resistance: perspectives from Britain and beyond Tony Evans	139

10	Systemic barriers to effective implementation of child protection reform in Israel *Ravit Alfandari*	155
11	Social workers implementing social assistance in Spain: reshaping poverty in a familialistic welfare state *Sergio Sánchez Castiñeira*	169
12	Layering, social risks and manufactured uncertainties in social work in Poland *Paweł Poławski*	185
13	'A little more humanity': placement officers in Germany between social work and social policy *Markus Gottwald and Frank Sowa*	201
14	Conclusion: social work and the making of social policy – lessons learned *Ute Klammer, Simone Leiber and Sigrid Leitner*	217

Index   229

List of figures and tables

Figures
1.1	Social work in the policy cycle of social policy making	4
5.1	The circle of social reform	75
5.2	The Chicago Reform Cohort & Network	79

Tables
4.1	Summary of in-depth studies carried out for the evaluation	55
4.2	Transposal level of requests reported by operators	63
5.1	The process from policy making to the creation of the Children's Bureau	77
14.1	Social work influencing the making of social policy: summary of furthering and inhibiting factors identified in the book's case studies	227

Notes on contributors

Ravit Alfandari is a researcher at the University of Haifa's School of Social Work. She is a qualified social worker with more than 15 years' experience in direct service delivery, programme development and research related to vulnerable children and families. She completed her doctoral research at the Social Policy Programme at the London School of Economics. Her main research interest lies in optimising child protection decision making, effective service delivery to children and families facing social exclusion and poverty, the role of technology in social work practice and client cyberbullying of social workers. She won the ESPAnet ISRAEL's Young Researcher Award for her paper on children's' participation in child protection decision making.

Francisco Branco is Associate Professor at the Catholic University of Portugal. He teaches social work history, social research and social policy, and coordinates the PhD in Social Work. Professor Branco is a member of the Catolica Research Centre for Individual, Family and Social Wellbeing at the Catholic University and a member of the Editorial Advisory Board of the international journal *Critical and Radical Social Work*. His research interests include the development of social work as a profession; social work history; policy practice in social work; and public policies, especially social assistance and social minimum policies.

Matteo D'Emilione is an expert in public policy evaluation. He is a researcher in the Social Inclusion Division of INAPP (National Institute for the Analysis of Public Policies). His research activity is mainly directed to the study and analysis of social policies, in particular those aimed at fighting poverty, understood as a multidimensional phenomenon. He was part of a research group that developed a model analysis of poverty, in line with the capability approach of Amartya Sen and Martha Nussbaum. The model has been tested in various contexts, in particular in the social service department of some Italian metropolitan areas. His major publications include 'Will children of social care services users be future users? Results of a pilot research in Rome', in *The Well-Being of Children Philosophical and Social Scientific Approaches*, ed. Gottfried Schweiger and Gunter Graf (De Gruiter, 2016).

Tony Evans is a registered social worker and Professor of Social Work at Royal Holloway University of London. His research focuses on discretion and policy work, ethical judgement and forms of knowledge and professional decision making. He is author of *Professional Discretion in Welfare Services: Beyond Street-level Bureaucracy* (Routledge, 2016) and editor, with Frank Keating, of *Social Work and Social Policy* (SAGE, 2015). His most recent edited volume is, with Peter Hupe, the *Palgrave Handbook of Discretion: The Quest for Controlled Freedom* (2019).

Megan Feely is an Assistant Professor at the University of Connecticut School of Social Work in the Community Organizing concentration. She holds an MA and PhD in Social Work from Washington University in St Louis and an MSc in Clinical Investigation from the Washington University School of Medicine. Dr Feely's work focuses on the prevention of child maltreatment, implementation science, and the role of the child welfare system in promoting child well-being. Her work is informed by her experience working in the non-profit sector with children in foster care.

John Gal is Full Professor and former Dean at the Paul Baerwald School of Social Work and Social Welfare at the Hebrew University of Jerusalem. He currently heads the welfare policy programme at the Taub Center for Social Policy Studies in Israel. His fields of interest include social policy in Israel and in the Mediterranean region, with an emphasis on poverty and unemployment; policy practice in social work; and the history of social work in Israel. Professor Gal has published extensively in academic journals and has been deeply involved in social policy formulation in Israel. He has served on numerous state commissions, among them the Committee on Combatting Poverty. Recent books include (with Idit Weiss-Gal, 2012), *Social Workers Affecting Social Policy: An International Perspective on Policy Practice* (Policy Press, 2013) and *Where Academia and Policy Meet* (Policy Press, 2017), both edited with Idit Weiss-Gal.

Giovannina Assunta Giuliano is an expert in statistics applied to social sciences. She is a researcher at INAPP. Her research mainly focuses on poverty and inequality, deprivation, social exclusion, with a special focus on social well-being, demographic changes, quality of life and quality of public services. She has also worked as manager of the monitoring and evaluation system of the Italian National Operation Programme for social inclusion 2014–2020. Among her publications is the co-authored paper (with Matteo D'Emilione,

Luca Fabrizi, Giovanna Giuliano, Paolo Raciti, Simona Tenaglia and Paloma Vera Vivaldi), 'Multidimensional approach to an analysis of individual deprivation: the MACaD model and the results of empirical investigation', *Forum for Social Economics*, 45(2–3): 256–82.

Markus Gottwald is a Senior Researcher at the Institute for Employment Research in Nuremberg and a Lecturer in Sociology at the Friedrich-Alexander University of Erlangen-Nuremberg and the University of Applied Science in Fulda. His research interests include social theory, sociology of knowledge, organisation theory and qualitative methods with a special focus on ethnography. His recent publications include '"Walking the line": an at-home ethnography of bureaucracy', *Journal of Organisational Ethnography*, 7(1), 2018: 87–102 (co-authored with Frank Sowa and Ronald Staples) and '(Extra)ordinary presence: social configurations and cultural repertoires' (co-edited with Kay Kirchmann and Heike Paul, transcript 2017).

Riccardo Guidi is Assistant Professor in Sociology at the Department of Political Science at University of Pisa where he teaches Organisation of Social Services and Sociology of the Third Sector. His research focuses on social work organisations and social workers' policy practice, welfare partnerships, volunteering and social participation. He is co-convenor of the Special Interest Group 'Research on Social Work and Policy Engagement' of the European Society for Social Work Research.

Ute Klammer is Professor of Sociology and Executive Director of the Institute for Work, Skills and Training, University of Duisburg-Essen, Germany. Her main fields of research are social policy (pension systems, health care systems, family policy), labour markets, European and comparative social policy, gender research. Her publications in English include 'Germany: deviating from the male breadwinner norm', in Gertrude Schaffner Goldberg (ed.), *Poor Women in Rich Countries: The Feminization of Poverty over the Life Course* (Oxford University Press, 2009), and (with Marie-Thérèse Letablier, 2007), 'Family policies in Germany and France: the role of enterprises and social partners', *Social Policy & Administration*, 41(6): 672–92.

Michael Lavalette is Professor of Social Work and Social Policy at Liverpool Hope University. He writes widely in the social work field. His recent book publications include (with Steve Cunningham) *Schools Out! The Hidden History of School Student Strikes* (Bookmarks, 2016) and (with Iain Ferguson and Vassilis Ioakimidis), *Global Social Work in* *a Political Context* (Policy Press, 2017). He is national convenor of the Social Work Action Network in the UK and Editor-in-Chief of the journal *Critical and Radical Social Work*.

Simone Leiber is a Professor for Social Policy at the Institute for Social Work and Social Policy of the University of Duisburg-Essen, Germany. Her research interests are comparative welfare state reform, particularly in field of elderly care, as well as the relationship of social policy and social work. Among her publications are (with Stephanie Heinemann and Stefan Greß, 2014): 'Explaining different paths in social health insurance countries: healthcare system change and cross-border lesson-drawing between Germany, Austria, and the Netherlands', *Social Policy and Administration*, 49(1), 48–108; (with Gerda Falkner, Oliver Treib and Miriam Hartlap) *Complying with Europe? The Impact of EU Minimum Harmonisation and Soft Law in the Member States* (Cambridge University Press, 2005).

Sigrid Leitner is Professor for Social Policy at the University of Applied Sciences Cologne. Main research interest: comparative social policy analysis. She specialises in the gender effects of social policy and has published extensively on varieties of familialism (first in 2003 in *European Societies* 5(4): 353–75). She also has a special interest in social workers' policy practice. Among her most recent publications in English are, in 2010, 'Germany outpaces Austria: the historical contingencies of conservative progressivism in family policy', *Journal of European Social Policy* 20(5): 456–67, and 'Reconciliation of employment and childcare in Austria, Germany and Iceland. Examples for gender equality in family life?', in Diana Auth, Jutta Hergenhan and Barbara Holland-Cunz (eds), *Gender and Family in European Economic Policy* (Palgrave Macmillan, 2017).

Rich Moth is a Senior Lecturer in Social Work at Liverpool Hope University. Before moving into his current post, he worked for 15 years in the social care field in a variety of voluntary sector roles and then as a mental health social worker in NHS services. Rich has been involved in a number of mental health, welfare and anti-austerity campaigns in recent years and is a member of the national steering committee of the Social Work Action Network in the UK. Rich's recent publications include *Understanding Mental Distress: Knowledge and Practice in Neoliberal Mental Health Services* (Policy Press) and *Resist the Punitive State: Grassroots Struggles across Welfare, Housing, Education and Prisons* (Pluto Press).

Jason Ostrander is Assistant Professor at Sacred Heart University and Coordinates the Online Education method. He has been a social work educator for more than ten years teaching face-to-face, blended and online (asynchronous and synchronous) courses. He has worked as a Member of Congress and remains very active in politics on the local, state and federal levels. His scholarly work focuses on political social work, the political participation of social workers, social and economic justice, and policy implications relating to marginalised and oppressed populations. He maintains professional affiliations with the National Association of Social Workers, Council on Social Work Education, the Association for Community Organization & Social Administration, and Influencing Social Policy. He also serves on the Research and Program Committees as well as a training consultant for the Nancy A. Humphreys Institute for Political Social Work.

Paweł Poławski is an Assistant Professor at the Institute of Labor and Social Affairs and at the Institute of Sociology, Warsaw University, Poland. His research interests include welfare state reforms, dynamics of social policy and social assistance, welfare conditionality, social citizenship, third sector and social economy. He also teaches public policy, social problems and sociology of deviance and social control courses. Recently he edited and co-authored Conditionality and Contractualism in Social Assistance (2018), *The Third Sector: Facades and Realities* (2013), and (with D. Zalewski) *Social Problems: Between Public Sociology and Social Policy* (2017).

Paolo Raciti is pedagogist and PhD in Social Service. He is a researcher in the Social Inclusion Division of INAPP. He conducts research in the field of anti-poverty policies according to a multidimensional perspective, welfare systems design, assessment of socio-emotional skills. He also works in international cooperation programs in Latin America in which he carries out technical assistance activities for governmental public institutions in the field of evaluation and training on socio-emotional skills. Among his publications are (with P. Vivaldi), 'A proposal for measuring children emotional well-being within an anti-poverty measure in Italy: psychometric characteristics and comparative verification of results', *Child Indicators Research* (2018).

Sergio Sánchez Castiñeira is a part-time lecturer in social work at University of Barcelona. He earned a PhD in sociology, with a dissertation based on local policies against poverty during the economic recession. His research interests are social assistance, social policy, poverty and inequality. He has worked in public social services in Spain and England for several years. He is currently working as a researcher for The Young Foundation on the B-MINCOME, a pilot project that is testing the efficacy of combining economic support with active social policies in disadvantaged areas of Barcelona.

Roger Smith is Professor of Social Work at Durham University, UK. In his early career he was a probation office before moving into a senior policy role with a children's organisation, and later becoming an academic. His research interests include the sociology of childhood: *A Universal Child* (Palgrave Macmillan, 2010), social work and power: *Social Work and Power* (Springer, 2008); social work education, and youth crime and justice. He has long advocated a children's rights approach to work with children and families: *Social Work with Young People* (Polity Press, 2008).

Frank Sowa is a Professor of Sociology at Nuremberg Tech Georg Simon Ohm, Germany. He worked for many years as senior researcher at the Institute for Employment Research. He is a sociologist specialising in qualitative and ethnographic methods. His past experiences have drawn his interest in organisational ethnography of public employment services, trends of globalisation of social policy, deviance and social control, homelessness as well as identity politics of the Greenlandic Inuit. His recent publications include (co-edited with Ronald Staples and Stefan Zapfel), *The Transformation of Work in Welfare State Organizations* (Routledge, 2018) and (co-edited with Ronald Staples), *Beratung und Vermittlung im Wohlfahrtsstaat* (Nomos, 2017).

Paloma Vivaldi Vera is psychologist and group psychoanalyst. She is a researcher at INAPP. She conducts research in the field of anti-poverty policies according to a multidimensional perspective. She also works in international cooperation programmes in Latin America in which she carries out technical assistance activities for governmental public institutions in the field of evaluation and training on socio-emotional skills. Her publications include (with P. P. Raciti), 'A proposal for measuring children emotional well-being within an anti-poverty measure in Italy: Psychometric characteristics and comparative verification of results', *Child Indicators Research* (2018).

Idit Weiss-Gal is Associate Professor and Head of the Bob Shapell School of Social Work at Tel Aviv University in Israel. Her fields of research and teaching include policy practice, critical perspectives in social work, and social work as a profession. She has published numerous articles in social work academic publications. Her Hebrew-language book, *Policy Practice in Social Work*, written with John Gal, was published in 2012. In addition, she has edited four cross-national comparative studies: (with John Gal) *Where Academia and Policy Meet* (2017); (with John Gal) *Social Workers Affecting Social Policy: An International Perspective* (2013); (with Penelope Wellbourne) *Social Work as a Profession: A Cross-National Perspective* (2007); and (with John Gal and John Dixon) *Professional Ideologies and Preferences in Social Work: A Global Study* (2003).

Lisa Werkmeister Rozas is an Associate Professor at the University of Connecticut School of Social Work, Director of the BSW programme, member of the Puerto Rican/Latin@ Studies Project, and Chair of the Human Oppression Curriculum Unit. Her research interests include health inequities, issues of oppression, discrimination, racism, critical consciousness and intergroup dialogue. Her teaching and consulting interests also focus around issues of oppression, power, privilege, implicit bias, intersectionality, culture, identity and stigma.

Acknowledgements

First ideas for this book evolved during workshops of the German doctoral research programme 'Living in the Transformed Welfare State' (TRANSSOZ), funded by the state of North Rhine-Westphalia between 2013 and 2017. This programme focused on the intersections of social policy and social work. While the participating doctoral students analysed social practices and social outcomes under the conditions of new welfare state paradigms in Western Europe since the 1990s, the 'inverse perspective' of social work as an actor actively shaping the making of social policy was identified as a desideratum for future research.

The project of 'social work and the making of social policy' was further developed during several panel sessions at the annual conferences of the European Network for Social Policy Analysis (ESPAnet) 2016 in Rotterdam, 2017 in Lisbon, as well as 2018 in Vilnius. We are very grateful to all members of the TRANSSOZ doctoral programme and all participants of the respective ESPAnet sessions for their very valuable contributions and comments. In particular, we would like to thank Idit Weiss-Gal and John Gal for their inspiring activities in the research field of policy practice, which have been and continue to be an important role model for us. We are also very grateful to John Gal and Ian Shaw for incorporating us into their book series 'Research in Social Work', and their very helpful advice throughout the editing process. Of course, we would also like to thank most warmly all contributors for presenting their research results, and for their willingness to relate these to the conceptual framework of the policy cycle we suggested for the book.

In addition, such a book requires plenty of work in terms of layout, which was brilliantly taken care of by Monika Spies, Elena Zeidler, Sarah Dickel and Charlotte Nebel. Thanks very much to all of you!

We hope that the contributions in this book will inspire both social work students and academics as well as social work professionals interested in the relationship of social work and social policy.

1

Introduction: social work and the making of social policy

Ute Klammer, Simone Leiber and Sigrid Leitner

> Social work is a systematic way of helping
> individuals and groups towards better adaptation
> to society. (Definition IFSW from 1957)[1]

> Social work is a practice-based profession and
> an academic discipline that promotes social
> change and development, social cohesion, and
> the empowerment and liberation of people.
> (Definition IFSW and IASSW from 2014)[2]

Ideas of social work's role in society have changed considerably over the last decades, as shown by the comparison of international social work definitions over time. At the level of discourse, social work is no longer considered a mere target of top-down policy and welfare reform, but has been assigned an active role in shaping the structural environment of clients and users of welfare programmes. This normative ideal seems internationally widespread, although national codes of ethics in social work still differ in detail as regards the acknowledgement of the political activities of social workers (Weiss-Gal & Gal, 2014: 185–90). In addition, there is a remarkable lack of knowledge on how the political function of social work actually plays out in practice. This is all the more important as the socio-political context of social work clients and welfare users has recently faced significant change. Contemporary welfare states of the 'global North' focused on in this volume are, among other things, characterised by an extension of 'welfare markets' (for example, Taylor-Gooby, 1999; Bode, 2008), new paradigms of social investment (for example, Morel et al, 2012) and enhanced individual responsibilities for welfare provision under different activation schemes (for example, Serrano Pascual & Magnusson, 2007). These changes have an important impact on the relationship among social work, its clients and the welfare state. In line with Simpson and Connor (2011, 1), we take a critical stance on positions where '[l]ike actors in front of a blue screen, those individuals and groups who provide and receive welfare services are just expected to accept this new backdrop to their lives and seek ways to adapt and rise to the challenge of this new context'. Instead, we share the idea that welfare professionals are an important part of and need to critically engage with social policy, and that there is a need to further the 'policy literacy'[3] of citizens and practitioners of social welfare alike. By presenting an international collection of social work's more or less successful activities in the making of social policy, this book seeks to contribute to that aim. However, it should not be taken for granted that social works' role in the making of social policy automatically aims at emancipatory and 'positive' developments from the viewpoint of the clients and welfare recipients. Although the contributions in this volume do not provide much evidence of such a 'negative' role of social work on social policy making, certain bias in the types of studies selected in the production of this book cannot be ruled out.

The aim of this book is also to link important perspectives of social work and social policy research, as they have often remained unconnected. Research on the politics of welfare state reform usually does not include a social work perspective at all, despite a growing interest in 'welfare state reforms seen from below' (Ebbinghaus & Naumann, 2018) and the interdependence of the two fields is framed as a one-way street: reforms in generalised schemes affect social work 'from above'. Additionally, the more retrenchment happens, the more people depend on individualised support from social work. By contrast, this book underscores the mutuality of the relationship between social policy and social work by focusing on the influence of social work on social policy.

Social work research, on the other hand, still rather seldom deals with social work professionals or social work organisations as political actors – although there is a growing interest in social workers' *policy practice*. The notion was first used by Jansson (1984), and the debate was initially strongly driven by the US, where social work is considered a 'policy-based profession' (Popple & Leighninger, 2014: 12) and where landmark textbooks are written in the manner of manuals on how to become 'an effective policy advocate' (Jansson, 2014; see also Rocha, 2007; Ritter, 2013; for UK perspectives on 'policy and social work practice', see Evans & Keating, 2015). In the meantime, the notion is also widespread in international comparisons when referring to 'activities undertaken by social workers as an integral part of their professional activity in diverse fields and types of practice, that focus on the formulation and implementation of new policies, as well as on existing policies and suggested changes in them' (Weiss-Gal & Gal, 2014: 4–5). This book strongly builds on this research, but goes beyond existing studies by looking at social work actors from different organisational perspectives, and by using the policy cycle as a core analytical framework (see also Güntner & Langer, 2014): how does social work, involving individual as well as corporate actors at different organisational levels, affect social policy along different stages of the policy cycle, and what explains success or failure? This volume examines and contrasts cases across different welfare models. It seeks to provide innovative theoretical as well as empirical insights into the roles of social work in the policy cycle of social policy making (Figure 1.1), whereby multiple theoretical perspectives from governance, implementation and interest representation theory will be applied.

Social work as a political actor

Speaking of social work as a political actor, we have to differentiate between different types of actors in social work and between different levels of policy making. On the one hand, individual social workers and their political engagement come into focus. Weiss-Gal (2017: 286) distinguishes between 'three major modes of social workers' policy involvement: voluntary political participation…, holding elected office, policy practice'. While the first two modes are executed by individual social workers in their role as active citizens within civil society and the general institutional framework of political participation, policy practice is part of their professional work tasks. In this book we are especially interested in policy practice since it refers to *professional activities* of social workers in order to influence the making of social policy along the different stages of the policy cycle.

This also implies that our perspective is narrower than a focus on *political participation* in general, which would include non-professional political activities, but also broader than the scope of community social work, which necessarily requires the active participation of the clients or users concerned (Gal & Weiss-Gal, 2014: 7). Our research interest thus includes activities of *empowerment* (by encouraging self-representation of the clients/users), *co-determination* (for example, by exercising co-determination rights in elected bodies of professional representation) and *social advocacy*, which goes beyond individual case advocacy and is generally understood as political activities on behalf of larger groups that share certain common problems or social features. Finally, the book's focus is above all on social work's/workers' political

Figure 1.1: Social work in the policy cycle of social policy making

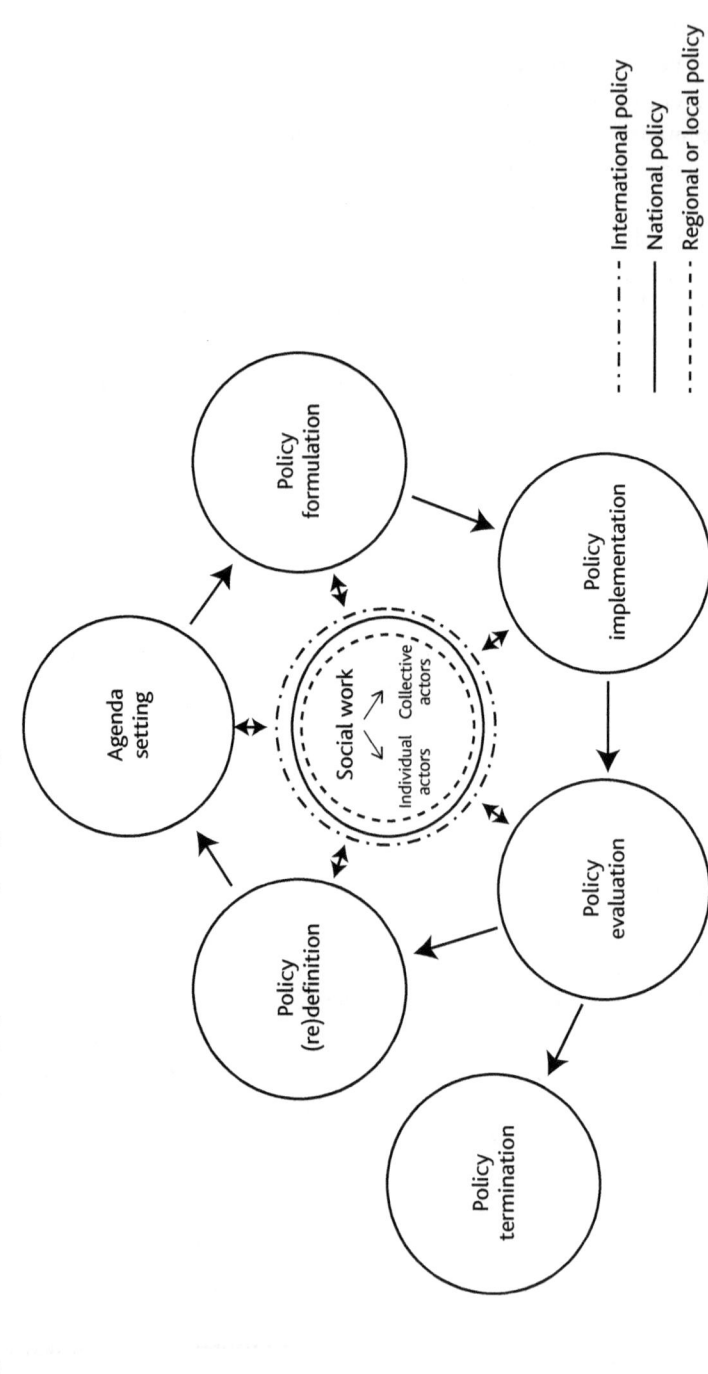

Source: Authors

activities in the client's name, whereas direct activities in their own interests, such as in terms of wages and working conditions, are not covered by the studies presented here.

In addition, differences among countries on the nature of the social work profession, education for policy practice and the (historical) 'institutional embeddedness' of social work(ers) in the public and welfare state system have to be taken into account (Weiss-Gal & Gal, 2014). The range of political action scrutinised in this book is often closely related to local community structures. Individual social workers can influence agenda setting and policy formulation processes at the municipal level by contacting administrators and politicians or by testifying to municipal committees. Social workers as street-level bureaucrats (Lipsky, 2010) certainly do have influence on the implementation of local and national policies.

On the other hand, in addition to individual social work professionals, there are different kinds of collective actors in social work. Professionals are organised in national social work associations which sometimes have regional subgroups, and there are also the International Federation of Social Workers (IFSW) and the International Council on Social Welfare (ICSW). Social work academics also have national organisations for the exchange of research and teaching and on the international level; for example, the European Association of Schools of Social Work (EASSW) fosters common political goals related to social work and social development. The impact of these actors probably concerns mostly the agenda-setting stage of the policy cycle, but national associations of social work might also affect policy formulation if they aim at the regulation of specific problems.

Furthermore, there also exists a broad range of consortia for specific areas of social work such as homelessness, psychiatry, sex work, drug abuse and the inclusion of handicapped people. These groups often consist of social workers and other professionals as well as clients, and they can engage in local, regional or national political action with the aim to bring relevant topics to the political agenda, to formulate policies and to influence political decision making.

Finally, the responsible bodies of social work institutions might also be important political actors, especially if they employ a large number of social workers and serve not only locally but on a national scale.

New paradigms in social policy

When attention is focused on the role of social work in the process of formulating, designing and implementing social policies, it should be borne in mind that social policy itself has fundamentally changed shape during the last decades in the context of the challenges of economic globalisation, the transformation of industrial to service-based societies and social modernisation (see Häusermann & Palier, 2008). This change cannot simply be described as a degradation or retrenchment of the welfare state (Bonoli et al, 2000), even if it seems to be a natural interpretation. Rather we see a profound transformation process of the welfare state, which has been taken either as a neo-social restructuring of social policy (Taylor-Gooby, 2016) or as a readjustment of the welfare state (Kessl, 2013). There are tendencies of change that reflect a very fundamental redefinition of the dominating socio-political objectives and ideological convictions on which the structure of the welfare state rests. This is also reflected in a new balancing of redistribution norms: performative justice tends to be strengthened while solidarity is weakened (Leitner, 2016), with new demarcations of inclusion and exclusion.

The transformation of the welfare state and its underlying principles can be characterised transnationally through several key paradigms (Klammer et al, 2017):

- The *activation paradigm* that has gained international importance aims at the (re)integration of employable persons in the labour market. It focuses either directly on expected participation through measures of activating labour market policy or manifests itself in its absence, in cuts to or the postponement of monetary ('passive') social benefits. The target groups of activation are manifold. Support from the community must be earned (deservingness) – it is no longer unconditionally based on citizenship. The paradigm of activation fundamentally changes the relationship between the individual and society: socialisation and social inclusion become a task for which every individual is responsible.
- The *self-responsibility paradigm* transfers the responsibility for provision in relation to health, labour market integration or retirement provision to the individual. Self-responsible action is demanded and rewarded, 'misconduct' or 'obstinacy' lead to benefit reduction or a lack of social protection.
- The *autonomy* or *self-determination paradigm*, on the other hand, focuses on the choice and co-determination of clients' possibilities and can therefore be described as the positive aspect of self-responsibility. As part of a shared decision-making process, clients are addressed as responsible citizens and become co-producers in welfare state arrangements.

- On the whole, tendencies of *economisation and privatisation* characterise the transformation of most developed welfare states: social services are increasingly geared to efficiency indicators and subject to the rules of the market, former state-regulated benefit systems are taken over by private sector organisations. In social services, the marketisation and privatisation of social security has been accompanied by the introduction of new governance models transferring economic efficiency criteria and management thinking to public administration and social organisations (Taylor-Gooby, 2016).

These international reform trends in the institutional framework of developed welfare states and their governance have dramatically changed the role of social work. As will be highlighted in the following sections, the changes influence not only the tasks and behaviours of social workers in concrete work with clients, but also the way social work is involved in the perception, formulation and implementation of social policy along the policy cycle.

Social work, problem definition and agenda setting

Social work is at the heart of pressing social problems. When new social risks arise, local social workers are among the first to be aware of them. They have the professional knowledge to deal with social problems on an individual level, but their work is also strongly related to the structural framework of the welfare state. Social workers and social work organisations have insight not only into individual needs but also into structural shortcomings and omissions. They may also be part of processes of an evaluation of existing interventions and raise their voice towards problem redefinition. Thus, social work can raise awareness of social problems and has the potential to draw attention to policy issues, which may then enter the political agenda.

We assume that in the realm of problem definition, and against the backdrop of the new social policy paradigms described above, individual as well as collective social work actors have a crucial role in public or political debates by arguing towards a shift of the perceived responsibility for social problems from individual clients to structural limitations of contemporary welfare capitalism. An important prerequisite for that seems to be consciousness raising among clients as well as social work professionals, as it is the aim of approaches such as critical (Gil, 2013) or structural social work (Moreau, 1990; Mullaly, 2007). As Moreau (1990: 54) puts it, the core aim of social work should be threefold:

> A key concern is to prevent clients from unduly scapegoating themselves or others for material situations that are largely out of their personal control, to collectivize rather than to individualize their situation, and, where possible, to change their material conditions prior to working together on personal change.

To us, one of the main tasks of social work at the stage of problem definition in the making of social policy, thus, could be to expand this consciousness-raising for structural problems from clients and social work professionals to other key stakeholders of the political debate and the political process in order to initiate policy change.

However, when it comes to the question of which (perceived) pressing social problems would actually make it onto governments' political agendas, we know that changes in problem perceptions are not sufficient. It seems that the seminal approach of Kingdon (1984) is still very useful and commonly used (for example in teaching policy practice, see Jansson, 2014: 178 ff), when it comes to understanding successful agenda setting. Kingdon (1984) distinguishes three so-called streams: problem recognition, policy proposals and politics. In the stream of problem recognition, the central question is why governments pay attention to some problems and not others. According to Kingdon, sudden shifts in the performance of systems regularly monitored by standard indicators – or focusing events, such as crisis – are particularly decisive for attracting politicians' attention. Social work actors involved in such situations (such as the recent 'refugee crisis' in many European countries) could make use of that.

In the stream of policy proposals, a policy community of specialists like bureaucrats, people in planning, evaluation and budgeting, academics, interest groups and researchers is constantly generating proposals. Social work – at this point most likely not individual social workers, but their collective representatives – although not mentioned explicitly by Kingdon, is part of that. In a selection process, some ideas or proposals are discarded and others are taken into consideration, especially when they are technically feasible, not too expensive and acceptable to the public.

For the third stream, politics, changes in the administration, partisan or ideological composition of parliament and interest group pressure are central factors influencing agenda setting. Only a policy window enhances the chance to actually influence the agenda. A policy window can open either because of change in the political stream or because new problems come to the attention of government officials.

Against this backdrop, analysts of social work actors should also be aware of such policy windows.

Roger Smith's conceptual contribution (Chapter 2) looks at 'social work as a policy innovator'. By comparing different policy fields, he explores inhibiting factors for the profession's capacity to publicly engage in key policy issues, as well as looking at factors of success and their underlying mechanisms.

Lisa Werkmeister Rozas, Megan Feely and Jason Ostrander (Chapter 3) present a case study from the United States showing how critical awareness raising among social workers has contributed to a changed public perception of sex-trafficked youth – from criminals to victims. In the course of awareness raising, this modified problem definition has also led to legal changes in favour of this particular vulnerable client group.

The contribution of Matteo D'Emilione et al (Chapter 4) shows how via evaluation of a regional pilot anti-poverty intervention, Italian social workers' voices have been taken into account when the intervention was redefined and adapted towards a nationwide policy measure.

Social work interests in policy formulation and decision making

While individual social workers might selectively gain influence over policy formulation and decision making (for example, see Ferguson & Woodward, 2009; Lavalette, 2017), it seems obvious that collective actors of social work play a more important part in this regard on all levels of the political system. A recently published thorough review of the literature on social workers' policy engagement states that '[d]espite the many differences in their design, all the studies, whether undertaken in the US, Israel or Canada, report low or very low levels of social workers' engagement in PP [policy practice]' (Weiss-Gal, 2017: 292). The policy practice engagement framework (Gal & Weiss-Gal, 2014) shows that different factors are responsible for engagement in PP: besides individual motivation, the employing organisation may or may not facilitate PP and institutional norms, and the accessibility of political institutions may or may not provide opportunities for PP.

As a matter of fact, different political systems provide different possibilities for participating in policy formulation and decision making: Whereas in *neo-corporatist systems* collective actors are given the opportunity to share their thoughts during the legislative process, in *pluralist systems* collective actors have to push their interests mainly through lobbying activities. Recent research on interest representation assumes that neo-corporatist structures lose importance due to new forms of governance while pluralist strategies of interest representation become more and more common (Holtmann & Voelzkow, 2000; Reutter, 2012). To build coalitions, to testify in expert hearings, to write comments on proposed legislation, to work with the media, to contact decision makers and to be consulted by them – these are core activities of collective actors like social work associations or schools. Becoming an active part of the *policy network* (Schneider et al, 2009) and to form *advocacy coalitions* (Weible et al, 2011) seems to be crucial for exerting political influence.

Little research exists on the political action of collective actors of social work. In early papers, Mathews (1983) reflected on the purpose and action strategies of social work Political Action Committees (PAC) by describing the example of the Michigan National Association of Social Workers PAC, and Northwood and Parker (1984) documented a legislative campaign undertaken at the University of Washington School of Social Work. Collective action and social struggle from below are important forces for the development of social policy, as literature on social movements suggests (Barker & Lavalette, 2015).

Although there must be a lot more collective political action taking place in social work, it is rarely a topic of research. The second part of this book presents four chapters that deal with the role of individual and collective actors in policy formulation and decision making.

Francisco Branco (Chapter 5) takes a historical approach and sheds light on early social reform in the United States. He explores the involvement of social work pioneers in the development of social work and social reform policies and examines their collective strategies to successfully influence decision making.

The relationship of academia and political advocacy is dealt with by Idit Weiss-Gal and John Gal in their study on academia, social work and social policy (Chapter 6). This chapter aims at a better understanding of the forms of social work academics' policy engagement, its perceived impact and associated opportunities and obstacles.

Against the backdrop of economic crisis in southern Europe, and by using a theoretical framework from social movements and critical policy analysis, Riccardo Guidi's study (Chapter 7) compares how social workers in Italy and Spain have followed different paths towards mobilisation against politics of austerity, and how this has affected political decision making in these countries.

Rich Moth and Michael Lavalette (Chapter 8) consider organising and networking methodologies of a collective actor in times of austerity and welfare reform, focusing on the Social Work Action Network (SWAN), a social movement organisation within the social work field in the UK. The authors analyse the way(s) that SWAN mobilises activist resources to maximise impact within the political opportunity structure.

Social work and implementation

A continuing theme in the relationship of social work and the welfare state is the role of social workers as practical policy actors implementing welfare policies. For a long time there has been consensus in the research debate that social policies – especially social insurance – serve to eliminate typical social risks and emergencies by providing generalised benefits and services, while social work deals with complex situations of need, taking into account the specific circumstances of individual cases through individualised benefits (see Kaufmann, 1973: 97). Within the described transformation of the welfare state, social work has received more recognition because it has increasingly been integrated into many subsystems of the 'activating' welfare state. With the change of social policy towards activation and the accompanying pedagogical turn in the transformed social welfare state (approach of 'promoting and demanding'), social work and socio-pedagogical terminology and concepts have been applied to areas that previously followed the logic of social insurance. Today, social work is increasingly involved within the framework of the 'activating labour market policy' and the restructuring of social security for the unemployed. In addition, the new logic of an investive and preventive social policy (Morel et al, 2012), which is reflected in different countries in the development of social services (in particular in the areas of education, health and employability), have led to an increased importance of social work.

At the same time, the conditions for professional action have changed fundamentally. The dismantling of benefit systems as well as the expansion in fields such as care and education takes place mostly under the changed premises of economic utility logic. Limitations and definitions of professional action through economic conditions often lead to conflicting goals and difficult working conditions for social workers. Therefore, many social work researchers (for example, Kessl, 2013; Evans, 2016) believe that the increasing recognition and appreciation that social work has experienced in the course of recent welfare state reforms actually questions their basic logic and limits their professional leeway.

In contrast to the topics that have been outlined above, the question of how social workers contribute to the implementation of social policy programmes has quite a long research tradition. Since Lipsky (1980) brought the concept of 'street-level bureaucracy' to the debate, numerous scholars have referred to his research,[4] and his revisions for the 30th anniversary, 2010 edition demonstrates the ongoing interest in the challenge of 'how to treat citizens alike in their claims on government and how at the same time to be responsive to the individual case when appropriate' (Lipsky, 2010: xii). Lipsky's analysis made clear that social workers not only must be sensitive in implementing social policy, but it also encouraged them to reflect on how to work differently. Gilson (2015), reviewing recent scholarship drawing on Lipsky's ideas, sees three key contributions to the field of public policy analysis: the recognition that (1) street-level bureaucrats have discretion and power in implementation, (2) that their behaviour is systematically influenced by the organisational and institutional environment in which they work and (3) that efforts to control their behaviour undermines their responsiveness to clients, so that new approaches are needed to support them as part of a responsive public bureaucracy.

In particular the issue of discretion – the room to make judgement and to choose between options in social work practice – has been investigated and questioned by social work researchers (Evans, 2012; Carson et al, 2015). Recent studies confirm that social workers in many countries engage in policy implementation at various levels and through diverse strategies (Strier & Feldman 2017). This holds particularly true for the field of the frontline delivery of welfare-to-work policies (see contributions in van Berkel et al, 2017).

Under the conditions of the transformed welfare state, the question of how social workers deal with the 'double mandate' remains crucial. How do they support their clients on the one hand while, on the other hand, being vicarious agents of a social benefits system that is increasingly focused on activation, self-responsibility, control and sanctions? Is there any leeway in the implementation of activating, controlling and sanctioning measures? And what factors – such as individual experiences, resources, professional values, characteristics of professional education, structural features of organisations or institutional frameworks – could explain observable differences in the implementation of social policy by social workers? The five contributions in the third part of this book seek to further close this research gap by investigating implementation practices of social work in different countries.

Tony Evans (Chapter 9) starts by exploring the ethics of social work policy practice in Britain, particularly the relationship between practitioners and the public welfare agencies within which they work. Based on his earlier work, Evans' contribution (again) brings one of the most debated issues to the fore: the conflict between many social workers' ideas of social justice on the one hand and their professional tasks in the reformed welfare state on the other, where their organisations expect them to implement the policies of welfare retrenchment and austerity.

Ravit Alfandari (Chapter 10) investigates the implementation of child protection reform in Israel, focusing on systemic barriers that have interfered with effective realisation of reform in the field. In her qualitative study based on the 'systems approach' as a conceptual framework, she scrutinises how the underlying organisational factors of the social services system interact with social workers' everyday work.

The following contribution by Sergio Sánchez Castiñeira (Chapter 11) focuses on the ambivalent role of social workers in the context of the reformed Spanish welfare state and the economic crisis. Given the fact that laws, organisations and professions of social assistance widely proclaim social inclusion to be the official goal, he asks whether resources are sufficient to realise this task and investigates how frontline social workers are mobilising available material, symbolic and relational resources to protect their own and their clients' dignity.

The contribution of Paweł Poławski (Chapter 12) draws our attention to the fact that some of the problems clients and social workers have to deal with are 'manufactured risks' produced by the reformed welfare state itself. Focusing on social assistance in Poland, the author is interested in whether or not and how the new layered welfare system translates into segmentation of entitlements, financial mechanisms, management methods and institutional responsibility. Based on qualitative data, he identifies different rules social workers apply to deal with tension and uncertainty.

Finally, in their study Markus Gottwald and Frank Sowa (Chapter 13) focus on the attitude and behaviour of placement professionals in Germany against the background of the so-called 'Hartz reforms' implemented in 2005, which shifted placement services towards the market economy and business practices. The chapter also contributes to the framework of the book by investigating and questioning the division between social policy and social work.

In sum, despite great differences between the country contexts, all contributions across the three parts of the book underline a great variety of (potential) activities as well as the general importance of social work(ers) in public policy making. To enhance systematic knowledge in the field is, thus, the core aim of this book.

Notes

1. IFSW: International Federation of Social Workers (see Truell, 2014).
2. IASSW: International Association of Schools of Social Work (definition adopted at the General Assembly in July 2014).
3. Understood as the 'ability to read (comprehend), write (create, design, produce) and perform policies' (Simpson & Connor, 2011: 2).
4. Gilson (2015) points to the nearly 7000 citations of the book on Google Scholar.

References

Barker, C. and Lavalette, M. (2015) 'Welfare changes and social movements', in D. della Porta and M. Diani (eds) *The Oxford Handbook of Social Movements*, Oxford: Oxford University Press, pp 711–28.

Bode, I. (2008) *The Culture of Welfare Markets. The International Recasting of Pension and Care Systems*, New York: Routledge.

Bonoli, G., Vic, G. and Taylor-Gooby, P. (2000) *European Welfare Futures. Towards a Theory of Retrenchment*, Cambridge: Polity Press.

Carson, E., Chung, D. and Evans, T. (2015) 'Complexities of discretion in human services in the third sector', *European Journal of Social Work*, 18: 167–84.

Ebbinghaus, B. and Naumann, E. (eds) (2018) *Welfare State Reforms Seen from Below. Comparing Public Attitudes and Organized Interests in Britain and Germany*, London: Palgrave Macmillan.

Evans, T. (2016) 'Street-level bureaucracy, management and the corrupted world of service', *European Journal of Social Work*, 19: 602-15.

Evans, T. (2012) 'Organisational rules and discretion in adult social work', *British Journal of Social Work*, 43: 739–58.

Evans, T. and Keating, F. (2015) *Policy and Social Work Practice*, London: Sage.

Ferguson, I. and Woodward, R. (2009) *Radical Social Work in Practice: Making a Difference*, Bristol: Policy Press.

Gal, J. and Weiss-Gal, I. (2014) 'Policy practice in social work: an introduction', in J. Gal and I. Weiss-Gal (eds) *Social Workers Affecting Social Policy. An International Perspective on Policy Practice*, Bristol: Policy Press, 1–16.

Gil, D. G. (2013) *Confronting Justice and Oppression: Concepts and Strategies for Social Workers*, New York: Columbia University Press.

Gilson, L. (2015) 'Michael Lipsky, street-level bureaucracy: dilemmas of the individual in public service', in E. Page, M. Lodge and S. Balla (eds) *Oxford Handbook of the Classics of Public Policy*, Oxford: Oxford University Press, pp 383–404.

Güntner, S. and Langer, A. (2014) 'Sozialarbeitspolitik zwischen Professionspolitik und Gesellschaftsgestaltung', in B. Benz, G. Rieger, W. Schönig and M. Többe-Schukalla (eds), *Politik Sozialer Arbeit*, 2: Akteure, Handlungsfelder und Methoden, Weinheim: Beltz Juventa, pp 238–54.

Häusermann, S. and Palier, B. (2008) 'The politics of employment-friendly welfare reforms in post-industrial economies', *Socio-Economic Review* 6(3): 559–86.

Holtmann, E. and Voelzkow, H. (eds) (2000) *Zwischen Wettbewerbs- und Verhandlungsdemokratie. Analysen zum Regierungssystem der Bundesrepublik Deutschland*, Wiesbaden: Springer VS.

Jansson, B. S. (1984) *Theory and Practice of Social Welfare Policy: Analysis, Process, and Current Issues*, Belmont, CA: Wadsworth.

Jansson, B. S. (2014) *Becoming an Effective Policy Advocate. From Policy Practice to Social Justice* (7th edn), Belmont, CA: Brooks/Cole.

Kaufmann, F.-X. (1973) 'Vom Verhältnis von Sozialarbeit und Sozialpädagogik', in H.-U. Otto and S. Schneider (eds) *Gesellschaftliche Perspektiven der Sozialarbeit*, Neuwied/Berlin: Luchterhand, pp 87–104.

Kessl, F. (2013) *Soziale Arbeit in der Transformation des Sozialen. Eine Ortsbestimmung*, Wiesbaden: Springer VS.

Kingdon, J. W. (1984) *Agendas, Alternatives and Public Policies*, Boston: Little, Brown.

Klammer, U., Leiber, S. and Leitner, S. (2017) 'Leben im transformierten Sozialstaat. Sozialpolitische Perspektiven auf Soziale Arbeit', *Soziale Passagen*, 1: 7–21.

Lavalette, M. (2017) 'Sylvia Pankhurst: suffragette, socialist, anti-imperialist… and social worker?', *Critical and Radical Social Work* 5(3): 369–82.

Leitner, S. (2016) 'Leistungs- und Bedarfsgerechtigkeit im Sozialstaat. Umverteilungsnormen im Wandel', in B. Aulenbacher, M. Dammayr, M. Dörre, W. Menz, B. Riegraf and H. Wolf (eds) *Leistung und Gerechtigkeit*, Weinheim/Basel: Beltz Juventa.

Lipsky, M. (1980) *Street-level Bureaucracy: Dilemmas of the Individual in Public Services*, New York: Sage.

Lipsky, M. (2010) *Street-Level Bureaucracy: Dilemmas of the Individual in Public Service, 30th Anniversary Expanded Edition*, New York: Russel Sage Foundation.

Mathews, G. (1983) 'Social work PAC's and state social work associations purpose, history, and action strategies', *Journal of Sociology & Social Welfare*, 10(2): 347–54.

Moreau, M. (1990) 'Empowerment through advocacy and consciousness-raising. Implications of a structural approach to social work', *Journal of Sociology & Social Welfare*, 17(2): 53–67.

Morel, N., Palier, B. and Palme, J. (eds) (2012) *Towards a Social Investment State? Ideas, Polies, and Challenges*, Bristol: Policy Press.

Mullaly, R. P. (2006) *The New Structural Social Work: Ideology, Theory, Practice* (3rd edn), Don Mills, Ontario: Oxford University Press.

Northwood, L. K. and Parker, M. (1984) 'The relative effectiveness of legislative campaigning in a school of social work', *Journal of Sociology & Social Welfare*, 11(3): 684–713.

Popple, P. R. and Leighninger, L. (2014) *The Policy Based Profession. An Introduction to Social Welfare Policy Analysis for Social Workers* (6th edn), Boston: Pearson.

Reutter, W. (ed) (2012) *Verbände und Interessengruppen in den Ländern der Europäischen Union*, Wiesbaden: Springer VS.

Ritter, J. A. (2013) *Social Work Policy Practice: Changing Our Community, Nation and the World*, Boston: Pearson.

Rocha, C. J. (2007) *Essentials of Social Work Policy Practice*, Hoboken, NJ: John Wiley.

Schneider, V., Janning, F., Leifeld, P. and Malang, T. (eds) (2009) *Politiknetzwerke. Modelle, Anwendungen und Visualisierungen*, Wiesbaden: Springer VS.

Serrano Pascual, A. S. and Magnusson, L. (eds) (2007) *Reshaping Welfare States and Activation Regimes in Europe*, Brussels: Peter Lang.

Simpson, G. and Connor, S. (2011) *Social Policy for Social Welfare Professionals. Tools for Understanding, Analysis, and Engagement*, Bristol: Policy Press.

Strier, R. and Feldman, G. (2017) 'Reengineering social work's political passion: policy practice and neo-liberalism', *British Journal of Social Work*, 48(3): 751–68.

Taylor-Gooby, P. (1999) 'Markets and motives. Trust and egoism in welfare markets', *Journal of Social Policy*, 28(1): 97–114.

Taylor-Gooby, P. (2016) 'The divisive welfare state', *Social Policy Administration*, 50(6): 712–33.

Truell, R. (2014) 'What is social work?', *The Guardian, International Edition*, 7 July. Available at: www.theguardian.com/social-care-network/2014/jul/07/what-is-social-work

Van Berkel, R., Caswell, D., Kupka, P. and Larsen, F. (eds) (2017) *Frontline Delivery of Welfare-to-Work Policies in Europe: Activating the Unemployed*, London: Routledge.

Weible, C., Sabatier, P., Jenkins-Smith, H., Nohrstedt, D., Douglas Henry, A. and de Leon, P. (2011) 'A quarter century of the advocacy coalition framework: an introduction to the special issue', *Policy Studies Journal*, 39(3): 349–60.

Weiss-Gal, I. (2017) 'Social workers' policy engagement: a review of the literature', *International Journal of Social Welfare*, 26: 285–98.

Weiss-Gal, I. and Gal, J. (2014) 'An international perspective on policy practice', in J. Gal and I. Weiss-Gal (eds) *Social Workers Affecting Social Policy. An International Perspective on Policy Practice*, Bristol: Policy Press, pp 183–209.

Part I
Social work, problem definition and agenda setting

2

Social work as policy innovator: challenges and possibilities in the UK

Roger Smith

Introduction

In social work practice settings, social problems are, by definition, centre stage. We can think of issues such as child poverty, violence and abuse, social exclusion, family breakdown and migration as closely intertwined with the contexts of social work practice. For social work, such issues are highly visible, and unquestionably associated with the tasks integral to professional practice. The key question for us to consider is how this relationship is played out, and how social work's 'natural' interest in such policy issues manifests itself in action to secure change. As the book's introductory chapter explained, this is a complex and challenging field for social work, but one where there are a number of opportunities arising from the obvious common ground between the 'project' of the profession itself and the lived experiences of those for whom it seeks to make a difference in their lives.

Social work can be considered a natural ally of those experiencing disadvantage and discrimination, but it is also faced with the paradoxical observation that often it is experienced by service users as 'part of the problem'. Others have written extensively about the complex and ambiguous 'positioning' of social work in the UK context, to which this chapter particularly refers. Here, social work is constituted as a formal state function, which must simultaneously represent the notional public interest, and intervene decisively (and divisively) to protect and promote the interests of vulnerable members of the population, in particular (Jordan & Drakeford, 2012).

So, 'Don't Even Get Us Started on Social Workers' appears in the title of a recent article focusing on the role of practitioners in working with the effects of domestic abuse (Robbins & Cook, 2017). Instead of finding social workers as natural allies in helping them resist and deal with violence, women interviewed for this study spoke of being threatened and judged, and held responsible for the harm they and their children were experiencing. Here, then, the fundamental question for social work of its relationship to service users on the one hand, and state power and dominant ideologies on the other, becomes acute:

> There was a perceived gulf of experience between the workers and their service users ... In a period of gross inequality, as currently in the UK, distances between groups are intensified and exaggerated ... The women in the [focus] groups saw social workers as alien in terms of experience, understanding and class. (Robbins & Cook, 2017: 13)

Issues of structural inequality, gender and oppression are unchallenged and, if anything, simply replicated in this portrayal of everyday social work practice; and yet social work values explicitly place these at the centre of the profession's framework for intervention.

In seeking to explore these apparent tensions, we need to consider the inhibiting factors which seem to limit the profession's capacity to 'speak out'. These are associated with the individualising frame for social work practice, and the associated tendency to problematise those with whom social work intervenes, rather than the external, systemic or structural issues which underlie their problems – the translation of the issue of poverty into a concern with 'child neglect', for example. In other words, there is a task to be undertaken by critically reflective practitioners to locate themselves (as well as their clients) within a context where external pressures shape not only the immediate practice environment but also the ways in which it (and those within it) are understood.

Additionally, social work itself has to face the challenge of asserting its legitimacy and gaining credibility for interventions in the policy sphere. It has to re-establish the connections between individual difficulties and social harms in order to translate 'people problems' into social policy issues. And, additionally, social work has to establish its own authority to comment about problems which are not seen as falling within its remit, or scope of expertise, such as the oppressive nature and consequences of income inequality, or the harm caused by discriminatory and divisive immigration rules.

For some, these constraints are at least partly self-imposed, and social work's limited role in policy debates may be attributable to:

> Its quest for recognition as a profession. It has been more anxious to establish its credentials as an exclusive expertise

in solving specific problems or ameliorating specific conflicts, rather than allowing itself to become associated with movements for social change, or with developments in society at large. (Jordan & Drakeford, 2012: 167)

It may also be the case that social work education, especially in England, is constructed and validated in ways which tend to foreground individualised models of problem identification and intervention and related skills and methods; and this is certainly a criticism levelled at the proliferating number of 'fast track' practice-based qualifying routes into the profession (Thoburn, 2017). Social work is held responsible for limiting its own sphere of expertise and therefore influence to a particular type of 'social' problem, constructed in a particular fashion, where concerns are focused on individuals, families and their personal and private issues, rather than their public dimensions.

We night surmise that social work has more success in raising policy concerns and achieving change in those areas where its role is viewed as more legitimate, such as child protection or adult care. Therefore, we could anticipate that there are likely to be concrete examples of progressive change in the form of both agenda setting and policy innovation where social work's claims to expertise are more credible. In England and Wales, the Children Act 1989, for example, could be seen as a piece of legislation that was very extensively informed through dialogue and consultation with 'experts' from within the professional field of child welfare; and, indeed, a similar case might even be made for the Care Act 2014, in relation to adult services.

But it will also be important to consider the means and mechanisms by which social workers and their representatives have sought to extend their 'sphere of credibility', to address shortcomings in mental health provision, for example, and the extent to which these may or may not have been successful.

And, finally, it will be helpful to conclude with a brief review of social work's policy achievements, in the UK context, and the necessary building blocks (such as sound organisation, effective communication, good knowledge base) which have underpinned its successes, while also still acknowledging the enormous challenges involved.

Social workers as activists: a long tradition

Social work practitioners and the wider social work community (agencies, non-governmental organisations and academics) have consistently argued that it is legitimate and necessary to maintain a distinctive voice in the policy arena, with very few overtly dissenting voices (Davies, 1994). This belief is manifested in the longstanding experience of practitioners in establishing collective fora with the aim of generating awareness of key issues affecting service users and carers, and then arguing for change. In the 1970s, for example, 'radical social work' (Bailey & Brake, 1976) became an identifiable body of ideas and practice within the social work profession, and the campaigning group Case Con was established to give collective voice to expressions of dissent, resistance and progressive agendas for change.

Despite the entrenchment of neoliberalism and persistent attacks on welfare in general, and social work and its clients in particular, there has remained a reservoir of activism within the profession, underpinned by its core values:

> Social workers recognise the fundamental principles of human rights and equality, and that these are protected in national and international law, conventions and policies. They ensure these principles underpin their practice. Social workers understand the importance of using and contributing to case law and applying these rights in their own practice. (From the Professional Capabilities Framework for Social Workers: BASW, 2018)

The notions of equality, social justice, respect for individuals and personal autonomy are deeply embedded in the operating philosophy of social workers and, of course, very often these cannot be realised simply or only thorough working one-to-one to achieve positive change for people, even though this lies at the heart of day-to-day practice.

Organisations such as the British Association of Social Workers (BASW) have consistently viewed their role as extending beyond acting as a professional body, overseeing and supporting the development of good practice and the maintenance of standards. BASW is a consistent presence in key policy debates concerning the future development of services for people in need or at risk. Other important organisations, too, such as the Social Work Action Network (SWAN) have come into being, inheriting the mantle of *Case Con* and maintaining the tradition of activism originating in the 1970s. *Case Con* was a radical magazine which acted as the focal point for academic and practitioner activists:

> The editorial of the first edition of 'Case Con' (June 1970), which had the sub-title 'for revolutionary social work',

stated that it had been produced 'by an ad hoc group of radicals – social workers and social work teachers – whose dissatisfaction with the way social work is practised and taught has finally reached creative proportions.' Its title derived from the belief that the problems social workers had to deal with could only be solved by replacing capitalism with socialism, as opposed to the casework approach of treating them as deviations from the norm.[1]

The achievements of those associated with the publication led to the subsequent conclusion that: 'Pressure groups such as Case Con for socialist social workers and Child Poverty Action Group have made valuable contributions' to making the case for social change (Bailey & Brake, 1976: 10).

Subsequent initiatives from within the social work profession have highlighted the importance of anti-oppressive practices across the range of public services. It was as a result of activist pressure, for example, that anti-racist practice skills and values came to be embedded in the social work educational curriculum during the 1980s, which at the time marked the profession out for its progressive aspirations (Lavalette & Penketh, 2013). Of course, it is important to acknowledge the subsequent dilution of this commitment, and the recurrent challenge of converting a progressive change agenda into material reality.

Currently, the Social Work Action Network, originating in 2004, has become established as a key and effective rallying group for social work activists, as discussed in detail in Chapter 8 by Moth and Lavalette, taking it as a matter of principle that the network should bring together social workers, service users, academics and others to demonstrate the principles of solidarity and collective change. Even in difficult times, social work retains the desire and the means to identify and challenge social injustices, and to act for change by setting (or at least influencing) the social policy agenda.

Both SWAN and BASW have, for example, maintained a prominent role in campaigns for better and fairer treatment of asylum seekers and refugees, connecting policy work to the direct practice of those who have interpreted their social work role as being grounded in principles of human rights and social justice, mirroring the direct action of their colleagues in Austria (Truell, 2015). UK social workers have travelled repeatedly to Calais to provide assistance to those stranded at the Channel port in terrible conditions while governments haggled over whose responsibility they were – as in Amy Norris' (2016) account of her experience.

In turn, these direct experiences and eye-witness accounts offer substantive evidence to inform campaigning work in support of those affected, and at least provide the ammunition required to make a case for change:

> BASW is calling on the British Government to receive those fleeing war, persecution, and devastation in their home countries with respect and dignity and is urging its members to sign a petition to up the number of refugees being accepted into the UK. (BASW, 4 September 2015, www.basw.co.uk/news/article/?id=1018)

The limits of change

Whether it is possible to trace a line from this tradition of campaigning for change through to specific and concrete achievements is more difficult. This is for several reasons, including: the sheer difficulty of ensuring that dissenting voices are heard in a hostile political and economic climate; the limited capacity to find time and space when confronted with the unceasing demands of the 'day job'; establishing credibility and claiming legitimacy to speak about critical issues, which may or may not fall within the conventional remit of social work; the problem of finding a common voice and overcoming the structural divisions between different interest groups (including people who use services); limited expertise and experience in engaging in the policy arena; and the associated practical tasks involved in setting up and maintaining an effective and responsive infrastructure to respond to policy issues as they emerge. In light of these obstacles, we should perhaps ask ourselves not why social work is not a more effective player in policy debates, but how it manages to be heard at all; this is preferable to the alternative of giving in to a mood of pessimistic self-criticism.

We can certainly make the case that social work has played a significant part in highlighting problems and achieving change in a number of key areas, where legitimacy and expertise are relatively easier to claim, such as safeguarding children, domestic violence and social care for adults and older people. Taking the long view, social work's very proximity to the serious and persistent needs identified among its clientele has helped to shed light on these, and at the very least has contributed to policy makers' wider awareness that 'something must be done', as in the case of domestic violence.

It is plausible to argue, for instance, that social work's very exposure to enduring aspects of inequality has been consistently significant simply in terms of bringing such issues to light and thereby, indeed, helping to set the policy agenda. It has been suggested that the relationship between a largely female social work workforce and an equally if not more heavily weighted population of women in caring roles has provided fertile ground for the recognition and calls for action to deal with the systemic disadvantages faced by women. Thus, ground-level discussion

> of the material welfare of women clients and women social workers swiftly uncovered questions about the need for profound changes in policies to income maintenance and the collectivisation of 'care' if women's material welfare and emotional wellbeing was not to be sacrificed. (Dominelli & McLeod, 1989: 153)

Problematically, though, the legitimacy for social work to comment upon and argue for change depends on the 'discourse' within which such arguments are framed. It is easier for social work to claim the professional standing and insight to promote improvements in child protection systems than it is to develop the more far-reaching argument that many of the issues of safeguarding and children's well-being are rooted not in poor parenting, but in inequality and poverty, despite attempts by social work academics to redress this omission (Bywaters et al, 2014).

It has been more difficult, therefore, when social work has pursued change in areas which fall outside its recognised areas of competence: in challenging the impacts of homelessness or poverty on its service users or in seeking to address discrimination and abuse in generic rather than individualised terms. This is partly to do with the way social work practice is organised and professional competences are delimited. Social injustices are not always immediately visible, as people's lives and their atomised problems come to the fore, and are effectively decontextualised and depoliticised. For social workers, there is an inherent challenge in being able to think (and act) 'outside the box'. There is, then, a task for those who do wish to redefine and address so-called personal problems as broader social issues. There is a preparatory task to be undertaken for those concerned with taking a 'social justice' value-based approach, and this is to redefine and reconnect the multiple forms of oppression experienced differently and disjointedly at individual level, simply in order to be able to claim the authority to articulate common concerns, and thereby to set an appropriate policy agenda.

Nonetheless, in 2017, the British Association of Social Workers initiated and supported the 'Boot Out Austerity' campaign in which social workers took action by way of a week-long march to highlight the effects of austerity in the UK:

> Between 19th and 25th April, a group of social workers and supporters walked the 100 miles from Birmingham to Liverpool, arriving the day before the British Association of Social Workers' Annual General Meeting and Conference there. The aim was to highlight the devastating effects of austerity measures and call for their end.[2]

And yet evidence suggests that, in the course of their day-to-day practice, social workers tend to underplay the effects of poverty. As Morris and colleagues (2018: 4) have argued, there appear to be 'various mechanisms by which attention to family policy was obscured, blocked or avoided in individual case work and social work decision making'. The conclusion is drawn that poverty was so pervasive among service users that it became just a 'normative backdrop, something unremarkable and unremarked upon'. In such circumstances, the differential capacity of families and their constituent members to cope with and transcend disadvantage invites practitioners to draw on a lexicon of more individualised and 'victim-blaming' explanations for things going wrong. This results in a 'moral muddle' where abstract and plausible explanations linking people's difficulties to entrenched poverty might make sense; but assessment and intervention excluded this and drew on a quite different repertoire of (individualised) explanations and justifications for social workers' case decisions: 'The absence of a mutually informing relationship between abstract hypotheses about the impact of poverty and social work practice is striking' (Morris et al, 2018: 8).

Similarly, Cummins (2018: 151) describes this as the 'poverty paradox' in social work, observing that 'the profession commits itself to social justice and therefore to tackling poverty and inequality'; yet at the same time 'social workers' awareness of the impact of poverty seems to be low. This creates a tendency to view the causes of poverty as individual rather than structural'. This validates the world view associated with individualisation of responsibility and neoliberalism, rather than reflecting the value base of social work.

Alongside these theoretical and moral confusions, social workers are discouraged from engaging in broad policy debates in a number of other ways. Their work is structured to compartmentalise social problems; they are often working in contexts where they are 'on the other side of the fence' from service users (rationing resources and imposing constraints on them); they are too busy to document or report injustice where it is identified; and they are vulnerable to the predictable demands of organisational expectations and overbearing managerial preoccupations.

Renewed arguments have been advanced for a more 'poverty-aware' approach to practice (Krumer-Nevo, 2016); this is the starting point for a rather different level of engagement of practitioners, with 'systems' and 'structures' as well as with individuals. Indeed, it is relatively easy to make the abstract argument for a holistic form of practice which encompasses speaking *up* to the agencies and agendas which shape the practice context as well as (or instead of?) *down* to those who are the focal point for interventions.

It is, though, difficult to achieve this vision of a politically informed, change-oriented form of 'practice'. Usually, social workers have to step out of their day-to-day roles in order to achieve the space and support necessary to engage in making the case for policy reforms and structural realignment, and there are good examples of this happening, either through finding a voice through academic research or establishing credible and resourceful representative bodies and campaigning groups. But, if anything, this would simply reinforce our concerns about the 'paradox' identified by Cummins (2018). Here, as campaigners, social workers find themselves more or less confronting themselves, as practitioners.

Social work and social policy: 'sites of engagement'

This then leads us to seek out a more fine-grained understanding of both the contexts of social work activity and the policy worlds with which the profession engages. Indeed, there are a number of existing examples of social workers taking action to achieve policy change, and these may help us to understand what is possible and under what circumstances. Simpson (2014: 50) describes a number of 'sites of engagement' for social work. One of these examples is, predictably perhaps, 'outside working hours', involving collaboration between service users, trade unions and practitioners to challenge a local decision (by Birmingham City Council) which would have had adverse consequences in terms of reduced access to services. In this case 'the council lost a court case brought against it by service user groups' (Simpson, 2014: 50), which itself was informed by the experience and expert knowledge of social workers. Here, then, is an example of social workers contributing to agenda setting, albeit outside their direct practice role.

More clearly grounded in their practice, as Simpson observes, are some of the choices social workers are able to make about how services are organised and delivered, and whether or not they are prepared to implement (and legitimise) market-driven approaches to service delivery – he cites an example of practitioners refusing to involve themselves in one such scheme, thereby throwing both the strategy and the underlying philosophy into question (Cardy, 2010).

Sometimes, too, social workers are accorded legitimacy as contributors to discussions, as Simpson points out; for example, their views were sought in relation to the implementation of recommendations arising from a recent review of practice in children's services (the Munro Review). Social workers have also been included in discussions about equality in the workplace: 'Many of these social workers report their views and opinions have not always been dismissed, which in itself induces a level of surprise' (Simpson, 2014: 51).

On the other hand, there are instances where social workers' views are not taken into account, or acted upon. This is possibly because their experiences are not accorded validity. Everyday encounters with social disadvantage may thus be discounted because practitioners lack the credentials afforded to a detailed research study. Or they may question the preferred characterisation of those in poverty among the mainstream media. We should not underestimate the challenge for social work, and, indeed, many other active campaigners, simply to gain a platform. Here, then, is one of the core tasks for practitioners, their allies and representative bodies: to establish a credible basis for influencing policy.

The case of the British Association of Social Workers is significant. The association has a large membership (over 20,000), and it seeks to combine a role as the professional representative body for social work with a much more active campaigning function, claiming the authority to speak with and on behalf of service users on issues which affect them. The organisation thus maintains an active role in commenting on the impacts of government funding decisions and 'austerity', both on the capacity of social work services to deliver effective interventions, and on the direct impact of withdrawal of benefits and other forms of welfare support (of which the Boot Out Austerity campaign mentioned previously is one example).

BASW has come to represent itself as in equal parts a campaigning organisation and a representative professional body. Of course, social work is in some senses in a quite distinctive position, in that it can claim that it is acting consistently with its 'professional' responsibilities and values precisely when it does present evidence of oppression and gives voice to the daily hardships of those for whom it provides services. This is an important message for those engaged in frontline practice as social workers, whether or not they are members of BASW. A policy-oriented approach to practice is integral to our understanding of what constitutes a rounded professional social work identity.

SWAN, too, represents an important development in the recent history of social work in the UK, not just in the undeniably important sense of being a focal point for progressive campaigns against injustices impacting on service users. Like BASW, SWAN can arguably be seen as a significant rallying point for the legitimation of policy-oriented activism on the part of social workers. These developments represent a concrete example of 'network-making' (Castells, 2007) which has been identified as a critical element of progressive practice and the renegotiation of apparently fixed power relations in and around social work (Smith, 2013). Thus, practitioners are offered both a concrete base from which to organise and raise policy issues collectively, and a potential source of justification for their framing of these activities as 'professional' initiatives. Political activism and professional responsibilities are thereby brought into alignment.

Legitimation and policy-oriented practice

Arguably, there has been a shift towards a recognition of the social worker as being more than a problem-solving caseworker, adept at dealing responsively and effectively with crises in human relationships and social care. In addition, the capable practitioner can reasonably and legitimately intervene in the policy sphere to address and challenge the harmful effects of failings in service planning, organisation and resourcing, as part of the job. Of course, in the real world this aspiration is highly circumscribed: by pressures of time and caseload demands; by organisational and structural constraints; by managerial and supervisory pressures; by fears of isolation and lack of support; and by the limited experience and confidence of those who set out on the difficult road of challenging 'the system'. Nonetheless, there is a case for developing a typology of policy activity in social work *as practice*.

So, for example, Wilks (2012) makes the case for advocacy as a strong central feature of good practice; in turn citing Davies, reputedly one of the most apolitical of social work commentators: 'The social worker acts on behalf of a harassed mother in a face-to-face confrontation with a housing manager or landlord wanting to evict her and her family for non-payment of rent' (Davies, 1994: 90). Although the central focus of this intervention is the individual and her immediate housing problem, the rights-based approach taken necessarily involves arguing for a change in policy, even if only on an exceptional basis. This could still provide justification for pursuing wider and more substantial changes subsequently.

Wilks (2012: 9) also endorses a wider definition of social work advocacy (policy work), such as 'lobbying for resources for a local community perhaps, or ... to meet particular types of service user need'. Certainly much has been written in recent years about the importance of engaging and including service users in determining and shaping the nature of the services they require; but here, importantly, this can be seen to extend beyond the individual to a form of partnership with service users as a collective interest: 'The type of advocacy envisaged within this model is one that engages with social campaigns and in which power is firmly in the hands of service users. So user-led approaches to advocacy are particularly important in this context' (Wilks, 2012: 10). Social workers might act in support of service users' self-identified common interests and priorities for change, as in the case of the joint anti-austerity campaign grouping 'Social Workers & Service Users against Austerity'.

Beyond this, in the more formalised policy sphere, there is still a role for the practising social worker in engaging with key issues and pursuing arguments for change (or retention of key provision) in support of service users. Thus, attempts by government to initiate a risky and potentially damaging legislative change to enable outsourcing (and thereby privatisation) of children's services in 2014 were contested by 'social work' from the ground up. This initiative had its roots in a planned programme of change in children's services in Birmingham which would ostensibly generate a wider range of resources and service options than had previously been available in that local authority area, and it was suggested by government ministers that this could be achieved by 'developing capacity for delivering children's services *outside of local authorities*' (Children's Minister, quoted in Tunstill & Willow, 2017: 52).

Opposition to these proposals was widespread, and notably involved social workers 'on the ground', working alongside academics, lawyers, politicians, children's organisations, self-advocacy and lobby groups. The threat of profit being put before children's interests was sufficiently acute and potentially damaging to inspire practitioner involvement. This action was largely successful and the proposed legislation to pave the way for privatisation was rejected: 'The campaign was won. Children's social care rights were secure' (Tunstill & Willow, 2017: 57).

Thus, the:

> apparent choice for social work between ownership of a wider collective model of responsibility as a profession, or acting as proponents of individualised responsibility is a false one and should be firmly rejected. Professional social workers must be able to recognise and respond to individual needs, circumstances and wishes; we must be ready to challenge (and help change) harmful individual behaviour; we must also have a deep understanding of the social, economic, political and cultural contexts of people's lives; and we must seek to reduce and remove societal harms. (Tunstill & Willow, 2017: 58)

Concluding thoughts: social workers as policy activists

In conclusion, the underlying principle is that it is impossible for anyone active in human service delivery to be policy neutral. In other words, it is impossible to opt out of the debate, even for those who would suggest that the overriding priority is to focus on delivering help to service users in the most timely and effective way. The role of social work as a vehicle for achieving change in human relationships and social functioning inevitably establishes it as a manifestation of welfare policy. To the extent that practitioners are simply receiving instructions and implementing rules in accordance with policy expectations, they are acting for the representation and realisation of state-sponsored political objectives. In this context, not to engage with the process of negotiating, questioning or challenging those policy objectives is effectively to endorse them. In practice, though, as Lipsky (2010) has famously shown, this is not what welfare professionals actually do. They are active agents in interpreting, reframing and possibly even subverting the messages passed down to them from government or official bodies; and this immanent capacity to influence the realisation of policy is of fundamental importance to those concerned with enacting progressive change and achieving social justice through their work.

As Milne and colleagues (2014: 33) put it, in relation to social work and policy for older people:

> Social workers are trained to think critically about their practice and the wider context in which it is shaped and delivered. They have a key role in highlighting tensions

between the realities of older people's lives and narrow interpretations of accepted policy discourses, such as 'personalisation' and 'active ageing'.

The question, then, is not 'if' social workers are to adopt an active role as policy makers but 'how' they are to do so. Outlined here are a number of ways in which practitioners can pursue policy objectives, consciously and deliberately: as advocates, as collaborators and as public campaigners. In each of these roles, though, they can be seen as embodying social work values and a spirit of professionalism; rather than being typified as disloyal to their organisations, or even harmful to the interests of service users. Indeed, probably the best test of whether or not social workers' policy activities are ultimately to be seen as valuable is the response of service users to their actions for progressive change, and in defence of welfare principles.

Notes

[1] From the Modern Records Centre, University of Warwick, http://mrc-catalogue.warwick.ac.uk/records/CSN

[2] www.boot-out-austerity.co.uk/

References

Bailey, R. and Brake, M. (1976) 'Introduction: social work in the welfare state', in R. Bailey and M. Brake (eds) *Radical Social Work*, New York: Random House, pp 1–12.

BASW (2018) *Professional Capabilities Framework*. Available at: www.basw.co.uk/pcf

Bywaters, P., Brady, G., Sparks, T. and Bos, E. (2014) 'Child welfare inequalities: new evidence, further questions', *Child & Family Social Work*, 21(3): 369–80.

Cardy, S. (2010) '"Care matters" and the privatization of looked after children's services in England and Wales: developing a critique of independent social work practices', *Critical Social Policy*, 30(3): 430–42.

Castells, M. (2007) 'Communication, power and counter-power in the network society', *International Journal of Communication*, 1: 238–66.

Cummins, I. (2018) *Poverty, Inequality and Social Work*, Bristol: Policy Press.

Davies, M. (1994) *The Essential Social Worker* (3rd edn), Aldershot: Ashgate.

Dominelli, L. and MacLeod, E. (1989) *Feminist Social Work*, Basingstoke: Macmillan.

Jordan, B. and Drakeford, M. (2012) *Social Work and Social Policy under Austerity*, Basingstoke: Palgrave Macmillan.

Krumer-Nevo, M. (2016) 'Poverty-aware social work: a paradigm for social work practice with people in poverty', *British Journal of Social Work*, 46(6): 1793–1808.

Lavalette, M. and Penketh, L. (eds) (2013) *Race, Racism and Social Work*, Bristol: Policy Press.

Lipsky, M. (2010) *Street-level Bureaucracy* (30th Anniversary Edition), New York: Russell Sage Foundation.

Milne, A., Sullivan, M., Tanner, D., Richards, S., Ray, M., Lloyd, L., Beech, C. and Phillips, J. (2014) *Social Work with Older People: A Vision for the Future*, London: The College of Social Work. Available at: www.cpa.org.uk/cpa-lga-evidence/College_of_Social_Work/Milneetal(2014)-Socialworkwitholderpeople-avisionforthefuture.pdf

Morris, K., Mason, W., Bywaters, P., Featherstone, B., Daniel, B., Brady, G., Bunting, L., Hooper, J., Mirza, N., Scourfield, J. and Webb, C. (2018) 'Social work, poverty and child welfare interventions', *Child & Family Social Work*, 23(3): 364–72.

Norris, A. (2016) 'Social work in the Calais Jungle: "Others disapproved, and tried to sabotage our work"'. Available at: www.communitycare.co.uk/2016/12/14/social-work-calais-jungle-others-disapproved-tried-sabotage-work/

Robbins, R. and Cook, K. (2017) '"Don't even get us started on social workers": domestic violence, social work and trust – an anecdote from research', *British Journal of Social Work*, 48(6): 1664–81.

Simpson, G. (2014) 'Social workers affecting social policy in England', in J. Gal and I. Weiss-Gal (eds) *Social Workers Affecting Social Policy*, Bristol: Policy Press, pp 39–57.

Smith, R. (2013) 'Castells, power and social work', *British Journal of Social Work*, 43: 1545–61.

Thoburn, J. (2017) 'In defence of a university social work education', *Journal of Children's Services*, 12(2/3): 97–106.

Truell, R. (2015) 'Social workers' response to Europe's refugee crisis a testament to human hope'. Available at: www.theguardian.com/social-care-network/2015/nov/23/refugee-crisis-europe-austria-social-work

Tunstill, J. and Willow, C. (2017) 'Professional social work and the defence of children's and their families' rights in a period of austerity: a case study', *Social Work & Social Sciences Review*, 19(1): 40–65.

Wilks, T. (2012) *Advocacy and Social Work Practice*, Maidenhead: Open University Press.

3

Social work, problem definition and policy change in the US: the case of sex-trafficked youth

Lisa Werkmeister Rozas, Megan Feely and Jason Ostrander

Introduction

Society comprises the social relations, social institutions and dominant ideologies that are present in and influence the social order. Social work is known for servicing populations that are the most vulnerable and oppressed within the construct of a particular social structure. The profession recognises the role people and social forces play in an individual's everyday life. One of its ethical standards is to create substantial and lasting change through social action and advocacy across all levels: micro, meso and macro. This can be challenging when access to each level is often limited based on the reach of a particular intervention. This is particularly relevant when addressing a social problem whose consequences are evident on multiple levels. One example is the social problem of domestic minor sex trafficking (DMST). In the United States, social workers in the state of Connecticut, a small state located in the north-eastern region of the United States, were influential in changing the way DMST was addressed. Working with local and state officials, social workers helped to redefine the problem and facilitate a more socially just way of addressing the plight in which the victims of this problem find themselves.

This chapter presents two theoretical frameworks, structural social work theory and critical consciousness theory, and discusses their relevance to social work practice and policy change, related to DMST. We use a critical lens to examine the social problem of youth sex trafficking in the United States and illustrate social workers' participation in defining the social problem and creating an agenda to change particular policies and procedures in order to produce a better outcome for the victims of this crime. Structural social work theory facilitates an understanding of the larger social forces, social relations, institutional and individual ideologies that, once recognised, need to be confronted and transformed in order to address the social problem and facilitate policy change. The theory of critical consciousness is used to illustrate the process of developing an awareness of the systems of domination and subjugation that exist in society that is vital to identifying and redefining a social problem.

Most social problems have more than one origin. Such is the case with DMST, where a fundamental, though not sole source, is gender oppression. An outgrowth of capitalism, such oppression views women as a commodity and obliges them to face exploitation, discrimination, marginalisation and exclusion on both systemic and individual levels. In a society where patriarchy is a dominant ideology, women and girls are subjected to patriarchal misogyny. Designating women as objects that exist for the pleasure of serving men rationalises oppressive acts such as DMST. Similarly, children have been exploited and endangered by abuse, coercion, deprivation and invalidation, denying them full protection because of their powerlessness. Experiences of subjugation and oppression are common to women and children in the US; therefore it is essential that social workers are able to assess the impact that structural forces have on individuals' well-being. Using a critical lens, it is possible to understand how to challenge the oppressive social structures and advocate for change. Without such a lens, social problems are often portrayed as the result of individual deficits, reducing the likelihood of greater social change.

A critical perspective can be difficult to maintain, particularly when individualism is a cultural norm. The United States has a federalist system of government: individual states retain a significant amount of autonomy, resulting in different laws in different states. Additionally, the federal government holds very few executive powers (such as declaring war and regulating interstate commerce). States are generally responsible for most of the functions of government, including education, social services and public safety. Even some of the health and social service programmes, such as health insurance for poor or low-income persons that are available in all states and receive some funding from the federal government, vary significantly across states. One advantage of this system is that state governments can decide to increase protection or services for particular groups within their state without agreement from other states. One disadvantage is that services and rights may vary and when the social problem easily crosses borders then having differing laws lessens the overall efforts to eliminate the problem. However, making changes to policies in one state can ultimately have an effect on others. This is the case of the growing social problem of youth sex trafficking in the US.

Critical theories in social work

As outlined in the introduction to this book, policy practice is an essential aspect of social workers' professional activities. Such activities in the context of the policy cycle of social policy making focus on social workers as both individual and collective actors in their respective areas of practice, working with and on behalf of their clients. The social work perspective values the understanding of the structural context in which individuals exist to appropriately define social problems and identify policy changes intended to alleviate these problems. This perspective enables the non-pathologising of individuals, families and communities for the challenges they encounter. Within this context, this chapter reveals how social workers identified adolescent victims of sex trafficking and worked with them to develop practice solutions and advocate for legislative change. This process and the strategies utilised as part of it speak directly to the critical theoretical frameworks for this chapter – structural social work and critical consciousness.

Theory of structural social work

Structural social work theory, conceptualised by Moreau (1979, 1990) and refined by Mullaly (2007), weaves radical perspectives such as Marxism, critical race theory, feminism and intersectionality into one approach. This theory's focus is the unequal distribution of power and the oppression of groups that are non-white, heterosexual, cisgender and male (Pyles, 2009), providing a framework for social work practitioners to understand how society's social structures cause social problems. Mullaly (2007) identifies structural social work as a theory and an approach that explains phenomena such as sexism and racism, and dominant ideologies such as patriarchy and white supremacy. Structural social work theory describes and defines the social problems derived from the superstructure – social relations and social institutions. It also identifies the ideological substructure that undergirds society, influences all social institutions, determines social relations and identifies how they, as the root of the problem, must be changed (Mullaly, 2007).

One strategy for such change is through critical consciousness-raising which is creating the awareness of the role that power, privilege and oppression play on creating and sustaining individual and social dysfunction (Freire, 2000). In this case, consciousness-raising happened through making victims of DMST and social workers who engage with them more aware of personal, social, economic and political issues and how those in power utilise these issues to oppress and marginalise segments of US society. Through this process of critical consciousness development, victims of DMST and their social workers define the social problem as it relates to the larger societal structural forces that limit their ability to be in control of their lives and identify forms of empowerment (Mullaly & Keating, 1991).

Critical consciousness theory

Critical consciousness is important for social workers engaged in addressing social problems that stem from socially sanctioned structural violence, such as DMST. As described by Freire (2000), critical consciousness involves an awareness of the following forces: power, critical discourse, de-socialisation of stereotypes and human agency. Developing an awareness of these forces enables the worker not only to define the problem but also to include the transformation of institutional policies and practices on a structural level. Recognising the mechanisms of power that operate on a structural level helps practitioners to understand how the interconnection between oppressive ideologies, social systems and interpersonal interactions create a social problem. As a result, in the cycle of policy making there are several places where critical consciousness is vital to the process, the first being problem recognition and definition.

Recognising a problem and creating a plan to address it requires an understanding of the larger social forces that play a role in the creation and maintenance of the problem. When sexism and other forms of oppression are examined only from an individual interpersonal level, the influence of durable social, political and economic structures undergirding social hierarchies are excluded. Conversely, only considering oppressions as the result of faceless systems can obscure the ways in which we create and recreate forms of oppression through our actions and inactions, as well as diminishing the role individual human agency has in confronting change.

Second, in order for policy makers to identify a social problem and formulate a policy that addresses the multiple factors contributing to the inequities, they must be able to engage in, and analyse, the critical discourse surrounding the problem. One must use this awareness of social forces to redefine the problem so that the victims are not blamed. Recognising the critical discourse present in the testimonies of the individuals directly affected by the problem and presenting them to critical stakeholders is key in this process. This gives voice and power to the people most invested in the policy outcomes and highlights the process of human agency requisite in the process of policy making.

A third component of critical consciousness that is fundamental in the policy-making cycle includes the necessary function of de-socialisation. Very often society has developed stereotypes of individuals affected by social problems. Mostly, this function comes about in the policy cycle when policy makers are determining how the problem is introduced and defined. A variety of constituents need to be involved in the manner in which a problem is framed, not only to the public but also to policy makers. Trainings that de-socialise common stereotypes of 'problem youth' and develop awareness of the larger social forces that create the problem are necessary for the individuals who are most likely to be involved in enforcing the policy.

Youth and domestic sex trafficking

The system of trafficking in persons is often referred to as 'modern-day slavery' and in US federal laws it is defined as 'a crime involving the exploitation of someone for the purposes of compelled labour or a commercial sex act through the use of force, fraud, or coercion' (22 USC § 7102). Human trafficking affects individuals across the world, including in the United States, and is regarded as one of the most pressing human rights issues of our time. Human trafficking affects every community in the United States across age, gender, ethnicity and socioeconomic backgrounds. It is divided into trafficking for labour and sex. Sex trafficking is defined as

> the recruitment, harbouring, transportation, provision, obtaining, patronizing, or soliciting of a person for the purposes of a commercial sex act, in which the commercial sex act is induced by force, fraud, or coercion, or in which the person induced to perform such an act has not attained 18 years of age. (22 USC § 7102)

Sex trafficking of a minor is defined as benefiting from the commercial sex act of a person who is not 18 years old, whether or not coercion is involved. The US federal definition of sex trafficking of children is:

> To recruit, entice, harbour, transport, provide, obtain, or maintain by any means a person, or to benefit financially from such action, knowing or in reckless disregard of the fact that the person has not attained the age of 18 years and will be caused to engage in a commercial sex act. (18 USC § 1591)

In 2016 5593 trafficking cases were reported in the US. According to the US State Department, approximately '600,000 to 800,000 people are trafficked across international borders every year ... 80% are females and half are children'. Awareness of this issue in the United States has been increasing over the last 20 years, including the implementation of the key federal law, Trafficking Victims Assistance Program (TVAP) in 2000.

The overwhelming majority of DMST are women and girls (Shigekane, 2007). Research has directly linked DMST to the child welfare system – including foster care and juvenile justice services – and lack of parental support (Fong & Berger-Cardoso, 2010; Kotrla, 2010). One study estimates that over 80% of girls forced into child trafficking are engaged with public child welfare and family services (Gibbs et al, 2010) and within these homes minors experience child maltreatment, including physical and sexual abuse (Kotrla, 2010; Institute of Medicine and National Research Council, 2013). A history of abuse and neglect heightens the risk of exploitation (Smith et al, 2009) and those who ran away from their home or a child welfare placement were at greater risk for trafficking (Kotrla, 2010). A study of New York agencies who work with DMST found that almost 50% of those under the age of 18 were involved with child welfare and juvenile justice systems (Gragg et al, 2007).

Framed within neoliberal, patriarchal and racial paradigms, the roots of child trafficking are embedded in cultural, political and economic structures that prioritise male power and pleasure over the rights of females. Through a structural social work lens, the exploitation and victimisation of trafficked youths will be viewed and understood.

Domestic minor sex trafficking: an emerging problem

In Connecticut, a 13-year effort took place to deter the trafficking and sexual exploitation of minors (DMST) by transforming the state's legal and social environment. Framing this effort within structural social work theory can help identify critical areas to target in order to bring about lasting change. It argues the necessity and limits of social services in effecting real change, illustrates the key role of social workers in cross-discipline collaborations, and exemplifies that in order to protect vulnerable populations, change must occur on multiple levels.

Connecticut has been at the forefront of providing services and changing the laws to provide better protection for child victims of sex trafficking and commercial sexual exploitation. The Department of Children and Families (DCF) was a central player throughout this process. DCF is the state-wide department responsible for child protection, investigation of maltreatment, foster care services and many services to families with alleged or confirmed cases of maltreatment. Social workers have been a critical voice at each stage of this process. It has taken a series of law and policy changes to slowly alter the dynamic in the state around how power and privilege are exercised and who is perceived as a victim and is deserving of access to services.

Protections for power and privilege

In the United States, criminal codes can vary between states, as do the classification of specific crimes. In most states, there are two categories of criminal charges: misdemeanours and felonies (civil charges are different and separate). Within each of these categories, most states have sub-classifications for these crimes. In Connecticut, the classes are identified by letters: A, B, C and D. The most serious charge is classified as a Class A felony, the least serious a Class D misdemeanour.

Sexism and racism are often codified into laws in ways that perpetuate the oppression of women and people of colour. In 2004, the Connecticut laws that pertained to sexually exploited youth reflected institutional oppression and protected the privileged. In 2004, Connecticut treated 16- and 17-year-olds who were being paid for sex as adult prostitutes potentially being charged with Class A misdemeanour. At the same time, buyers were also charged with a Class A misdemeanour if the youth was at least 16 years old. The structure of the laws perpetuates existing systems of power and oppression, by race, age and gender. The majority of people who buy sex from minors are the most privileged in our society, white men between the ages of 30 and 50. Among youth who are sold for sex, Black and Latina girls are overrepresented (Farley et al, 2017). Additionally, while most sexually exploited youth are cis-gendered, heterosexual women, sexual minority youth, particularly transgender youth, are at very high risk of being exploited (Gangama et al, 2008; Wilson et al, 2009).

Social workers' changing policy

The current legal and services framework created to protect victims and punish perpetrators of DMST in the state of Connecticut is the result of a series of successive and overlapping cycles of social policy making. The concurrent cycles focus on different aspects of this complex problem. Comprehensively addressing the issue of DMST requires changes in criminal laws pertaining to: prostitution, patronising a prostitute and human trafficking. In addition, changes are also essential in civil laws, child welfare service eligibility, reporting requirements within and to child welfare, and awareness training for police and other professions. In Connecticut, each of these domains was addressed through successive cycles of social policy making to produce incremental, but consistent, legal changes.

The changes in Connecticut were led by the Trafficking in Persons (TIP) Council. The TIP council is currently led by a social worker, and many of the positions on the Council are held either by social workers or by representatives of agencies that employ many social workers. The TIP Council has been a critical player in shaping the cycle of social policy making at many stages in that process. Using stories and data from frontline agencies, many of which were staffed by social workers, the TIP Council developed strategic recommendations to effect gradual but dramatic changes to state statutes in four key areas of social policy. From the definition of the problem through to implementation of policy, and using critical discourse supported by examples from different agencies, social workers played a key role in the TIP Council. Social workers brought the experiences of trafficked youth and the implications of different policy changes back to the council. This helped to identify emerging issues in the field and bring the voices of victims to the fore.

Identified below is the iterative process through which state-level policy change occurred. There are three separate but interrelated problems with their corresponding cycles of change. Within each problem, a cycle was a successful effort in changing the state statute. Individually, each change was a small victory; collectively they have revolutionised the approach to DMST in Connecticut.

Problem definition 1: There were many domestic youths in Connecticut who were the victims of sex trafficking. These youth needed to be identified, treated as victims and engaged in services to address their trauma.

Cycle 1. DCF could provide services for suspected DMST youth, regardless of the perpetrator. Internally, DCF developed procedures for appropriate service provision. This change was important because prior to 2010, DCF was limited to cases involving child abuse or neglect, which involves a perpetrator who is the legal guardian or other person responsible for the child's care and custody. However, victims of DMST were often abused by persons other than a parent or guardian; therefore, they were not eligible for services. Internally, DCF developed procedures for appropriate service provision.

Cycle 2. Police had to alert DCF when they arrested a youth for suspected prostitution. Prior to this change, it was up to the individual officers whether they alerted DCF so the youth could receive services.

Cycle 3. Signage detailing the services available to victims of human trafficking and the toll-free numbers for state and federal anti-trafficking hotlines had to be posted at truck stops and certain establishments selling alcohol. The intent of this change was to increase the awareness of services among victims.

Cycle 4. Mandatory training was implemented for police and other professionals who may observe DMST. An important set of recommendations and policy changes included mandatory training for people, such as police, emergency room workers, judges or hotel/motel workers, who were likely to come into contact with DMST and could identify possible trafficking occurrences (Public Act 06-43). Police needed to be trained to screen youth for DMST rather than simply arresting them or returning them to their homes. Hotel and motel workers were identified for awareness training because their establishments were used by traffickers as a meeting point between the trafficked youth and buyers. Increased awareness was a successful approach, reflected by the dramatic increase in the number of youths referred to DCF from 4 in 2008 to over 150 in 2016 (DCF, 2017).

Cycle 5. The state government designated an agency or department to develop a comprehensive plan to address the mental health issues, substance abuse problems and other support needs for victims of trafficking.

Problem definition 2: Teenagers were not voluntarily working as prostitutes and the coercion they experienced, such as physical violence, was not obvious.

In other areas of the law 18 is considered the earliest age to be treated as an adult (for example, at 18 one can legally vote in the US). Under the age of 18, youth are considered to be less culpable for their actions. Raising the age at which someone could be charged with prostitution, or the age at which they could be assumed to be making a voluntary choice about their actions, to 18 took three cycles of change.

Cycle 1. Youth could be charged with prostitution at 16 years of age, but if the sexual acts were coerced the youth could apply to the Superior Court of the state to have the charges dropped. Preventing youth from having a criminal record for prostitution under this law required the youth to be informed and/or for the youth to have access to legal counsel. Additionally, the youth had to demonstrate they were a victim of trafficking to have the charges dropped.

Cycle 2. A criminal record of crimes committed while trafficked could be expunged. Although only a slight improvement from the first cycle, this allowed youth who were trafficked to have their charges removed from their record.

Cycle 3. The age at which someone can be charged with prostitution was raised from 16 to 18. This change made the age of culpability more consistent with other laws.

Problem definition 3: Paying for sex with a minor is a serious crime and should be punished accordingly. Under the state laws in 2006, buyers of sex from anyone 16 years and older, or who claimed they thought the person was older, had relatively low criminal charges and were only charged with a misdemeanour. Enticing a minor was a separate crime and could only be used if the youth was under 16 years of age. Additionally, the buyer could claim he was unaware of the person's age, avoiding the charge of a more serious crime.

Cycle 1. The charge of 'Patronizing a Prostitute' was increased from a misdemeanour to a Class C felony if the person being paid for sex was 16 or 17 years old. However, that still allowed for a loophole stating 'knew or reasonably should have known' the person was under 18 or the victim of trafficking.

Cycle 2. The more serious charge of 'Commercial Sexual Abuse of a Minor' replaced 'Patronizing a Prostitute' if the youth was under 18 years of age. This change reframed the action of paying for sex with a minor from one that was sanctioned by society (frequenting a prostitute) to one that was taboo (sexual abuse). The buyer could be charged with a Class A or B felony depending on the victimised youth's age. Additionally, as a result of these legal changes, the line between buyer and trafficker was blurred in this cycle because the definition of trafficking was expanded to include 'commissioning a sex act'.

By 2017, through the tireless efforts of many people, and social workers in particular, the laws no longer protected the powerful at the expense of vulnerable youth. The laws now protect youth, and the penalties have increased for the buyers of sex and for those who profit from selling sex with minors.

Discussion

Social workers in the United States are expected to be attuned to the myriad of structural forces that oppress based on economic, gender and/or racial status, as outlined in our Code of Ethics (National Association of Social Workers, 2008). In the case of sex trafficking, capitalism, patriarchy and gender oppression as well as white supremacy all play an important role in maintaining and perpetuating this social problem. These forces of oppression also have an influence on the way many social service workers interact with and conceptualise DMST youth.

Social workers employed within the Connecticut child welfare system are constrained by the types of interventions they can implement because of larger social and institutional policies. However, through successive cycles of change, the behaviour of DMST youth that previously had been categorised as 'running away' or being a 'rule breaker' is now perceived as a coerced action. To share this new perspective, the Department of Children and Families has been holding internal and external monthly training courses on DMST since 2009. These policies, along with expanding the understanding of child maltreatment to include abuse or neglect committed not only by a parent or legal guardian but also by individuals to whom they are not legally bound, have given youth greater protection and access to DCF services by allowing them to be categorised as 'uncared for'. Once the issue of DMST was identified in closely monitored youth, the full extent of the problem could be explored and identified in the general population of youth.

Such stereotypes and categorisations of youth involved in what has been perceived as criminal or deviant behaviour allows for a domino effect of how further actions are interpreted. Such implicit bias is firmly embedded in US society. Individuals who break the law are seen as morally weak and when such behaviour occurs in childhood or adolescence the individual is often seen as hopeless or unlikely to rehabilitate. In the case presented here, social workers working with victims of sex trafficking made it a point to analyse some of the dominant cultural norms, values and ideas about DMST youth that caused them to be categorised as criminals. Social work education in the United States has always stressed the importance of developing a critical consciousness to be used as a skill. Generally, this is taught in the foundation year of a social worker's education. This skill is particularly useful when social workers are taught policy analysis and advocacy.

The social workers in this case were skilled in their ability to recognise how socially sanctioned structural violence can manifest due to their social location and non-dominant status. They focused on how many dominant culture-centred institutions communicated and interacted with them differently and unfairly due to this status. What was often seen as the youth's lack of interest in being educated or their misplaced desire for material things was recognised as a child's developmental need to feel valued, cared for, protected and to feel a sense of belonging. Many youths experienced their pimp as providing these much-needed elements. Having this perspective in mind allowed the social workers to utilise critical consciousness when listening to the narratives of these marginalised youth, which are often misunderstood, ignored or unrecognised because they fail to follow the dominant cultural norms. Thus, these social workers not only understood cultural differences that existed between the youth and individuals who worked for and within the institutions, but the social relations of racism, sexism and ageism that created them. This allowed social workers to perceive critical laws and policies affecting DMST youth as mutable instead of unalterable constructs of societal mores. Using their skills, social workers develop language used with both DCF and the police that explained the social environmental impact on clients: a language of victimisation rather than criminalisation when referring to the youth who were engaging in commercial sex. This shift culminated in the change in the state laws to refer to purchasing sex from a minor from 'Patronizing a Prostitute', to the creation of the new legal charge of 'Commercial Sexual Abuse of a Minor'.

Critical consciousness was developed not only in social workers but also in the victims of DMST. They used their human agency to develop testimonials shared with policy makers. Having become aware of the socially sanctioned structural violence that was integral to their situation, these youth became engaged in the advocacy process. Activating awareness and engagement in advocacy is often difficult with highly stigmatised adolescents. However, their voices were included in the public testimony before the Connecticut General Assembly when the 2017 Act Concerning Human Trafficking was being debated. During the time for public testimony before the General Assembly, a survivor of DMST submitted testimony about her personal experience and also discussed the role of prior laws in law enforcement's ability to prosecute her traffickers. This demonstrated a sophisticated/high level of awareness about the laws and legal process and the role of advocacy in changing policies. Additionally, youth from the Center for Youth Leadership in Norwalk, Connecticut and the Mayor's Youth Leadership Council from the Stamford, Connecticut Youth Services Bureau submitted testimony. These youth organisations were advocating for specific changes to the required signage and reinforced the importance of DMST awareness training in high schools.

Conclusion

Critical theoretical frameworks provide a lens for both understanding how structural contexts negatively impact the well-being of marginalised populations and for identifying practices that promote structural change. In this chapter, we have presented two critical theoretical frameworks and have discussed their relevance for defining DMST as a problem needing a policy-based solution. We have used a critical lens to examine how earlier DCF policies and service delivery systems, which are interconnected, were unprepared to address the needs of the emerging and growing DMST youth population. Simultaneously, legislation in conjunction with law enforcement attitudes and behaviours had to be transformed in order to no longer perpetuate structural violence. We suggest that when social workers are educated about these theories, they will be able to engage in social justice-oriented emancipatory practice through appropriate problem definition and implementation of interventions that promote personal healing while simultaneously challenging oppressive elements of social systems and their underlying ideologies.

References

DCF (Connecticut State Department of Children and Families) (2017) *Human Anti-Trafficking Team*, HART 2016 Data, January–December 2016.

Farley, M., Golding, J. M., Matthews, E. S., Malamuth, N. M. and Jarrett, L. (2017) 'Comparing sex buyers with men who do not buy sex: new data on prostitution and trafficking', *Journal of Interpersonal Violence*, 32(23): 3601–25.

Fong, R. and Berger-Cardoso, J. B. (2010) 'Child human trafficking victims: challenges for the child welfare system', *Evaluation and Program Planning*, 33: 311–16.

Freire, P. (2000) *Pedagogy of the Oppressed* (Translated by M. Ramos, 30th anniversary edition), New York: Continuum.

Gangamma, R., Slesnick, N., Toviessi, P. and Serovich, J. M. (2008) 'Comparison of HIV risks among gay, lesbian, bisexual and heterosexual homeless youth', *Journal of Youth and Adolescence*, 37(4): 456–64.

Gibbs, D., Hardison Walters, J., Lutnick, A., Miller, S. and Kluckman, M. (2010) 'Services to domestic minor victims of sex trafficking: opportunities for engagement and support', *Children and Youth Services Review*, 54: 1–7.

Gragg, F., Petta, I., Bernstein, H., Eisen, K. and Quinn, L. (2007) *New York Prevalence Study of Commercially Exploited Children. Final Report*, Rockville, MD: Westat.

IOM (Institute of Medicine) and NRC (National Research Council). (2013) Confronting commercial sexual exploitation and sex trafficking of minors in the United States. Washington, DC: The National Academies Press.

Kotrla, K. (2010) 'Domestic minor sex trafficking in the United States', *Social Work*, 55(2): 181–87.

Logan, T. K., Walker, R. and Hunt, G. (2009) 'Understanding human trafficking in the United States', *Trauma, Violence, and Abuse*, 10(1): 3–30.

Moreau, M. J. (1979) 'A structural approach to social work practice', *Canadian Journal of Social Work Education*, 5(1): 78–94.

Moreau, M. J. (1990) 'Empowerment through advocacy and consciousness-raising: implications of a structural approach to social work', *Journal of Sociology and Social Welfare*, 17(2): 53–67.

Mullaly, R. (2007) *The NEW STRUCTURAL SOCIAL WORK* (3rd edn). Don Mills, Ontario: Oxford University Press.

Mullaly, R. and Keating, E. (1991) 'Similarities, differences and dialectics of radical social work', *Journal of Progressive Human Services*, 2(2): 49–78.

National Association of Social Workers (NASW) (2008) Code of ethics. Retrieved from https://www.socialworkers.org/About/Ethics/Code-of-Ethics/Code-of-Ethics-English

Pyles, L. (2009) *Progressive Community Organizing*, New York: Routledge.

Shigekane, R. (2007) 'Rehabilitation and community integration of trafficking survivors in the United States', *Human Rights Quarterly*, 29: 112–36.

Smith, L. A., Vardaman, S. A. and Snow, M. A. (2009) *The National Report on Domestic Minor Sex Trafficking: America's Prostituted Children*, Arlington, VA: Shared Hope International.

Wilson, E. C., Garofalo, R., Harris, R. D., Herrick, A., Martinez, M., Martinez, J. and Belzer, M. (2009) 'Transgender female youth and sex work: HIV risk and a comparison of life factors related to engagement in sex work', *AIDS and Behavior*, 13(5): 902–13.

4

The voices of Italian social workers: from a pilot anti-poverty intervention to a national policy

*Matteo D'Emilione, Giovannina Assunta Giuliano,
Paolo Raciti and Paloma Vivaldi Vera*

Introduction

According to the indicators commonly used at the European level, the period in which the economic crisis was at its peak in Europe was between 2012 and 2013. In Italy, this is especially true in terms of child poverty but also in terms of absolute poverty for different types of households.

In a situation of extreme difficulty, economic resources available for the welfare system in order to protect the most vulnerable showed a reducing trend, making the situation even more complicated to manage for the social services at local level.

With a view to turn the tide and reopen the debate on the need for a minimum income scheme in Italy, between 2013 and 2015 the Italian Ministry of Labour and Social Policies implemented an experimental measure to fight poverty in 12 metropolitan cities.[1]

Therefore, it could be argued that, triggered by the economic crisis and the lack of a national measure to fight poverty, poverty became a prominent subject on the policy agenda (Kingdon, 1984; Beland & Howlett, 2016).

The intervention provided economic support and a personalised social and employment inclusion project for families with children living in conditions of economic hardship (or families with a disabled child or a pregnant woman) and low work intensity. This personalised project was a contract between the family and the local service system, involving *co-responsibility* in its implementation: the integrated services system committed to provide one or more services and the beneficiary, the family, committed to act on the basis of the personalised project.

The measure, the so-called *Carta Acquisti Sperimentale* (CAS; experimental social card or new social card in English) was designed as an experimental measure in view of the implementation of the national measure to fight poverty, called *Sostegno per l'Inclusione Attiva* (SIA, support for active inclusion) recently changed to *Reddito di Inclusione* (REI, inclusion income).

According to a mixed evaluation approach (Bamberger, 2012), complementary to the counterfactual one,[3] a qualitative evaluation of the measure's implementation process was developed in order to analyse and understand the different stakeholders' perspectives (White & Day, 2016).

Taking into account the elements briefly described above, this chapter proposes two different interpretations: on the one hand it provides the main findings from the evaluation activity; on the other, it tries to provide a first interpretation of 'if and how' some of the instances and problems expressed by social workers involved in the implementation of the measure were taken into account by political decision makers during the transition between the experimental step and implementation at national level.

The opportunity to also take part in the institutional round tables where the new national measure was drawn up (although it was not a specific objective of our research project) made it possible for the research group to be part of a process of a developing policy.

Therefore, if we read the facts through the lens of the policy learning theory (Heclo, 1974; Trein 2015), we could provide a very wide picture of the situation: we explored the three levels of analysis (micro, meso and macro) used within this theoretical framework (Moyson et al, 2017).

The aim of this chapter is therefore to provide insights about an evaluation that has seen social workers strongly involved as 'policy implementers',[4] pointing out how and why some lessons have been conducive to policy change at national level and others have not.

The chapter consists of four sections. The first briefly presents the research approach and the content analysis methodology (grounded theory and the hermeneutic analysis of texts) used for the analysis of the narrative material collected and the main features of the institutional context in which the pilot scheme (the new social card) took place, testing the adaptability of local services to the new measure. The second section focuses mainly on social workers' views on the measure's overall implementation (in particular, governance and conditionality), providing significant evidence for the third section, where we analyse if and how the experience and evaluation of social workers were considered in the measures introduced at national level, viewing the evaluation process as an opportunity structure for social workers to influence the policy process. The last section is dedicated to highlighting the lessons learned from this experience.

Methodological framework and institutional context: key features

Before entering into the details of the positions and perceptions expressed by social workers during the focus groups, it is fitting to provide some indications of the type of work carried out within the evaluation activity and some clarifications on the main characteristics of the functioning of the Italian local welfare system.

The qualitative evaluation of the measure was carried out through: (i) semi-structured interviews with the project manager of the Ministry of Labour and Social Policies (MLSP), with the project staff members of the National Institute for Social Security (INPS) and with the CAS Municipal officials; (ii) focus groups with local social workers in each of the cities involved (Table 4.1).

The interview with the MLSP's project manager covered the different steps of the implementation process pointing out problems and strengths found for each of them and any corrections to be made to the national measure, as an extension of the experiment throughout the country.[5]

The interview with the INPS staff members aimed at describing the functions and tasks performed by the implementing body, its managing structure for the execution of the functions envisaged by the measure and the management of information flows activated. It is important to underline that INPS was the body responsible for conducting the means-test procedure and the provision of the cash benefit to the eligible households.

Concerning the municipal officials responsible for the intervention, the following aspects were investigated:

Table 4.1: Summary of in-depth studies carried out for the evaluation

Semi-structured interviews	Focus groups
• 1 Interview with the policy-maker (MLSP)	• 11 Focus groups set up
• 1 Interview with the Implementing Body (INPS)	• 87 Social workers involved
• 11 Interviews with the measure's local officials and their staff	• 19 Hours and 43 minutes of recorded and transcribed discussions
	• Use of Atlas.ti specialised software with theoretical reference to *Grounded Theory* and the *Hermeneutic Process*

1. The identification and selection criteria for the beneficiaries of the measure; new users identified and their specific characteristics.
2. The method of household supervision, based on the family's project and how conditionality had been applied.
3. The method for managing the measure: intervention areas with highest investments; monetary disbursement; integration of services for social and employment inclusion; human resources put in place for the creation of multidisciplinary teams; use of additional resources in the implementation of measures.
4. The communication and information flow system implemented by the institutional network (Poste Italiane and the MLSP).
5. The monitoring and evaluation plan of the CAS: positive aspects and problems.

In this chapter we will specifically concentrate on the analysis of the focus groups' narrative material. The analysis was carried out using the Grounded Theory methodology (Glaser & Strauss, 1967). In fact, almost 90 workers from different public services involved in the implementation of the measure (social services, employment services, health services, schools and the third sector) participated in 11 focus groups, during which the main topics introduced by the experiment were examined in depth: the multidimensional analysis of needs and the creation of multidisciplinary teams; children's wellbeing; conditionality versus co-responsibility; and the effectiveness of the projects implemented.

When we look at a brief description of the institutional context in which the measure was developed, in most territories the intervention was launched through the involvement of existing services and the use of the municipalities' own resources. The design and management of the social services system in Italy involves different public responsibility levels, mainly regional and municipal (Bifulco & Centemeri, 2008). At municipal level, most of the resources were allocated to families with children, disabled and elderly people and, residually, to fight poverty and social exclusion, to support immigrants and people with addictions.

It is necessary to highlight the fundamental role that municipalities have in the planning and management of the social service system at local level in light of the number of municipalities (about 8000). This 'administrative issue' is obviously a core problem when a national social policy is supposed to guarantee homogeneity at the territorial level in terms of quality of public services (and among these, social services). The so-called 'minimum levels of assistance', regulated by specific laws in the past, had never actually been applied in practice (OECD, 2017).

At the regional level, specific programmes to fight poverty have been developed over the last few years, increasing the heterogeneity of welfare systems and the complexity of coordinating a national measure with different regional measures. As a general consideration, it could be argued that geography matters and therefore being poor in different Italian cities or regions implies quite different levels of welfare support.

As already mentioned in the introduction to this chapter, the interplay between economic crisis, social policy budget constraints (at all levels) and complex governance represents the context in which the local services found themselves working.

Furthermore, other factors than budget constraints that negatively affect social work practice should be highlighted: the limited public acknowledgment of their role; their professional boundaries; the need for better integration between different fields of intervention (Barberis & Boccagni, 2014).

By making the CAS an opportunity for reflection and learning in view of the launch of the SIA, the main findings that emerged from interviews with the officials responsible for the experiment can be summarised as follows:

1. The administrative and organisational capacity and the ability to identify new solutions to meet the management challenges imposed by the process to implement the measure are identified as a success factor.
2. The supervision of new users previously unknown to social services is recognised as an added value to the process.
3. If reinterpreted in a non-sanctioning manner, conditionality may be an effective tool for users' access to services.
4. It is necessary to restore centrality to social services in the families' choice to undertake the assessment by integrating the multidisciplinary team with employment service employees in those cases where supporting families only require training and/or employment guidance.

Furthermore, in view of the experiment's planned expansion throughout the country, local officials in charge of the implementing the measure reported the need for investment in training services, thus enriching activation paths.

Eventually, a robust national and regional direction in overall management of the measure was strongly advocated to foster the connections required at the welfare, employment and local system training levels. Without this support the sustainability of social and economic reintegration paths will be reduced.

As we will see later, several of the main indications expressed during interviews and in inter-institutional discussion meetings by the authorities pioneering the CAS were incorporated in the regulatory act which extends the SIA to the entire country. In particular, the experiment's implementation system was amended by abolishing strict job requirements in the selection of beneficiary households.

Implementation of the measure: social workers' points of view

According to social workers, the CAS, as a measure of economic relief and social support through supervision and support towards social and employment autonomy, was an additional tool at the disposal of social services in the framework of their institutional action. In this sense, the implementation of the measure has strengthened actions against poverty based on the provision of economic subsidies, enabling significant 'system learning' and the consolidation of intervention centred on the activation of the beneficiaries. The same motivation approach has pushed social services to improve and strengthen the level of cooperation and collaboration with other services, in particular with employment services (public or private) and profit and non-profit organisations. Moreover, the CAS' management has fostered the development and consolidation of multidisciplinary teams. By stimulating intra- and inter-services collaboration, the CAS has provided the opportunity to repair the fragmentation that often exists in local welfare systems, with overlapping and uncoordinated interventions. However, it was not possible to create multidisciplinary teams in all cities, especially in school and health services. It was clear that the weaker the local network, the more likely was the intervention to be ineffective in some contexts.

Concerning the governance of the implementation of the measure, several weaknesses were highlighted by the social workers. Many were linked to the temporal misalignment of the complex implementation process (Rogers, 2008). The lack of connection between the provision of the economic benefit and the start of social services support caused some important problems in the management of the measure: (i) difficulty of combining social work practice with conditionality; (ii) duration of the household projects often too limited to obtain appreciable results; (iii) impossibility of monitoring and checking the progress of personalised projects; (iv) delays and demotivation of users; (v) complications in the administrative management of the CAS; (vi) delays in the administration of the evaluation tools, including the impossibility of administering the ex post questionnaire to beneficiary households once the economic benefit had been received.

This time lag had a major impact on social services which, in many cases, generated significant extra work causing a work overload which sometimes led to social workers' progressive lack of commitment and demotivation.

Deepening some of the abovementioned issues, it can be pointed out that one of the principal matters that emerged during the focus groups was the compatibility between social work practice and some characteristics of the measure, particularly those connected to the use of conditionality, the annual limit constraints, the randomisation and the heavy workloads for social workers.

The methodological choice of randomly generating two groups of beneficiaries that were distinct from one another by the presence or absence of a personalised project (in-kind intervention), generated significant difficulties for the service employees: (i) users who did not need to be supported were included in the treatment group; (ii) beneficiaries with needs and issues that would have effectively required support by the services were included in the control group.

The consequence of this choice was, on the one hand, the 'bureaucratic' implementation of social service support in those cases where this was not necessary; on the other hand, the increase of mistrust among some new users who saw themselves as being obliged to accept a supervised process despite not having expressed the need for it.

From an implementation point of view, according to the social workers there was a presence of two seemingly contradictory interpretative elements: the evaluation and monitoring phase has been predominantly interpreted as extra work, while the tools used have been recognised as a resource for the supervision work and support routinely carried out by the services. This apparent contradiction can be explained by considering, in a complementary manner, some descriptive elements of the social workers' experience in the social services system: (i) being unaccustomed to the writing and use of structured tools; (ii) lack of staff and work overload of social workers; (iii) the widespread disposition to learn and innovate their own operating practices.

Randomisation, as certain social workers have pointed out, has had a significant impact on the definition of the personalised project and especially on the reporting of macro types of users generated by the CAS access criteria: *long-term users* already in the care of services and *new users* predominantly characterised by the need for work also as a result of the recent economic crisis. The *annual limit constraint* was considered to be a contradiction according to the perspective of a relationship-based approach (Wilson et al, 2011): time is needed for the service user to build and maintain trust and for the practitioner to engage with and intervene in the complexity of the individual's world. In this perspective, the experimental intervention confirmed how the duration of the interventions cannot be defined a priori on administrative or regulatory bases, but should be made driven by the needs of disadvantaged people, taking into account their biography, their needs and the material and non-material resources available.

The annual limit was possible to contain and manage in a system perspective to the extent that: (i) the CAS was inserted into a pre-existing working procedure and rooted in a system where local services were functioning and effective; (ii) it was possible to consider the measure as an additional resource for services within a process already in place and independent of the life cycle of the CAS.

As a final point emerging from the analysis of the debate, linked to the supervision process, *conditionality* is analysed by predominantly highlighting its methodological limitations.

These limitations (see also Fletcher et al, 2016) and their relationship with the supervision process are at the source of two opposing methods of application of conditionality. Conditionality was applied in a bureaucratic manner, complying with the indications of the regulatory act establishing the measure; at the same time, this was interpreted in a soft, non-rigid and functional manner according to the specific dynamics of supervising the individual beneficiary.

With regard to the first method, the obligation linked to conditionality was limited to the mere signing of the contract with the users, given that this signature provided entitlement to receive the economic benefit. Therefore, conditionality was limited to the fulfilment of bureaucratic and administrative formalities.

In contrast, the *soft application* of conditionality envisaged an approach that used conditionality as a tool for user engagement by setting up the relationship on the basis of dialogue and negotiation, allowing sanction to be residual. A *soft approach* to conditionality has been endorsed, favouring more effective support for the most vulnerable families that could not fulfil some of the commitments made, thus avoiding the imposition of prescriptive models. In this sense, the experience gained in previous experiments was important in some contexts, making it possible to circumscribe the matter of conditionality not as a vexatious fulfilment of a contractual form (or essentially as a sanction agreement), but as an engagement and incentive mechanism for users, and exercised in a relationship based on the principles of co-responsibility between the social worker and the beneficiary. In particular, the provision of tools and various measures (ancillary work, educational services, training courses and internships) was decisive for social and employment inclusion. The conditional mechanism was also mitigated where the institutional offer was weaker or the conditions of the beneficiary families were fragile.

From micro to macro: how much were the social operators heard?

The SIA measure officially entered into force about one year after the end of the CAS experiment (June 2015) and, with some important remedial actions, would have extended the pilot measure at national level. Specifically, from early September 2016, social services opened their doors to the SIA's potential beneficiaries. To what extent, therefore, has the SIA's implementation actually taken into account the requests for change made by social workers and the local officials of the services involved in the experimental intervention? To answer this question it is necessary to highlight at least two significant aspects that characterise the phase of transition from one measure to the other.

The first aspect concerns the Ministry of Labour and Social Policy's establishment, since the end of 2015, of a Coordination Round Table for the launch of the SIA ('National Round Table for Social Planners'[6]) involving a diversity of stakeholders charged with defining the fundamental guidelines for the implementation of the national measure.[7]

This coordination mechanism represented a real *political arena* (Lowi, 1964) where representatives of the central government, the regions, the main metropolitan areas, the association of Italian municipalities and the national social security institution periodically met. The involvement of the central level of the various participants was obviously voluntary, therefore not all the Italian regions decided to be actively involved. With the creation of this coordinating body the Ministry sought to define the 'rules of the game' given the new significant financial resources dedicated to fight poverty dealing with deeply different regional welfare systems. In this perspective, we could usefully recall the words of Wildavsky (1973: 143) when he states that 'coordination thus becomes a form of coercive power' or 'another word for consent' which, in our case, could help in achieving what you don't have: homogeneity.

The second significant aspect, related to the first, is the launch of a national plan dedicated to the strengthening of social services financed by the European Community.[8] While this makes it possible to imagine an overall improvement in the level of social services involved in the SIA provision, it also renders the measure's institutional system extremely complex.

As mentioned above, in addition to the region's institutional focal points, some representatives of the metropolitan areas' social services involved in the experiment also participated in the work of the national round table. They were very active in covering the role of experimenters and, simultaneously, implementers of the new measure under discussion. They were, therefore, witnesses of a series of lessons learned during the pilot intervention and promoters of change with respect to problematic issues to be addressed and resolved.

In order to summarise the central level's ability to consider the requests for change made by the social workers involved in the experiment and, subsequently, in the work of the institutional round table, we have constructed a simple reading table (Table 4.2) that links the main requests and the associated transposal level in implementing the new measure.

As observed in Table 4.2, most of the issues have been transposed, or partly addressed, in the national measure's extension phase. So why were some demands of social workers and other stakeholders fulfilled and others were not?

If we refer to the job requirement, whose rigidity and restriction had created significant problems in access to the experimental measure, the decision maker (the Ministry of Welfare) could not help but recognise the evidence available, making these requirements less stringent within the individual/household assessment process. From the social workers' point of view, too many people in need had not been considered eligible because of these requirements.

A similar argument can be made regarding the establishment of a national steering committee, a recommendation implemented through the setting up of the round table for social planners and the focus on strengthening social services through a dedicated national operational programme. With respect to the latter point, as already discussed, the use of European financial resources has made this measure's governance even more complex, potentially replicating governance problems that already emerged during the experiment. Thus, a coordinating body was perceived as essential by the policy maker, although a

Table 4.2: Transposal level of requests reported by operators

Requests for change	Considered	Only partially considered	Not considered
Change job requirement	X		
Adoption of a model for access to the measure at the counter		X	
Definition of the supervision duration depending on necessity		X	
Intercept extreme poverty situations		X	
Need to strengthen services	X		
Establishment of a national steering committee	X		
Better use of prepaid card		X	
Mitigate conditionality			X
Improve the management of information flows			X
Careful use of the counterfactual approach		X	
Greater attention to communication role	X		
Greater integration with employment services		X	

Source: Elab. INAPP

specific method of coordination had not been developed, making its functioning less effective than it could have been.

The request regarding the application of conditionality seems, instead, to have been almost completely ignored, although reinforced in some respects. With respect to the issue of conditionality, it can be argued that the approach towards a stronger (or better, hyper-regulated) conditionality seems to be in line with what happens in other European countries (especially the UK), in the fallacious belief that more conditionality necessarily means more effectiveness (Griggs & Evans, 2010) or that welfare dependency is a trap to avoid in order to fight the poor's laziness (Banerjee et al, 2016). In this sense, the point of view of social workers and employment service employees is more oriented towards the capacity of the welfare system to guarantee, upstream, the social reintegration of disadvantaged individuals or households than to provide sanctions.

The management of information flows is still greatly lacking to date. The difficulty in dealing with the issue of management of information flows among the many actors involved in the implementation of the measure is essentially connected to two aspects: first, the development complexity of a single IT platform valid for a very large number of administrations; secondly, more relevant to the practice of the social workers themselves, the significant digital divide all over the country. In many cases, especially (but not only) in the south of Italy, the presence of an updated computer, enabling efficient working, cannot be taken for granted. From this point of view, the policy maker and the many administrations involved were faced with an extremely complex issue with limited room for action in the short term.

Finally, some brief recommendations with regard to requests *only partially* taken into consideration, a category that groups most of the recommendations identified: the solutions found in the measure's extension phase only partially resolve the problems highlighted. For example, in the case of the request for greater flexibility in managing the duration of users' supervision based on the actual needs, the SIA provides for a non-extendable fixed duration for the disbursement of cash (12 months). From the social services' point of view, this remains a fixed variable that affects the construction of the personalised project. Therefore, financial constraints are the most plausible explanation for a failure to extend the duration of the personalised project.

Another example concerns the ability to create a network with the employment service system. In this respect, the Ministry of Labour has moved forward by establishing an additional institutional round table for the coordination of social services and employment services (systems that relate to the management of different types of entities): however, almost a year after the beginning of the work no tangible operating results had been achieved. In the Italian context, the integration (or even the simple coordination) between social and employment services has always represented a delicate and difficult situation for two main reasons: the first concerns the different administrative responsibilities between the two type of services, at municipal level for the social services and at regional level for the employment public services; the second involves the different types of users they work with. In the first case, different administrative bodies mean different management and different work codes, which leads to more complicated relationships. Regarding the second question, although in recent years due to the economic crisis there has been a certain overlap between users of social services and employment services, social workers and employment service employees have different approaches and different objectives, depending on users' needs. Consistent with these differences, one of the foremost issues that emerged within the institutional coordination mechanism was the need for specific training for both types of employees.

Lessons learned

The CAS has been a considerable challenge for the 11 metropolitan cities, for the institutional stakeholders involved, for the social workers and even for the recipients.

The policy maker (Ministry of Labour) had to address issues that were only partly predictable at the time of drawing up the measure: the difficulty of reconciling the ambitious objectives with the times and the practice of political and administrative processes as well as social work practice; the subsequent difficulty of establishing and complying with the timescales envisaged by the legislation; the complexity associated with the construction of an effective information system and its repercussions for the management, monitoring and evaluation capacity of the measure itself; the heterogeneity of the regional contexts and its effects on a policy's implementation. The integrated approach between different services has been fostered within a complex governance structure which could sometimes create serious challenges to quick and effective integration of social service delivery (OECD, 2015).

However, alongside the management of these problems, the high level of commitment should be stressed, which developed within the implementation process of the measure in a logic of 'mutual learning' between institutions. Consistent with this approach, the national coordination mechanism of social planners represented a policy arena in which exchange of knowledge among different stakeholders occurred, fostering the so-called 'policy transfer' (Benson & Jordan, 2011).

In this context, the point of view of the social workers has found, not without difficulties, an institutional space in which to lay claim to the specificities and autonomy of social work practice, supported by the experience of the pilot intervention and by some outcomes of the evaluation process.

Taking into account the financial constraints and the complex governance of the national measure, we have highlighted in this chapter how some aspects have nevertheless been taken into consideration by the policy maker, demonstrating an openness to change and to policy reformulation.

The path that has just started to reinforce the national anti-poverty measure (Raitano et al, 2018) in which the role of social services continues to be fundamental is not only an incentive for research on the policy process (and its effects) but also for the social workers themselves. As a matter of fact, they will increasingly need to adjust to new ways of working, fostering integration with other services and developing new skills: will they be able to do it? Or rather, will the conditions be created for them to succeed? According to our work, a step forward has been made, but we will see how the process develops in the future.

Notes

[1] The research data refers to 11 cities (Bari, Bologna, Catania, Florence, Genoa, Palermo, Milan, Naples, Turin, Venice and Verona). Details are contained in the evaluation report by INAPP 'Verso il Sostegno per l'inclusione attiva: il processo di implementazione della Carta acquisti sperimentale (un'indagine qualitativa)'. The city of Rome, which started its experimental intervention in June 2016, has not been taken into account in this research.

[2] A monthly subsidy (between €230 and €400 depending on the household's composition) was paid to beneficiaries for one year.

[3] The experiment's design, based on a logic of counterfactual assessment, envisaged that not all beneficiary households (BHs) would be supported through a personalised project since this arrangement was planned for at least half and not more than two-thirds of BHs. The so-called 'treatment group' received cash and in-kind services; the control group received only the monetary subsidy.

[4] In Italy, social workers (known as 'assistenti sociali') are specific practitioners with tertiary-level qualifications enrolled in a specific register and working mainly in the public sector. The Italian Social Workers Association (CNOAS) was established by law in 1993.

[5] Data and general information about SIA from the point of view of the Ministry of Labour are available at: http://cdss.sta.uniroma1.it/files/site/Abstract/Tangorra_Raffaele.pdf

[6] The round table met twice in 2015 and once in 2016.

[7] The members of the research group, as mentioned in the introduction, had the opportunity to participate as experts, having also carried out the evaluation of the pilot intervention.

[8] National Operational Programme for Inclusion 2014–20 funded by the European Social Fund (ESF).

References

Bamberger, M. (2012) 'Introduction to mixed methods in impact evaluation', Inter Action and Rockfeller Foundation. Available at: www.alnap.org/resource/8079

Banerjee, A., Hanna, R., Kreindler, G. and Olken, B. A. (2016) 'Debunking the stereotype of the lazy welfare recipient: evidence from cash transfer programs'. Available at: https://economics.mit.edu/files/12488

Barberis, E. and Boccagni, P. (2014) 'Blurred rights, local practices: social work and immigration in Italy', *British Journal of Social Work*, 44, Supplement 1: 70–87.

Beland, D. and Howlett, M. (2016) 'The role and impact of the multiple-streams approach in comparative policy analysis', *Journal of Comparative Policy Analysis: Research and Practice*, 18(3): 221–27.

Benson, D. and Jordan, A. (2011) 'What have we learned from policy transfer research? Dolowitz and Marsh revisited', *Political Studies Review*, 9: 366–78.

Bifulco, L. and Centemeri, L. (2008) 'Governance and participation in local welfare: the case of the Italian Piani di Zona', *Social Policy Administration*, 42(3): 211–27. Available at: https://doi.org/10.1111/j.1467-9515.2007.00593.x

Fletcher, D., Flint, J., Batty, E. and McNeill, J. (2016) 'Gamers or victims of the system? Welfare reform, cynical manipulation and vulnerability', *Journal of Poverty and Social Justice*, 24(2): 171–85. Available at: http://shura.shu.ac.uk/12232/

Glaser, B. G. and Strauss, A., L. (1967) *The Discovery of Grounded Theory: Strategies for Qualitative Research*, New Brunswick, NJ: Aldine Transaction.

Griggs, J. and Evans, M. (2010) 'A review of benefit sanctions. The impact of sanctions in benefit systems, how they have been used and the experiences of claimants'. Available at: www.jrf.org.uk/report/review-benefit-sanctions

Heclo, H. (1974) *Modern Social Policy in Britain and Sweden: From Relief to Income Maintenance*, New Haven, CT: Yale University Press.

Kingdon, J. W. (1984) *Agendas, Alternatives and Public Policies*, Boston: Little, Brown.

Lowi, T. (1964) 'American business, public policy, case-studies, and political theory', *World Politics*, XVI: 677–715.

Moyson, S., Scholten, P. and Weible, M. (2017) 'Policy learning and policy change: theorizing their relations from different perspectives', *Policy and Society*, 36(2): 161–77.

OECD (2015) *Integrating Social Services for Vulnerable Groups: Bridging Sectors for Better Service Delivery*, Paris: OECD Publishing. Available at: http://dx.doi.org/10.1787/9789264233775-en

OECD (2017) *Economic Surveys Italy. Overview*. Available at: http://www.oecd.org/eco/surveys/italy-2017-OECD-economic-survey-overview.pdf

Raitano, M., Natili, M. and Jessoula, M. (2018) 'Two decades on, Italy finally introduces a national minimum income scheme', ESPN Flash Report 2018/6.

Rogers, P. (2008) *Using Programme Theory to Evaluate Complicated and Complex Aspects of Interventions*, Los Angeles, London, New Delhi and Singapore: SAGE Publications. Available at: https://journals.sagepub.com/doi/pdf/10.1177/1356389007084674

Trein, P. (2015) 'Literature report: a review of policy learning in five strands of political science research', INSPIRES Working Paper. Available at: https://ssrn.com/abstract=2707344

White, C. and Day, L. (2016) *National Evaluation of the Troubled Families Programme Process evaluation. Final Report*, London: Department for Communities and Local Government. Available at: www.gov.uk/government/uploads/system/uploads/attachment_data/file/560500/Troubled_Families_Evaluation_Process_Evaluation.pdf

Wildavsky, A. (1973) 'If planning is everything, maybe it's nothing', *Policy Sciences*, 4(2): 127–53.

Wilson, K., Ruch, G., Lymbery, M. and Cooper, A. (eds) (2011) *Social Work: An Introduction to Contemporary Practice*, Harlow: Pearson.

Part II
Social work interests in policy formulation and decision making

Part II

5

Social reform in the US: lessons from the Progressive Era

Francisco Branco

Social casework and social reform

As argued in previous work (Branco, 2016), social reform was, to paraphrase Richmond (1922: 223), one of the forms of social work present in the thoughts of the most prominent and seminal pioneers of social work in the Progressive Era.[1] Whereas the conceptualisation of and engagement in social reform of Jane Addams is relativity well known and recognised (compare, among others, Muncy, 1991; Lengermann & Niebrugge, 1998, 2007; Lengermann & Niebrugge-Brantley, 2002; MacLean & Williams, 2012; Williams & MacLean, 2016), this vision was not exclusive to the settlement workers. It could also be observed, albeit differently, as present in the thought and work of Mary Richmond and other social case workers (Richmond, 1906/1930; Pittman-Munke, 1985; Agnew, 2004).

A legacy of the social work pioneers of the Progressive Era, policy making (or the socio-political approach) is considered to be an intrinsic element of social work and one of the two faces of social work – the other being individual and family social work (or the psychosocial approach). In this sense, it is important to point out two key ideas of the pioneers' conceptualisation of social reform. First, they envisaged social reform as a research-based action. Second, their idea of 'the cycle of social reform' was an expression of the awareness of the complexity and different levels of the public policy process.

Policy practice as a component of social work

For Jane Addams, the Hull-House residents and other settlement workers, policy-oriented practice was an intrinsic and central element of social work. This was clearly expressed in Hull-House's motto: 'Research, Reform, Residence'.

Addams developed an influential leadership of policy making in the Progressive Years, a pivotal task not only in the establishment of several public agencies at state and federal levels, but also the establishment of minimum standards of industry work conditions for working-class men, regulation of employment for women and child labour protection, and a system of accident, old age and unemployment insurance (Franklin, 1986: 513). A strong commitment to social reform activities is well documented in biographies and essays about several Hull-House residents and settlement workers: namely, Florence Kelley, Edith and Grace Abbot, Julia Lathrop, Lillian Wald (Addams, 1935/2004; Sklar, 1985, 2001; Coss, 1989; Lengermann & Niebrugge, 1998; Costin, 2003; Cohen, 2017).

Despite the fact that, in the official history of social work in the United States and also across the world, Richmond is not considered to be a social reformer, but essentially a social case worker with a relevant contribution to the foundation of the social work profession, her involvement in social reform activities is undeniable, specifically during her years (1900–1909) as secretary of the Philadelphia Society for Organizing Charity. In this period, she exercised a leading role in campaigns for the adoption of legislation in the areas of education, employment, housing, healthcare and public health and women's status. Richmond was particularly active with regard to the welfare of children and women; she elaborated the draft of the Wife Desertion Law which aimed to provide relief to women facing poverty and deprivation as a result of their husbands' desertion. She also contributed to the foundation of the Pennsylvania Child Labour Committee and child labour legislation, to the establishment of the Juvenile Court and Children's Bureau and to the reform of the Society to Protect Children from Cruelty (Richmond, 1930: 217; Pittman-Munke, 1985: 163–64; Agnew, 2004: 6, 97, 113; Barga, 2013). Later, during her years in New York in the 1910s, Richmond not only remained involved in social reform activities – such as using her studies as evidence to advocate for reforms related to health, old-age and unemployment insurance (Agnew, 2004: 126–27) – but also conceptualised the relation between social work with individuals and social work for the whole society (compare Richmond, 1930: 375). As she discussed in her address to the National Conference of Charities and Correction in 1915:

> Social case work does different things for and with different people – it specializes and differentiates; social reform generalizes and simplifies by discovering ways of doing the same thing for everybody. Together it is possible for them to achieve social well-being; acting separately and more

or less at cross purposes they achieve only the most partial and transitory results. The only kind of social case work in which I believe, therefore, and the only kind to which I shall refer today, may be defined as the art of doing different things for and with people by co-operating with them to achieve at one and the same time their own and society's betterment. (Richmond, 1930: 374–75)

Her mature work, *What Is Social Case Work?*, shows Richmond's vision of the relevance of policy-oriented practice in social work:

> The other forms of social work, all of which interplay with case work, are three – group work, social reform, and social research. … By a method different from that employed in either case or group work, though with the same end in view, social reform seeks to improve conditions in the mass, chiefly through social propaganda and social legislation. (Richmond, 1922: 223)

Social reform as a research-based action

The use of research as a source of evidence to support social reform, or the policy-making process, according to the language in use in current public policy theory, is one of the distinctive features of the social pioneers' approach in this domain and can be seen as a contribution to the development of grounded social policies, as pointed out by Lengermann and Niebrugge:

> To be a successful advocate, settlement sociologists needed to build up, out of what they learned as neighbours, information that would be accepted by a wider public as valid … They concretized social problems in terms of empirical experiences of human pain. They analytically demonstrated that that pain occurred not randomly but in a pattern caused by social structure. They presented their information and analysis in an accessible form for a general public. And they concluded their research with proposals for change – actions to be taken and policies to be enacted. (Lengermann & Niebrugge, 2007: 102–3)

This point of view is also stressed in other research on the settlements (for example, MacLean & Williams, 2012; Williams & MacLean, 2016).

As these studies point out, the settlements not only provided education services, cultural activities and community group support, but 'also collected data in the form of statistics and systematic observations to advocate for needed services and social reforms' (MacLean & Williams, 2012: 238).

Probably the most paradigmatic example of this orientation is the collective work of the Hull-House residents, *Hull-House Maps and Papers* (1895), inspired by Charles Booth's *Descriptive Map of London Poverty*, one of the volumes of *Life and Labour of the People in London* (Sklar, 1998). This work is a compilation of maps of the nationalities and wages of the immigrant population and essays about sweatshops, wage-earning children, cloak makers and other social and public health problems in settlement neighbourhoods (compare Schultz, 2007). Also, in *Twenty Years at Hull-House*, Addams (1912/1990, especially chapter 3: 'Public activities and investigations') describes not only her vision of the place of research, but presents several examples of research activity that covered issues from the influence of health conditions on environmental and living conditions of immigrants, studies on children and young people in school settings and in factory work, as well as in many other areas such as housing conditions; these studies were understood as an essential support for social reforms.

The link between research and social reform was presented by several other settlement residents and members of the Charities Movement, such as Mary Richmond. Her involvement during her position as director of the Russell Sage Foundation in New York is exemplified by the 'Study of nine hundred and eighty-five widows known to certain Charity Organization Societies in 1910', which drove Richmond to advocate for reforms related to health, old-age and unemployment insurance (Agnew, 2004: 126–7). For example, early in her tenure as secretary of the Philadelphia Charity Organization Society, Richmond sponsored, in partnership with the University of Pennsylvania, a study of vagrancy and homeless men (Pittman-Munke, 1985: 163; Agnew, 2004: 107–8).

The cycle of social reform and the policy-making process

Another relevant contribution to the policy-making process by the social work pioneers was, as Branco (2016) argues, Richmond's conception of the circle of social reform.

In a relatively unknown article published in the *International Journal of Ethics* in 1906 called 'The Retail Method of Reform', Richmond supports the idea that an effective social reform implies a double circular movement beginning with the direct intervention at the micro-level (the 'retail' method), and returning to the idea again, following the legislative process or policy measures (the 'wholesale' process), thus forming two curves: one ascending and one descending, completing the circle (Figure 5.1):

> Pushed upward by our interest in some retail task toward a wholesale remedy for evils of the same class, we are pulled back, our remedy once secured, into the particular again, to complete the work there begun. The healthy and well-rounded reform movement usually begins in the retail method and returns to it again, forming in the two curves of its upward push and downward pull a complete circle. (Richmond, 1906/1930: 216)

In this article illustrating her conceptualisation Richmond (1906/1930) explains her own involvement in and experience of the child labour campaign in Pennsylvania, stressing the centrality of small tasks of direct intervention and administration for the effectiveness of social reforms, which represent, according to Pittman-Munke (1985: 165), an emphasis on the need for societal reform.

> The campaign was an instructive one. For seven months before the new bill was drafted, schedules of individual working children had been gathered in from those who

Figure 5.1: The circle of social reform

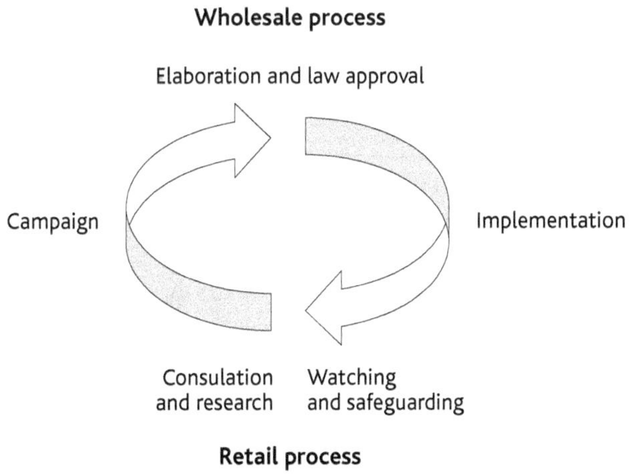

Wholesale process

Elaboration and law approval

Campaign — Implementation

Consulation and research — Watching and safeguarding

Retail process

Source: Own elaboration based on Richmond (1906/1930)

knew them in clubs, classes, homes, and reformatories. ... The bill became a law, but let no one imagine that child labour reforms have been secured in Pennsylvania; they have been made possible, but their securing must be by a tedious retail process upon which the friends of the law have just entered. The movement drew its best life from an interest in individual children, and it returns to them again, watching and safeguarding their interests, explaining the law and its enforcement to their employers, teachers, and parents, co-operating with the factory inspectors and with the school authorities. (Richmond, 1906/1930: 217–20)

This policy-making approach contributes to the understanding of the different levels involved in the policy practice in social work and values the relevance and potential of the micro-level activities (consultation, watching and safeguarding) in the role of social workers as *implementers* to the efficiency of the public policy measures.

The social work pioneers' methods of policy making in the Progressive Years

The social work pioneers' experience reveals a wide diversity of methods affecting public and social policies, with special emphasis on the networks and coalitions articulating different actors and social movements.

Addams was the central figure of the Chicago reforming cohort[2] (Muncy, 1991; Maclean & Williams, 2012), developing an influential leadership in the founding of a dominion of policy-making (Muncy, 1991). This task was pivotal to the establishment of several public agencies at state and federal levels in the United States.

According to Muncy (1991: xii) 'at the head of this dominion stood the *Children's Bureau in the Federal Department of Labor*, an agency created by Congress in 1912 at the urging of child welfare advocates. Settlement culture was partly responsible for the idea of a federal bureau devoted exclusively to children'.

The process of policy making that is the basis of the Children's Bureau clearly demonstrates the social reformers' strategies of networking, coalition, and lobbying, as shown in Table 5.1 and Figure 5.2.

As Muncy (1991: chapter 2) also details, there was intense networking involving Florence Kelley, Jane Addams, Lillian Wald, activists from the Settlement Movement and, particularly, from Hull-

Table 5.1: The process from policy making to the creation of the Children's Bureau

1874	The New York Society for the Prevention of Cruelty to Children (NYSPCC) was founded as a nongovernmental agency, by Henry Bergh and Elbridge Gerry, in the context of the rescue of Mary Ellen Wilson, a nine-year-old girl.
1882	Children's Aid Society of Pennsylvania (CAS of PA) was formed in 1882. The organisation's work has combined policy and direct service over the years. In the early twentieth century, Mary Richmond, secretary of the Charity Organization Society of Philadelphia, helped reform the organisation to match the latest progress of the scientific charity movement through collaboration and research.
1902	Florence Kelley, head of the National Consumers League, joined with Lillian Wald, the founder of Henry Street Settlement, to influence the Association of Neighborhood Workers to establish a child labour committee in New York. This committee was organised as the New York Child Labor Committee.
1903	At the 1903 meeting of the National Conference of Charities and Corrections (NCCC), a section was devoted to child labour. Jane Addams, Florence Kelley, Edgar Gardner Murphy (Rev.), among others, addressed the conference about different child labour topics.
	Following this event, Edgar Gardner Murphy (Rev.) made contact with the leaders of the New York Child Labor Committee to plan the foundation of a national organisation on child labour reform.
	Lillian Wald, in conversation with Florence Kelley of the Henry Street Settlement, expressed the idea: 'If the Government can have a department to look out after the nation's farm crops, why can't it have a bureau to look after the nation's child crop?' (Muncy, 1991: 39)
1904	National Child Labor Committee (NCLC) was created in New York City. Lillian Wald, Florence Kelley, Homer Folks (Secretary of the State Charities Aid Society of New York and advocate for child welfare), Edward Devine (Columbia University sociologist, member of Charity Organization Society of New York and child labour advocate), Graham Taylor (Chicago Commons Settlement House) were among the founding members.
1905	Lillian Wald presented the idea of a Children's Bureau to Edward Devine.
	Edward T. Devine, politically associated with President Theodore Roosevelt, introduced Wald's proposal to the president.
	Florence Kelley published her book *Some Ethical Gains Through Legislation*, in which she described evidence showing why federal action on behalf of children was needed. Kelley's book was a key tool in the policy-making process and in gaining support for the initiative, particularly from women's organisations.
	Wald, Devine, Jane Addams, Mary McDowell (University of Chicago Settlement and former Hull-House resident) met the president to discuss the proposal. President Roosevelt endorsed the idea, but declined to publicly support the proposal. The advocacy group established contact with the NCLC to support the initiative (March 1905).
	Wald, Kelley, Addams, and Samuel McCune Lindsay from NCLC draft legislation proposal.

(continued)

Table 5.1: The process from policy making to the creation of the Children's Bureau (continued)

1906	Senator W. Murray Crane and Representative John J. Gardner introduced bills to establish a children's bureau at NCLC's urging, but without success in the legislative process.
	Aiming to attract more attention to the cause, the NCLC adopted a coalition strategy joining efforts by women's groups including the National Consumers' League (chartered in 1899 by Jane Addams and Josephine Lowell – founder of the New York Charity Organization Society – and with Florence Kelley as first general secretary), the General Federation of Women's Clubs (founded in 1890, with clubwomen Jane Addams, Julia Lathrop and Eleanor Roosevelt, among others), the National Congress of Mothers (1897) and the Daughters of the American Revolution (1896).
1908	In 1908, Lewis Hine was hired by the NCLC to photograph children as young as three years working for long hours and in dangerous conditions, in factories, mines and fields across the US.
	From 1910 to 1920, the Committee published and disseminated Hine's photographs while promoting state and federal laws to ban most forms of child labour and encouraging compulsory education.
1909	White House Conference on the Care of Dependent Children (January 1909). Wald, Addams, Lathrop, Booker T. Washington, Devine, and Folks participated in the two-day conference and heard the president's opening address about 'children as the nation's future'. The conference debated different proposals to improve the condition of children, specifically the expansion of foster family care, adoption agencies, mother's pension, and there was a unanimous call for the creation of a federal children's bureau.
	President Roosevelt wrote to Congress, urging it to pass legislation to create the bureau (February 1909). Despite the president's recommendation and the support of high-level government officials, the bill failed to pass.
	Hine published the first photo essays depicting working children at risk. Hine's photographs helped to stimulate the nation's conscience and garner support for the NCLC's cause.
1910	The new president, William Howard Taft, gave his endorsement to the proposal in 1910.
1912	The bill passed the Senate (January 1912) and the House (April 1912) and President Taft signed it into law (9 April). The Children's Bureau was officially established.
	Julia Lathrop was appointed head of the Children's Bureau following her proposal by the NCLC and the influence of Jane Addams. She became the first woman ever to be appointed head of a federal bureau.
	Lathrop introduced research-based investigations to evaluate infant and maternal mortality, child labour and other social ills.
1913	First Annual Report of the Chief, Children's Bureau, to the Secretary of Labor for the fiscal year (30 June).
1921	Grace Abbott named second chief of the Children's Bureau (1921–34).

Note: Eleven bills (eight in the House and three in the Senate) were introduced between 1906 and 1912 to establish a federal children's bureau.

Source: Own elaboration based on The History Place (1998); Myers (2008); Children's Bureau (2013a, 2013b); Barga (2013); The Welfare History Project (2011)

House (Lengermann & Niebrugge, 1998: figure 7.1) and other relevant figures, such as Edward Devine (Columbia University, Charity Organization Society of New York and director of the journal *Charities*), Graham Taylor (Chicago Commons Settlement House), Homer Folks (Secretary of the State Charities Aid Society of New York and advocate for child welfare). There were also endorsements of organisations such as the National Consumers' League, the National Conference of Charities and Corrections, and other federal organisations and local child welfare societies (compare Muncy, 1991: 40) (see Table 5.1 and Figure 5.2). Of these, the National Child Labor Committee (NCLC) played a very important role. As discussed, Florence Kelley and Lillian Wald in particular assumed a leading role in the Child Labor Committee, a private organisation that grew into the NCLC in 1904, recognised by the Senate in 1907, and which gained wide support from the progressive reform movement. Within the field of children's well-being, the social reformers advanced remarkable advocacy work. This advocacy work was prominent in state campaigns, such as that developed by Mary Richmond in Pennsylvania, or in advocacy of legal reforms and the creation of federal organisations responsible for this area.

Figure 5.2: The Chicago Reform Cohort & Network

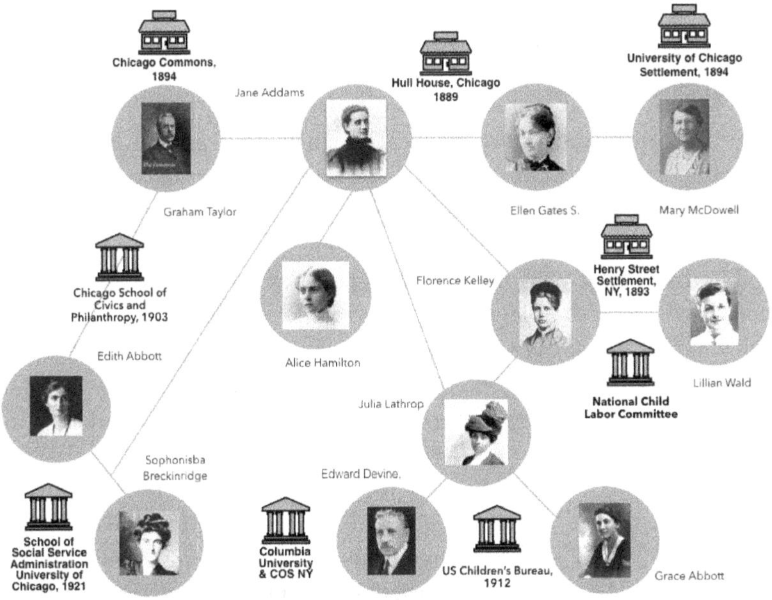

Source: Own elaboration based on MacLean and Williams (2012), Lengermann and Niebrugge (2007), and other reference sources

The new federal agency received a broad mandate, which was to 'investigate and report upon all matters pertaining to the welfare of children and child life among all classes of our people'. Among the issues suggested for study were 'infant mortality, the birth rate, orphanage, juvenile courts, desertion, dangerous occupations, accidents and diseases of children in the several states and territories' (Children's Bureau, 2013b: 22).

Julia Lathrop became the first woman to head a federal bureau and this child welfare territory represents the first position of official authority in the national government. She exercised strong leadership and contributed decisively to the important mission that the agency would play, but also to the consolidation of a female domain in American social policy. She had an important role in the formation of female leaders who shared the same values. From 1912 to 1921, research-based investigation on the welfare of children and their lives was the marker of Lathrop, her staff and the Bureau advisory committees. The impact of this orientation on legislation and programmes in child labour, maternal and infant mortality, juvenile delinquency, mothers' pensions and illegitimacy earned the Children's Bureau a huge reputation for its responsiveness to requests for help and care, showing a clear presence of the 'ethos of settlement' and an exercise of its mission well beyond its legal powers (see Muncy, 1991, chapter).

Social work education and public policy training in the Progressive Years

The history of social work education in the US in the Progressive Years is another strand that will be explored for its relevance to understanding the role of public policy training in the social worker's professional profile.

The first social work training programmes had their beginnings in autumn 1904 at the New York School of Philanthropy, in association with the local Charity Organization Society. In the same year, thanks to the initiative of Boston's Associated Charities, Simmons College and Harvard University, the Boston School for Social Workers was founded.

By 1907, succeeding the course founded by Graham Taylor and Jane Addams in 1903 – 'Social Science and Arts Training for Philanthropic and Social Work' – the Chicago School of Civics and Philanthropy was established with the involvement of the Hull-House residents Julia Lathrop, Sophonisba Breckinridge and Edith Abbott. In 1908, the St Louis School of Philanthropy and the Philadelphia Training School for

Social Work were also created (Lubov, 1971; Muncy, 1991, chapter ; Trattner, 1994; Costin, 2003).

The history of the Chicago School of Civics and Philanthropy (CSCP), involving key actors Graham Taylor, Sophonisba Breckinridge and Edith Abbott, constitutes a very heuristic realm for research into the relationship between social work and social policy in the Progressive Era. One relevant aspect of this topic is the divergences that emerged between the two generations involved in the CSCP project and its transition to the Chicago University.

> Strains were rooted in the diverging visions of Taylor versus Breckinridge and Abbott's quests for professional training and education. *It was the strain between experiential community-based versus professional education* that led to the School's merger with the University of Chicago and played a key role in the differentiation of sociology and social work. (MacLean & Williams, 2012: 247, emphasis added)

According to Muncy's analysis, Taylor's proposal at the Chicago School 'aimed almost exclusively to transform the nineteenth century's friendly visitors into the twentieth century's caseworkers' (Muncy, 1991: 74) in close relationship with the social service agencies of Chicago. As Muncy (1991: 75) emphasises, this commitment to practical training and an organic relationship with the field is a philosophy shared by his generation of settlement residents who valued the knowledge derived from the experience of 'living among the human beings they hoped to help'.

Julia Lathrop and Grace and Edith Abbott attempted to develop at the Chicago School of Civics and Philanthropy a professional social work education which had a greater focus on social policy and was public welfare oriented. This philosophy, 'stressing research, social policy, and public administration' (Trattner, 1994: 243), was reinforced at the school's successor institution, the School of Social Service Administration.

However, as Edith Abbott's 1941 paper 'Twenty-one Years of University Education for the Social Services, 1920–41' reveals, some of the settlement's residents, but also many leaders from the Charity Organizations movement expressed their criticism based on two interrelated arguments: the university affiliation and the model of social work education. The resistance to university integration was grounded in its research-oriented nature, which was regarded as not suitable for students' practical fieldwork and the devaluation of social work methods in the curriculum (Costin, 1983: 102). For Edith Abbott, Breckinridge and other Chicago colleagues, the narrow scope of social work education was the central point, as Abbott argued in her 1931 article, 'Social Welfare and Professional Education'.

> The academic curriculum of most of the professional schools [of social work] is now poor and slight and covers ... only the various aspects of a single field – casework. None of us will deny the importance of casework. It is as necessary to the social worker as, for example, the study of contracts is to the law student. But casework is very far from being the whole story. There are great reaches of territory, some of them yet unexplored and stretching out to a kind of no man's land – the great fields of public charitable organization, of law and government in relation to social work, of social economics, of social insurance, of modern social politics – all of which are required if the social worker is to be an efficient servant of the state. (Quoted in Trattner, 1994: 243–44, emphasis added)

For many years, notwithstanding the common interest in the development of social work education, tension and divergence remained. It wasn't until 1930 that the first steps could be observed towards greater convergence and uniformity. At the end of 1932, the Association of Professional Social Work adopted a minimum curriculum divided into four areas. Group A included courses in casework, medical and psychiatric information. Group B contained courses in community organisation, specialised casework and group work (two required). Group C contained courses in the field of social work, public welfare administration, child welfare and labour or industry problems (two required). Group D included courses in social statistics, social research, social legislation and legal aspects of social work (one required) (Lubov, 1971: 151–52).

From this point of view, there was also a relevant argument with regard to the need to avoid the dilution of social work into sociology in the academic context, which Abbott and Breckinridge referred to as 'recreating casework'. 'The message of their textbooks was that *well-educated caseworkers could transform their door-to-door experiences into scientific data and learn to become the policymakers* that Abbott and Breckinridge hoped to produce at their school'; this represented 'an attempt to reconcile factions within the profession' (Muncy, 1991: 81–82, emphasis added).

Conclusion

Revisiting our argument with regard to the social reform methods adopted by the Children's Bureau advocates (Wald, Kelley, Addams and others), we can establish a connection between the networking, coalition and lobbying approaches adopted, their roles as actors/policy entrepreneurs and some public policy theories, such as the models related to agenda setting and coalition building (Garraud, 2014).

Considering this process of policy making, we can argue that this case is illustrative of future public policy theories of agenda setting such as the *outside initiative model* by Cobb and colleagues (1976) or the *model of external mobilisation* (Garraud, 2014), which refers to when organised groups manage to transform a problem into a public interest issue, form a cause coalition and establish it in the public agenda to urge public authorities to put it on the governmental agenda in order to make a decision (compare Garraud, 2014).

In the same sense, the social work pioneers' attempts at social reform can be interpreted in the light of the advocacy coalition framework (ACF) proposed by Sabatier and Jenkins-Smith, which seeks to explain changes in public policy in periods of 10 or more years (compare Sabatier, 2014), as we have observed in the initiatives for the creation of the Children's Bureau (see Figure 5.2). According to this analytical model, 'the basic principle is that actors are grouped into one or more cause coalitions, whose members share a set of normative beliefs and perceptions of the world, and that they act together to translate their beliefs into public policy' (Sabatier, 2014: 49). In the Children's Bureau case, we can observe the role played by beliefs, relational and political resources, as well as the strategies used to broaden the coalition with the alliance of several groups from American civil society such as charities, women's associations and clubs, the Consumers' League and so on.

We can also discern the convergence of Richmond's conception of the social reform cycle with the thought of different public policy theory authors who emphasise the relevance of implementation in the social policy process, which affects the original conception of the policy (Hill, 1990/2003) and influences the real impact of a social policy, because social policy measures are often just guidelines and abstract policy orientations (Jansson, 1990). Richmond's conceptualisation is also aligned, in some respects, with the bottom-up models of policy implementation which do not recognise as pertinent the division between policy formulation and implementation. As Lipsky (1980/2010) and other bottom-up theorists (compare Hill & Hupe,

2009) argue, the relationship between the design and implementation of a given public policy is not characterised by simplicity and linearity, but by complexity.

In this perspective, implementation is the most complex and rich part of the process of public policy. Indeed, this phase of the 'policy life cycle' implies a direct relationship between public actors in the political and administrative structure, the target groups, the final beneficiaries and the groups constituting third parties (positively and negatively affected) (Knoepfel et al, 2011, figure 4). In a similar perspective, Knill and Tosun (2012) emphasise that *implementation is far from a trivial activity* because it involves a diversity of actors and different entities with different possible views about the implementation of a specified public policy (Knoepfel et al, 2011: 151).

Regarding social work education in the Progressive Years, and specifically the tension between casework-based and social welfare administration, the evolution of that debate is clear, as is its relevance to the perspective of social work affecting social policy. Even today, 'The social worker meets at every turn questions of social legislation, proposals for social reform, and even the more immediate problems [...] and the social worker should be able to give sound advice' (Edith Abbot, 1931, *Social Welfare and Professional Education*, quoted by Muncy, 1991: 78–79).

Notes

[1] The Progressive Era is usually defined as roughly from the 1890s to 1920 (compare Williams & MacLean, 2016).

[2] Formed by, among others, Edith and Grace Abbot, Sophonisba Breckinridge, Julia Lathrop and Florence Kelley, who came to exercise significant positions in several government services. It also included other settlement leaders including Graham Taylor of Chicago Commons and Mary McDowell of the University of Chicago Settlement (Muncy, 1991; Lengermann & Niebrugge, 2007; Maclean & Williams; 2012).

References

Abbott, E. (1941) 'Twenty-one years of university education for the social services, 1920-41', *Social Service Review*, 15(4): 670–705.

Addams, J. (1912/1990) *Twenty Years at Hull-House*, Chicago, IL: University of Illinois Press.

Addams, J. (1935/2004) *My Friend, Julia Lathrop*, Urbana, IL: University of Illinois Press.

Agnew, E. (2004) *From Charity to Social Work: Mary E. Richmond and the Creation of an American Profession*, Chicago, IL: University of Illinois Press.

Barga, M. (2013) 'Children's Aid Society of Pennsylvania'. Available at: http://socialwelfare.library.vcu.edu/programs/child-welfarechild-labor/childrens-aid-society-of-pennsylvania/

Branco, F. (2016) 'The circle of social reform: The relationship social work–social policy in Addams and Richmond', *European Journal of Social Work*, 19(3–4): 405–19.

Children's Bureau (2013a) 'Children's Bureau timeline'. Available at: https://cb100.acf.hhs.gov/childrens-bureau-timeline

Children's Bureau (2013b) *The Children's Bureau Legacy: Ensuring the Right to Childhood*. Available at: https://cb100.acf.hhs.gov/sites/default/files/cb_ebook/cb_ebook.pdf

Cobb, R., Ross, J.-K. and Ross, M. H. (1976) 'Agenda building as a comparative political process', *The American Political Science Review*, 70(1): 126–38.

Cohen, M. (2017) *Julia Lathrop – Social Service and Progressive Government*, Philadelphia, PA: Westview Press.

Coss, C. (ed) (1989) *Lillian Wald – Progressive Activist*, New York: The Feminist Press.

Costin, L. (1983) 'Edith Abbott and the Chicago influence on social work education', *Social Service Review*, 57(1): 94–111.

Costin, L. (2003) *Two Sisters for Social Justice*, Urbana, IL: University of Illinois Press.

Franklin, D. L. (1986) 'Mary Richmond and Jane Addams: from moral certainty to rational inquiry in social work practice', *Social Service Review*, 60(4): 504–25.

Garraud, P. (2014) 'Agenda/Émergence', in L. Boussaguet, S. Jacquot and P. Ravinet (eds) *Dictionnaire des politiques publiques. 4e édition précédée d'un nouvel avant-propos* (4th edn), Paris: Presses de Sciences Po, pp 58–67.

Hill, M. (1990/2003) *Understanding social policy* (7th edn), Oxford: Blackwell.

Hill, M. and Hupe, P. (2009) *Implementing Public Policy* (2nd edn), London: Sage.

Jansson, B. S. (1990) *Social Welfare Policy: From Theory to Policy Practice*, Belmont, CA: Wadsworth Publishing Company.

Knill, C. and Tosun, J. (2012) *Public Policy. A New Introduction*, Basingstoke: Palgrave Macmillan.

Knoepfel, P., Larrue, C., Varone, F. and Hill, M. (2011) *Public Policy Analysis*, Bristol: Policy Press.

Lengermann, P. and Niebrugge, G. (1998) *The Women Founders: Sociology and Social Theory 1830–1930*, Long Grove, IL: Waveland Press.

Lengermann, P. and Niebrugge, G. (2007) 'Three trice told: narratives of sociology's relation to social work', in C. Calhoun (ed) *Sociology in America*, Chicago, IL: University of Chicago Press, pp 63–114.

Lengermann, P. and Niebrugge-Brantley, J. (2002) 'Back to the future: settlement sociology, 1885–1930', *The American Sociologist*, 33(3), 5–20.

Lipsky, M. (1980/2010) *Street-level Bureaucracy. Dilemmas of the Individual in Public Services*, New York: Russel Sage Foundation.

Lubov, R. (1971) *The Professional Altruist: The Emergence of Social Work as Career*, Cambridge, MA: Harvard University Press.

MacLean, V. M. and Williams, J. E. (2012) '"Ghosts of sociologies past": settlement sociology in the progressive era at the Chicago School of Civics and Philanthropy', *The American Sociologist*, 43(3), 235–63.

Muncy, R. (1991) *Creating a Female Dominion in American Reform 1890–1935*, New York: Oxford University Press.

Myers, J. E. B. (2008) 'A short history of child protection in America', *Family Law Quarterly*, 42(3): 449–63.

Pittman-Munke, P. (1985) 'Mary E. Richmond: the Philadelphia years', *Social Casework*, 66(3): 160–66.

Richmond, M. (1930) *The Long View*, New York: Russell Sage Foundation.

Richmond, M. (1922) *What is Social Case Work?*, New York: Russell Sage Foundation.

Richmond, M. (1906/1930) 'The retail method of reform', in *The Long View*, New York: Russell Sage Foundation, pp 214–21.

Sabatier, P. A. (2014) 'Advocacy Coalition Framework (ACF)', in L. Boussaguet, L. Boussaguet, S. Jacquot and P. Ravinet (eds) *Dictionnaire des politiques publiques*, Paris: Presses de Sciences Po (P.F.N.S.P.).9782724615500, pp 49–57.

Schultz, R. L. (2007) 'Introduction', in R. Schultz (ed), *Hull-House Maps and Papers*, Chicago, IL: University of Illinois Press, pp 1–42.

Sklar, K. K. (1985) 'Hull House in the 1890s: a community of women reformers', *Signs,* 10(4): 658-77.

Sklar, K. K. (1998) 'Hull-House maps and papers: social sciences as women's work in the 1980s', in H. Silverberg (ed) *Gender and American Social Science: The Formative Years*, Princeton, NJ: Princeton University Press, pp 127–54.

Sklar, K. K. (2001) 'Florence Kelley', in R. L. Schultz and A. Hast (eds) *Women Building Chicago 1790–1990: A Biographical Dictionary*, Bloomington, IN: Indiana University Press, pp 460–68.

The History Place (1998) *Child Labour in America 1908–1912: Photographs of Lewis W. Hine.* www.historyplace.com/unitedstates/childlabor/

The Welfare History Project (2011) 'National Child Labor Committee (NCLC)'. Available at: https://socialwelfare.library.vcu.edu/programs/child-welfarechild-labor/national-child-labor-committee/

Trattner, W. (1994) *From Poor Law to Welfare State, 6th Edition: A History of Social Welfare in America* (5th edn), New York: The Free Press.

Williams, J. and MacLean, V. (2016) *Settlement Sociology in Progressive Years.* Chicago, IL: Brill Academics Publishers.

6

Social work academia and social policy in Israel: on the role of social work academics in the policy process

Idit Weiss-Gal and John Gal

Introduction

In social work discourse it is not only practitioners that are called on to engage in policy practice in order to further social justice (Gal & Weiss-Gal, 2013; Jansson, 2014; McBeath, 2016; Reisch, 2016) but also social work scholars (Howard, 2010). As the individuals responsible for educating future social workers, social work faculty members are expected to serve as role models for their students in addressing disadvantage and injustice. Moreover, social work academics can better achieve the social justice goals of the profession because they enjoy the prestige, the knowledge, the autonomy and the employment security that facilitate greater access to the policy-making process.

The importance ascribed to this involvement has generated interest in the participation of social work faculty in policy formulation processes (Karger & Hernández, 2004; MacKinnon, 2009; Weiss-Gal, 2016). The findings of quantitative studies indicate that social work faculty do engage in policy practice (Mary, 2001). Though their overall level of engagement is described as moderate to low (Weiss-Gal & Gal, 2017), it is greater than academics in other disciplines (Landry et al, 2001; Weiss-Gal & Gal, 2019).

Similarly, the factors associated with policy practice have been the subject of scholarly interest. One result of this effort was the formulation of the Policy Practice Engagement (PPE) conceptual framework, which was developed to explain the engagement of social workers in policy practice (Gal & Weiss-Gal, 2015). This framework posits that there are three types of factors related to policy practice engagement by social workers. The first of these is *motivation*, which underscores individuals' sense that involvement in policy change is an integral part of their professional role and that they have the knowledge and tools to engage in this. Second, *facilitation* pertains to the organisational context in which social workers are employed and the degree to which it supports their efforts to engage in policy practice. Finally, *opportunity* focuses upon the access that social workers have to the institutions in which policy is formulated and to policy-makers in them. A study of social work academics' engagement in policy in 12 nations found that, despite differences across nations, significant positive relationships were found between faculty involvement in policy and motivational factors such as attitudes towards the social role of academia, the faculty members' personal roles as social work academics and their sense that they had the personal capacity to engage in policy. By contrast, institutional support for policy engagement was associated with actual engagement in policy in only a small number of countries (Weiss-Gal & Gal, 2017).

This chapter contributes to knowledge on policy practice by focusing on social work academics who engage in policy formulation and decision making despite the neoliberal context in which higher education now operates and the growing emphasis on academic excellence, competition over resources and collaboration with market forces (Olssen & Peters, 2005). It draws upon the PPE conceptual framework described above. By exploring the policy engagement of members of this distinctive group, the study seeks to learn more about the form that their policy practice takes, why certain faculty members engage in policy practice and how they combine this with their other academic responsibilities. Qualitative tools are employed in order to better understand this involvement in policy.[1]

Method

The participants in the study included 24 faculty members of eight schools of social work, all of whom are, or were, involved in policy formulation. Half (12) were identified in an online questionnaire disseminated in a previous study (Weiss-Gal et al, 2017). The authors identified an additional eight faculty members who engaged in policy formulation, and another four were recommended by other interviewees. Only four of the faculty members invited to take part in the study did not participate.

The participants comprised a diverse group with regard to institutional affiliation, academic rank and years of teaching. Most of the interviewees (16) were women. A majority (18) were employed at universities, the rest (6) at academic colleges. Three held the rank of full professor, six held the rank of associate professor, seven were senior lecturers, five were lecturers and three were adjunct faculty. Thirteen of the interviewees had tenure. All but three held undergraduate degrees in social work. The interviewees' periods of employment at their respective schools of social work ranged from 25 to 35 years.

The interviews

After approval was received from the Tel Aviv University Ethics Committee, interviews were conducted between December 2014 and October 2015. A research assistant conducted 22 of the interviews; the study authors conducted the remaining two. The interviewees chose the interview locations: 21 were interviewed in their offices, two in their homes, and one by telephone. The interview durations ranged from 17 to 60 minutes.

The interviews were structured and based on the following questions:

1. Are you currently, or have you in the past, engaged in influencing social policy? If so, describe the area of your involvement and the form that it takes?
2. Do you think that you affected social policy? If so, how was this success manifested?
3. Is there a connection between your research or teaching and your involvement in policy formulation?
4. What factors motivated you to be involved? Were there factors during any specific periods that deterred you from being involved in social policy formulation?

Analysis of the interviews

All of the interviews were recorded and transcribed. The participants were informed that any identifying details would be concealed, and that the interview transcripts would be kept in a secure place.

A content analysis of the interviews was undertaken (Esterberg, 2002; Krippendorf, 1980). Initially, an open coding approach was adopted in the analysis of the interviewees' responses. On the basis of this initial analysis, we identified a number of common themes. We then grouped the responses to each question based on these common themes. The third stage entailed the two authors jointly grouping the themes identified into a smaller number of themes. The final stage was a reading by each author of the quotes by category, with no indication of the theme of each category, so as to enable us to conceptualise the theme based on the quotes. The themes that comprised the answers to each question were then reconsolidated and reformulated.

Findings

Areas of involvement

Personal social services was the most common area of faculty policy involvement (17 faculty members). This took three forms:

1. Developing policy with regard to work methods, new social service interventions or technologies. Examples of this are developing policies for new social work strategies to address the needs of people living in poverty and implementing them, and formulating policies for work methods based on partnership or strength-based practice (10).
2. Involvement in shaping social welfare service policy. Primarily, this took the form of participation in the design of reforms in social services (10).
3. Advancing the development of new social services or expanding services to geographic areas where vulnerable populations reside (5).

The second most common area of engagement was that of policy on poverty, exclusion or inequality (7). This form of involvement was broad-based and cut across more specific policy areas, such as formulating policy on social welfare services and the social security system, as well as housing policy in the context of poverty.

The third most prevalent area of involvement was social security. Six faculty members reported involvement that included activity aimed at affecting benefit eligibility conditions and increasing take-up of benefits.

Among other areas mentioned were policy on professional social work issues, policy towards specific populations (particularly people with disabilities), urban policy and relations with civil society.

An analysis of the policy areas revealed two recurrent motifs. The first was an emphasis on innovation, in that faculty underscored their involvement in developing new services or identifying social problems or policy problems not previously on the agenda. Second, the areas of involvement overlapped with the faculty members' fields of expertise in research and/or teaching.

Strategies for action

The policy activities described by faculty members can be divided between formal-institutional and social action. The former encompasses direct involvement in arenas in which policy deliberations and decisions occur, while the latter includes indirect social action aimed at affecting policy. All of the faculty members combined formal-institutional strategies with social action.

Formal-institutional policy activities included four main modes of action:

1. Fifteen faculty members participated in policy-making committees. Most were members of ministerial committees, internal governmental committees or municipal committees, or they spoke in parliamentary committee deliberations.
2. Ten faculty members met with policy makers, often on a regular basis. These included Members of Parliament (MPs), ministers and senior officials in government ministries, governmental authorities, local authorities or civil society organisations. At these meetings the faculty members expressed their views on existing policy and discussed desired policy changes. For example: a faculty member met with Ministry of Labour and Welfare officials regarding the need to formulate policy on behalf of an underserved population group.
3. Nine faculty members wrote policy papers or disseminated research findings to policy makers, including MPs and senior staff in government ministries and the social security institution. These papers drew upon studies conducted by the faculty members themselves, and were written at the initiative of the faculty member, in response to the request of others, or as part of the faculty member's involvement in groups, coalitions or research institutes. In half of the cases the faculty members cooperated with students or practitioners in writing the policy papers.
4. Two faculty members participated in government policy formulation teams. One faculty member was also appointed by a government ministry to a formal position in a welfare organisation that entailed involvement in policy-making processes.

Social action encompassed indirect activities intended to influence policy through the engagement of other policy actors (such as advocacy organisations, the media, professionals in the relevant fields) or by participating in civil society forums. Sometimes professionals in local government or civil society were also involved in these. They were undertaken in order to encourage discussion of a social or policy problem, raise awareness or motivate policy actors to take part in policy change.

This category contains five modes of action:

1. Ten faculty members reported involvement that included working with students to effect policy change, guiding students on policy change efforts within existing courses and creating study programmes or special action forums to effect policy change within the social work school, with the participation of faculty, students, practitioners, community activists and advocacy organisations.
2. Nine faculty members took part in civil society coalitions. They joined forces with practitioners in social work agencies and with advocacy groups or social service providers in order to promote policy.
3. Seven faculty members reported using the media: radio or television interviews; opinion pieces in the printed media, or information dissemination to media personnel.
4. Four faculty members held formal positions in advocacy organisations, generally as members of the executive committee.
5. Three faculty members disseminated social policy research to the public via conferences or social media.

Policy impact

All but one of the social work faculty members interviewed said they felt that they had influenced policy. Of these, only three also reported situations where they had not succeeded in affecting policy.

Most faculty members (16) reported success at the national policy level, while some mentioned success at the local level. They noted that their efforts led to policy change that took the form of the creation of a new service, new legislation, the beginnings of legislative change, or the initiation of policy change on the part of a governmental ministry, a local authority, a specific social service or public entity. From the academics' perspective, success could also mean thwarting policy change (such as preventing the privatisation of social services), influencing rulings that shape the interpretation of legislation, or placing an issue on the public agenda:[2] "Today the XX issue is on the social workers' agenda, it's a regular, acknowledged issue. It's not some esoteric issue, like it used to be. [...] Clearly there's an impact" (Professor, University).

Five other faculty members referred in their responses to the impact of their involvement on the school of social work and their students:

> 'I think I also had a major impact on the school in the sense that it understands that this issue is important, and this year

I was asked to teach the subject at the undergraduate level, which is something that hasn't happened here up to now.' (Senior lecturer, University)

Three faculty members also described their failure to advance policy within government ministries or to bring about change in social policy.

The relationship between research, teaching, and involvement in policy

All of the faculty members, except for two not involved in research, attested to a relationship between their research and their policy involvement. Ten described a close, all-encompassing and multidimensional relationship. They reported great overlap between their research and their policy involvement, describing it as intertwined and mutually reinforcing. This took different forms: (1) research identified a policy problem or desirable policy changes, and motivated them to become involved; (2) research as a tool in the process of influencing policy makers; (3) involvement drove research, as it exposed the faculty member to issues requiring empirical investigation; (4) involvement served as a basis for the conceptualisation of ideas and theoretical knowledge; (5) involvement fostered access to data and study participants, or facilitated policy-maker consent to research activity. This intimate relationship is reflected in the following quote:

> 'I feel a very strong, close connection that reinforces itself. I feel that much of my research is due to lacunae that I discerned at the policy level and I said to myself, "Okay, that's a change that has to be made, but I can't do it because I haven't actually studied it, so I study it and get back to the policy." […] I feel that research isn't just publishing or accumulating knowledge. It's also a tool for change.' (Senior lecturer, University)

All but one of the faculty members attested to a close relationship between policy involvement and teaching. This took the form of including policy issues in class discussions or incorporating material relating to policy practice in courses. Eight faculty members referred to involvement as an instructional tool. They discussed their involvement and its contribution in class and gave examples of dilemmas that arose in the course of their involvement. Several faculty members said that these classroom discussions encouraged their involvement.

'I often try [...] to give them examples from interventions at various levels, and then give them a sense of my own interventions. My students were totally involved. Totally. I'd give them case examples from what happened to me [...] and "What do you say", and share doubts, and involve them.' (Adjunct faculty member, College)

Six faculty members noted that involvement in policy change led them to create new courses, while another six noted that it had led them to develop assignments that required the students themselves to be involved in policy formulation, generally 'in the real world':

'The assignment was to write a [policy] paper [...], to take an issue from their practical training and write a policy paper about it, and then create a plan of action for how to change it. [...] I know that later on the instructors really liked these position papers.' (Lecturer, College)

The timing of their initial policy engagement and the initiative for policy involvement

Two-thirds of the interviewees (15) reported that their involvement in policy formulation began prior to their becoming faculty members. Sometimes this was when they were high school pupils, for others their policy engagement had its roots in their university studies, while the remainder first became engaged in policy when they were social workers or academics.

When asked to describe the initiative for their policy engagement, the faculty members identified different sources for this. Some said that they had taken the initiative while others noted that they had responded to requests from others to play a policy role, such as joining a policy committee, being interviewed on radio, or joining a team discussing policy. The requests came from both formal policy actors, such as ministers, MPs or government officials, and informal actors – civil society organisations or social work students.

Explaining involvement: prompting and inhibiting factors

Three categories of factors emerged from the faculty responses as to what prompted or impeded their involvement: *motivation* (individual-level factors), *facilitation* (factors related to the academic institution's organisational culture) and *opportunity* (factors relating to access to the policy process).

All of the faculty members explained their involvement in terms of motivational factors, with seven of them adding opportunity factors. More than half (13) linked their involvement to their views on the role of academia, their role as social work faculty and the role of the social work profession. They perceived involvement in policy formulation as a tool for social impact. "I see it as part of my professional role as a social work faculty member, to use my accumulated knowledge to exert an impact. [...] I view it as part of my academic work, not as something separate from it" (Professor, University).

Some faculty members said that involvement and impact on policy was a main goal of their academic role: "As far as I'm concerned, it's my job. That's my job in the academic world. That's how I perceive it. That's why I'm in academia, to make use of academia, the status, the privilege that academia provides" (Professor, University).

The second factor, mentioned by eight faculty members, related to identifying policy problems. Through their research and their familiarity with the professional literature, or by way of meetings with professionals in the field, students or community representatives, they became aware of policy failures, and this induced them to act:

> 'It started with an academic issue related to a topic on which I was conducting research. [...] While writing on the topic, I became aware of the need for policy change, warned that there is no policy and insisted that policy be formulated as soon as possible.' (Professor, University)

Seven faculty members mentioned a third factor – the relationship between involvement in policy formulation and social action as a personal characteristic. They viewed social involvement as something 'natural', or as a personality trait: "Something in [my] DNA; I've always felt that it's something natural to me. It's like something built into my attitude and my personality. [...] I like being involved in this area" (Lecturer, University).

Six faculty members described their involvement as reflecting a commitment to values. They emphasised their commitment to social justice and linked this commitment to their involvement:

> 'I was motivated by a very social-democratic concept. I think it's a matter of socialism. I think many of my

outlooks come from social responsibility. This element of mutual responsibility, of being socially responsible, is a very significant thing.' (Professor, University)

Five faculty members also mentioned the example set by other academics that had inspired them to become involved. These other academics exemplified the idea that one can integrate policy engagement with academic activity:

'In time, my personal and personality-based motivations were supplemented by the literature to which I was exposed, and I think the [role] models, the people I saw around me and I saw them as role models, greatly strengthened my desire to be involved.' (Lecturer, University)

Five faculty members connected their policy involvement with engagement that preceded their arrival at the academic institution: "I went from the field to academia, so it was very natural for me to continue" (Adjunct faculty member, University).

Four faculty members included among the factors driving their involvement an emerging theoretical understanding of the social roots of problems and distress. With their professional development as social workers or academics came a clearer structural understanding of problems and social ills, and this reinforced their desire or sense of obligation to strive for policy change:

'I'm always becoming more and more convinced that XX is something that's related, that it's a social problem and in order to deal with it [...] you can't deal with it only by helping individuals. Academic engagement with this sphere both raised awareness and awakened in me [...] gave me tools for thinking in this way.' (Professor, University)

A small number of faculty members mentioned other factors, such as specific protest events, a desire to serve as a role model for students and socioeconomic background that created the drive to seek social change.

The second category of factors prompting involvement was that of opportunity. Seven faculty members mentioned these factors in addition to motivational factors. They referred to situations in which opportunities arose for their participation in policy formulation, mainly in response to stakeholder appeals (for example, serving on policy committees or advising senior officials in the Ministry of Labour and Welfare): "I was invited to take part in a national committee dealing with the X plan, and now I've been invited to write a policy paper on the topic" (Lecturer, College).

The interviewees were also asked what factors hampered their involvement in policy formulation. Six faculty members in university settings, all professors, maintained that there were no factors of any kind that had made it hard for them to be involved. By contrast, other faculty mentioned factors that can be placed, for the most part, in the category of facilitation. The most common inhibiting factor, mentioned by ten faculty members, was the organisational culture of their academic institution, which encourages research and academic writing, with less emphasis, if any, on activity aimed at having a social impact:

> 'I think that at the personal level there were never any such factors that held me back. There were systemic factors related to the job, the place where I am, that sometimes there was a feeling that they didn't really support it. That is: the academic university structure, put very simply, doesn't appreciate that kind of activity; [...] People who advised me, out of the goodness of their hearts, and came and said, "Tell me what you're doing", and the moment you go into detail, they said, "Put it on hold, wait with that, you don't need that right now. Invest in the other things".' (Senior lecturer, University)

Two faculty members mentioned, as an inhibiting factor, colleagues' ambiguous attitude toward the nature of the involvement, due to disagreement with the political stand taken.

The academic institution's explicit opposition to involvement on a specific topic was also mentioned as an involvement-inhibiting factor, though it did not ultimately prevent involvement:

> 'I can say [that] only in one event, at XX, were there signals from XX and also position-holders at XX, that it could be a bit of a problem, my involvement, if it's something that would be interpreted [as] against the government or something, since we're supported as an academic institution by the government. [...] But that was dropped from the agenda very quickly. I removed it very quickly from the agenda, I held a discussion with the administration where I explained that it's inconceivable that I wouldn't support it.' (Senior lecturer, College)

Besides the enabling factors, three motivational factors were noted that inhibit involvement: parental duties; difficulties related to the process itself, such as opposition on the part of politicians, the dissolution of a policy committee before its recommendations were submitted; and weariness of fighting on behalf of social causes.

Discussion

This study focused on Israeli social work faculty engaged in policy formulation. It offers insights into the dynamics and the factors that lead social work faculty to become policy actors. The first of these factors is the faculty's perception regarding the organisational message transmitted to the faculty members and the degree to which it facilitates (or impedes) policy involvement. The interviews show that, while institutions of higher education regard involvement in policy formulation as an extra academic activity of secondary importance, there is also generally a message of academic freedom that fosters choice. The faculty members expressed, in various ways, a sense of broad autonomy for their activity, and a high degree of job security. In other words, they act within an academic environment that may not remunerate policy involvement, but nevertheless sees it as legitimate.

Here motivational factors come into play. Faculty members involved in policy formulation drew legitimacy for their actions from inner sources of ideology, personality and values. They regarded efforts to influence policy as an obligation of social work academics and strongly identified with social work's commitment to advance social justice by developing appropriate social policy. Most of the faculty members felt that they had an impact, that they had advanced policy or a new service, or that a problem had been placed on the agenda.

The close links that the academics interviewed forged between research, teaching and social engagement enabled them to succeed in realising their motivation to deal with policy and to devote resources to this involvement. This link is reflected in the fact that the faculty members were active in policy spheres that overlap with their areas of research. It is also reflected in the fact that their research fed into their teaching, and that their involvement and their contact with policy makers fed into their research. This integrated activity fosters resource and effort pooling, and made policy involvement possible in an environment that is poor in the resources necessary for such activity.

As faculty of schools of social work, the academics could avail themselves of diverse means of involvement and options through which to realize their sense of academic freedom and inner motivation:

forums for policy change established within the schools and facilitating joint activity with students and practitioners; student initiatives that mobilise faculty for action on behalf of policy change; courses that included assignments which required students to be involved in policy formulation. Although most of the study participants did not perceive the social work schools as institutions that encourage activity in the policy sphere, the schools created an environment that offered them a broad array of options for realising their values.

The faculty members' affiliation with schools of social work had consequences for their patterns of policy involvement. The areas of involvement were also influenced by this closeness to the field and the faculty members' affiliation with professional schools. The interviewees' tendency was to focus on policy areas with which Israeli social work is engaged.

Alongside these factors, opportunities for policy practice were also crucial. Thus, the characteristics of the Israeli policy formulation process, and the degree of access enjoyed by unofficial policy actors to policy-making arenas, also appear to be relevant to our understanding of social work faculty involvement in policy. The faculty interviews indicate that to policy makers they constitute an almost self-evident source of input regarding policy. A large majority of the faculty members reported that some of their involvement was at the initiative of policy makers, who asked them for assistance with policy formulation. In other words, political culture also comes into play and has an impact on faculty involvement. It is likely that these faculty members, more than others, tend to act on requests that they participate in policy processes (due to their inner motivation), or else they acquired a reputation for willingness to engage in consulting, which led policy actors to invite them to participate.

This access to policy-making processes is also linked to a policy legacy that established the role of social work academics in social policy formulation in Israel. In the early 1960s, just a few years after the first university-based school of social work was established, social work faculty began to play a role in social policy formulation. Given the paucity of researchers specialising in social policy, they have been a major source of knowledge and have provided the country's policy makers with academic legitimacy.

The functions fulfilled by social work faculty have often been part of the formal institutions in which policy is made. They have included heading or participating in public committees, conducting studies for policy formulation purposes and, at times, formal involvement in the policy-making process (Jaffe, 1973). Israeli social work academics also have a tradition of involvement in social action, especially in the form of advising protest movements (Bargal, 1972). The close reciprocal relations between social work academics and policy makers continue today, as reflected, for example, in their major role in the State Committee for the War Against Poverty in Israel (Ministry of Social Affairs and Social Services, 2014) and in government committees (Rimmerman & Soffer, 2016).

Unlike the findings of studies on the policy practice of social workers that have underscored the crucial impact of the organisational context in which they operate upon their engagement in policy practice (Gvirtz-Meidany et al, 2016), organisational support does not appear to be a major factor in the policy activities of social work academics. Indeed, even though the academic environment does not necessarily encourage the policy engagement of social work academics, the findings of this study indicate that social work faculty involvement in policy is a result of a combination of motivational factors, their ability to optimise their resources by combining teaching, research and policy involvement, and opportunity factors. Social work academics engaged in policy practice comprise a group of faculty members who are committed to the social justice goals of the social work profession and perceive policy change as an integral part of their academic role. They can undertake, and maintain, their policy engagement because they manage to successfully balance their involvement, their research and their teaching. In other words, instead of regarding policy engagement as an impediment to other academic endeavours, social work academics find ways to integrate this with their research and teaching and indeed regard this type of activity as a useful source of insights for research and teaching. When this takes place in the context of opportunities for involvement on the part of policy makers, policy engagement is possible.

Notes

[1] The site of this study is Israel, in which social work has existed for more than eight decades (Spiro, 2001). The academisation of social work in Israel began with the establishment of the first university-based school of social work in 1958. There are currently 13 schools of social work in universities and academic colleges across the country. Social policy has always had an important place in social work programmes in Israel. Policy practice has featured increasingly in social work education and is now integrated into undergraduate and graduate social work programmes at all the country's schools of social work (Weiss-Gal, 2013).

2   All the quotes are translated from the original Hebrew into English. At the end of each quote, the respondent's academic status and institutional affiliation are noted in parentheses. Full and associate professors were grouped into a single rank (professor).

References

Bargal, D. (1972) 'Social workers and the welfare policy of the Jerusalem municipality', *Saad*, 7: 235–41. (Hebrew)

Esterberg, K. G. (2002) *Qualitative Methods in Social Research*, Boston: McGraw-Hill.

Gal, J. and Weiss-Gal, I. (eds) (2013) *Social Workers Influencing Social Policy: An International Perspective on Policy Practice*, Bristol: Policy Press.

Gal, J. and Weiss-Gal, I. (2015) 'The "why" and the "how" of policy practice', *British Journal of Social Work*, 45: 1083–101.

Gvirtz-Meidany, A., Weiss-Gal, I. and Gal, J. (2016) 'Social workers' policy practice in nonprofit human service organizations in Israel', *British Journal of Social Work*, 46: 1890–1908.

Howard, M. O. (2010) 'Social workers as public intellectuals', *Social Work Research*, 34(3): 131–33.

Jaffe, E. D. (1973) 'Separation in Jerusalem', *Public Welfare*, 31(1): 33–38.

Jansson, B. S. (2014) *Becoming an Effective Policy Advocate: From Policy Practice to Social Justice* (7th edn), Belmont: Brooks/Cole.

Karger, H. J. and Hernández, M. T. (2004) 'The decline of the public intellectual in social work', *Journal of Sociology and Social Welfare*, 31(3): 51-68.

Krippendorff, K. (1980) *Content Analysis*, Newbury Park: Sage.

Landry, R., Amara, N. and Lamari, M. (2001) 'Utilization of social science research knowledge in Canada', *Research Policy*, 30(2): 333–49.

MacKinnon, S. T. (2009) 'Social work intellectuals in the twenty first century: critical social work theory, critical social work and public engagement', *Social Work Education*, 28(5): 512–27.

Mary, N. L. (2001) 'Political activism of social work educators', *Journal of Community Practice*, 9(4): 1–20.

McBeath, B. (2016) 'Re-envisioning macro social work practice', *Families in Society: The Journal of Contemporary Social Sciences*, 97(1): 5–14.

Ministry of Social Affairs and Social Services (2014) *Report by the Israel Committee for the War against Poverty*. Retrieved from https://brookdale.jdc.org.il/wp-content/uploads/2014/07/The-War-against-Poverty.pdf

Olssen, M. and Peters, M. A. (2005) 'Neoliberalism, higher education and the knowledge economy: from the free market to knowledge capitalism', *Journal of Education Policy*, 20(3): 313–45.

Reisch, M. (2016) 'Why macro practice matters', *Journal of Social Work Education*, 52(3): 258–68.

Rimmerman, A. and Soffer, M. (2016) 'The making of disability policy in Israel: ad hoc advisory expert panels', in G. Menachem and A. Zehavi (eds) *Policy Analysis in Israel*, Bristol: Policy Press, pp 109–22.

Spiro, S. (2001) 'Social work education in Israel: trends and issues', *Social Work Education*, 20(1): 89–99.

Weiss-Gal, I. (2013) 'Social workers affecting social policy in Israel', in J. Gal and I. Weiss-Gal (eds) *Social Workers Affecting Social Policy*, Bristol: Policy Press, pp 59–78.

Weiss-Gal, I. (2016) 'Policy practice education: Literature review', *International Journal of Social Welfare*, 25(3): 290–303.

Weiss-Gal, I. and Gal, J. (2017) 'Where academia and policy meet: a cross-national perspective', in J. Gal and I. Weiss-Gal (eds) *Where Academia and Policy Meet*, Bristol: Policy Press, pp 243–62.

Weiss-Gal, I. and Gal, J. (2019) 'Social work educators and social policy: a cross-professional perspective', *European Journal of Social Work*, 22(1): 145–57.

Weiss-Gal, I., Gal, J. and Schwartz-Tayri, T. M. (2017) 'Teacher, researcher and … policy actor? On social work faculty and the policy processes', *Social Policy and Administration*, 51(5): 776–95.

7

Social workers' collective policy practice in times of austerity: Italy and Spain compared[1]

Riccardo Guidi

Situating social workers' political responsibility

Although professional history and ethical codes clearly assign social workers to a political responsibility, putting it into effective practice appears all but obvious in contemporary contexts for at least two connected reasons.

First, the orientation towards so-called 'policy practice' (Gal & Weiss-Gal, 2013) may clash with micro-level routine professional activities. Although the fight for social justice can be significantly embedded in daily work with single users (Dominelli, 2002), social and political change in contemporary complex societies is not realistically achievable through the sum of individual, episodic actions alone; rather it requires some form of upscaling and coordination. To be effective political actors, social workers seem called to develop a multifaceted collective agency linking the professional and the political.

Second, the contexts of professional social work in Europe have changed so much in the last 25 years that social workers' political acting faces an unprecedented challenge today. Social services organisations have been called to tackle growing, changing and more complex social demands (Taylor-Gooby, 2004) under the pressure of new managerialism (Clarke et al, 2000) and 'permanent austerity' (Pierson, 2001). This institutional context has been proven to have a 'corrosive' (Healy, 2009) and 'deforming' (Rogowski, 2011) effect on professional social work (Kessl, 2009; Stark, 2010; Branco & Amaro, 2011) and has reduced social workers' possibility to empower users and act on social structures (Rogowski, 2011; Jordan, 2012). Critics have also observed that in this scenario social professions seem to have sought an institutional legitimation by developing 'both a distancing from "politics" and an emphasis on clinical approaches' (Ferguson &

Lavalette, 2013: 106). Nevertheless, neoliberalism is supposed to have 'opened up such disillusionment and discontent within the profession that it has created the space for the rebirth of radicalism in social work' (Lavalette, 2011: 7), mainly possible through a new collective agency of practitioners (Ferguson & Lavalette, 2013: 107).

While literature has robustly focused on how crucial aspects of professional social work have been hit by neoliberal and austerity politics (for example, Jordan & Drakeford, 2012), recently increasing attention has been to paid to the *agency side* of the coin, namely social workers' collective action facing this adverse context and affecting the political processes of austerity (so far on this issue: Harlow et al, 2012; Pentaraki, 2013, 2015; Ioakimidis et al, 2014; Martínez-Román & Mateo-Pérez, 2015). Further, the study of social workers' collective policy practice in a (permanent) austerity age can benefit from a theoretical frame shaped by the literature on policy making and political mobilisation as well as comparative analysis. Accordingly, these are here used to shed light on the peculiar features of collective social workers' policy practice in Italy and Spain and interpret differences and similarities.

Framing social workers' collective policy practice

Social workers exert their own political responsibility mainly against public policies. They are currently multidimensional, multi-level, multi-actorial 'ongoing processes whereby social and political problems are defined, public decisions are taken and attempts made to implement them, and the outcome and the impact on the real world are perceived and assessed' (Capano & Howlett, 2009: 1). The policy process is conflictual and highly institutionalised (Capano, 2009) and conventionally develops along an ideal-type model, the *policy cycle*, connecting the different stages of policy making (Howlett & Ramesh, 1995; see also the Introduction to this volume).

Considering public policies in terms of conflictual and institutional processes urges framing professional social workers' policy practice within the analysis of interplay between actors and institutions (Hay 2002). Two well-known perspectives of interplay between actors and institutions in contemporary policy making can help to interpret the different kinds of collective social workers' policy practice. These perspectives can be conceived as two poles in a continuum, with many hybrid logics mixing elements from both perspectives.

The first perspective (institutionalised political exchange – PE) comes from the 1960s/1970s neo-corporatist trends of European policy making (Schmitter, 1974), later developed and more recently reinterpreted by Molina and Rhodes (2002), according to whom neo-corporatism is currently a typical form of policy making based on political exchanges between state agencies and interest organisations that structure policy networks. In these networks, as Pizzorno (1978) originally wrote, state agencies exchange goods against the political consensus that another collective actor can give (or give back). This form of networked governance can have more or less high levels of integration providing social partners only with access to information or a real influence on policy design (Molina & Rhodes, 2002: 323). Within this perspective, social workers are supposed to act as an organised group promoting and defending professional interests in the institutionalised negotiations and outside, namely acting in a 'self-interested' way and generating 'categoric goods' (Streeck & Schmitter, 1985: 128–29). The latter may be 'compatible or identical to collective goods', depending on 'the way on which group interests are organised into associative structures and processes' as well as the characteristics of the bargaining process between the interest organisations and between these and the state (Streeck & Schmitter, 1985: 129). For the social work profession, the fight to strengthen the profession may overlap with the fight for social justice in so far as increasing the quantity of social workers and the quality of their work (education, workloads and remuneration etc.) may give users more real chances to be empowered. Moreover, given their own ethical mandate, organised social workers are supposed to reconcile the socio-political and professional demands within the negotiations. However, the overlap between the particular/professional and the universal/political is all but obvious.

On the opposite pole, collective social workers' policy practice can be framed in a social movement perspective (SM). Social movements can be conceived as a form of non-institutional collective action aimed at promoting or resisting change against an authority (Snow et al, 2004). They operate non-episodically with some degree of organisation and by networking between different actors (organisations, groups and individuals) based on a shared identity (della Porta & Diani, 1999). Unlike interest groups, social movements are neither defined in relation to the government nor embedded in the political arena. They 'bring ordinary people' – not the elites – 'into confrontation with opponents, elites or authorities' (Tarrow, 2011: 8). Literature has shown that social movements' action and success are influenced by many factors, such as the overall political opportunities structure (Tarrow, 2011), cultural changes (Touraine, 1977; Melucci, 1996; della Porta & Diani, 1999), the existence and quality of resources (skills, organisation, money, and so on) owned by the protesters (McCarthy & Zald 1977), the ways of legitimising their collective action (Snow et al, 1986) and the network of actors (activists, groups and organisations) (Diani, 2000). Within the SM perspective, professional social workers are supposed to act as political advocates for the rights of disadvantaged people and/or as enablers of users' participation. This political-professional action can be very important: users often experience a politically detrimental condition of weakness because they have fewer resources to mobilise compared with other social groups (Milbrath, 1965). Moreover, since social service users often have few standardisable needs and tend to be assisted by local agencies with a high level of self-government, they have a peculiar difficulty in coordinating and legitimating their collective action, resulting in greater problems in successfully representing their own interests in the conventional political arena (Trumbull, 2012).

The aforementioned perspectives clarify that social workers' collective policy practice can have a high (PE) or low (SM) institutionalisation level and be more particularly/professionally (PE) or universally/politically (SM) oriented. A common problem concerns the relations between social services users and social workers: within the PE logics, public advantages risk being a by-product of the political exchanges between self-interested social workers' organisations and the state, while within the SM logics the professionals have to face the dilemmas of a spurious representation because they are not legitimated to represent users.

Social workers' collective policy practice in the austerity age: a comparative analysis

European social workers' policy practice has appeared to be weak thus far. Although differentiated by country, the most recent comparative study concludes that 'the involvement of social workers tends to be marginal and there is a wide discrepancy between discourse and practice' (Weiss-Gal & Gal, 2013: 194). The interplay of four factors can explain this situation: the socio-political context, the profession, the work setting and individual characteristics and perceptions (Weiss-Gal & Gal, 2013: 199–204).

Starting from this evidence, one can wonder whether something has changed in the recent critical juncture and which directions collective social workers' policy practice has taken. The economic crisis and austerity politics – which have significantly affected social rights, policies and services – can be conceived as a dramatic test for the political responsibility of social workers as well as their endurance.

In addressing this question as part of a wider ongoing comparative project, I will focus on two national cases – Italy and Spain – based on document analysis, in-depth interviews with the leaders of social workers' organisations and a qualitative/quantitative analysis of news releases of the most active and representative Italian organisation.

Italy and Spain present some common points as well as differences. A late transition to democracy (later in Spain), large families and regional differences are some structural traits that differentiate them from central and northern Europe. Both belong to the so-called 'Southern Model' of welfare (Ferrera, 1996) and since the 1980s/1990s professional social workers have experienced a similar organisational structure: the *trabajadores sociales* in Spain and the *assistenti sociali* in Italy are represented at two levels, namely the regional (36 *Colegios Profesionales* in Spain; 20 *Consigli regionali* in Italy) and national (through *Consejo General del Trabajo Social* – CGTS and *Consiglio Nazionale Ordine Assistenti Sociali* – CNOAS). The boards of regional and national organisations are elected by social workers.

Italy and Spain have been severely hit by the economic crisis and austerity politics. Both have experienced a dramatic increase in the number of people at risk of poverty or social exclusion and they have significantly reformed their own welfare policies and retrenched social budgets under the pressure of the so-called 'Troika' (European Commission, European Central Bank, International Monetary Fund) without any real negotiation with domestic social partners (Pavolini et al, 2015). Nevertheless, austerity politics has been more shocking in Spain. Unlike in Italy, in 2012 Spain requested external financial assistance, which implied a higher intrusiveness of the EU in domestic policies (Pavolini et al, 2015: 9–10). Moreover, the austerity measures in Spain have interrupted a decade of welfare state recalibration, whereas in Italy they have followed the usual reform path started in the 1990s (Pavolini et al, 2015: 18).

Spain and Italy also clearly differ in terms of contentious policies against austerity. While in Italy social movement organisations have only developed intermittent and not very original mobilisations, an innovative and widespread protest dealing with welfare retrenchment and democracy has distinguished Spain (Alberich Nistal, 2016). The emerging new social movement organisations (the *Plataforma de Afectados por la Hipoteca*, *Plataforma Democracia Real Ya*, *Juventud sin Futuro* and the best-known *Movimiento 15-M*) have spoken for excluded and vulnerable people better than other collective actors through a radical and innovative action repertoire (for example, the *Acampadas*, the *Cumbre Social* and the *Mareas*).

Similarities and differences between Spain and Italy can be also considered regarding the collective policy practice social workers have developed. According to the former president, the Italian CNOAS has always acted on social policies since its establishment but with different orientations:

> 'sometimes it has been more centred on the profession, sometimes had a more general attention [...] historically CNOAS has worked more in the first direction and it has then been gradually opened to the second. It has been partially physiological because CNOAS had to start with the professional "ABC" at the beginning'.

The path towards 'professional empowerment' (Current CNOAS President) still seems incomplete and it significantly intersects the policy practice path. According to the current president, recent CNOAS activities (2014–18) have been mainly oriented to:

> 'promote a cultural movement [...] building a wider professional culture than the limited daily work context [...] making the profession more aware about its mandate and acting under the assumption that how the profession is exerted in a context makes a difference on the efficacy, efficiency and equity of a social policy'.

Dissatisfaction with the slow and laborious development of the social work profession in Italy and the (self-)representation of the latter as technically weak, with public services embedded, unable to link casework and societal trends, clearly shapes this strategic priority. It has implied working towards strengthening the professional community (internal side) and making it publicly count (external side), sometimes through specific activities for each side, sometimes by using the same instruments in both directions. However, the two sides are considered 'inseparable from each other' (Current CNOAS President).

Digital communication – beyond training and education – has recently been the most effective new activity line for 'professional empowerment'. In 2013–14, a new CNOAS website and a bimonthly newsletter were launched; in 2016, CNOAS opened its own Facebook page (9500 followers), and more recently it has produced a television series displayed on its WebTv. 'Creating a common feeling among our members', 'giving the public the idea about what our profession actually is' and 'developing the relationships with the institutional stakeholders' (Current CNOAS Communication Manager) are the interconnected priorities of CNOAS communication.

Digital communication instruments have also supported the efforts to position the profession in the public arena, namely through official stances. Analysis of the CNOAS website reveals that the number of news releases (2004–16) has increased exponentially since 2013. Both professionally (CNOAS positioning on the profession) and socio-politically oriented (CNOAS positioning on socio-political issues) news releases have grown in number. Professional claims are low and stable in the period (with only a minor peak in 2013), whereas socio-political claims have grown significantly from 2013 onwards. Migration policies have been the most frequent topic, followed by child policies, social policies, poverty and social rights, whereas the most frequent professionally oriented news releases are about internal communications, training and social workers' media representation.

Official stances are often preceded by elaboration of documents and coalition-building and followed by activities exerting political pressure. This has happened especially for social policies, about which CNOAS has produced the most structured documents (for example, CNOAS, 2013) and has repeatedly pressed governments and political parties through public expression of dissent on measures, open letters and public exchanges with candidates on their electoral programmes (for example, CNOAS, 2014). In 2016, CNOAS also promoted the constitution of a working group comprising 16 social workers' organisations, whose 'Manifesto for Welfare' (CNOAS, 2016) has held the last national governments accountable for the deficiencies of Welfare system, suggested reforms and announced future mobilisations.

Among the policy practice, the participation of CNOAS in institutional policy-making processes (for example, justice system reform, professions' reform, minimum income measure design, and so on) has been significant and increasing. Taking part in and influencing these processes confirms that CNOAS has successfully developed its own political capability, although it also poses questions about the social workers' representation.

> 'Firstly we have looked for being recognised by institutions through an informal lobbying. […] Now institutions look for us because they need to know what happens in the social field. We don't protest only but propose too. […] We

have positioned ourselves where we had to stay.' (Current CNOAS President)

'Participating in the institutional tables has been an achievement. For a long time institutions did not consider us a political actor. Now nobody forgets us. In the last years, *assistenti sociali* collective agency on policies has increased and now it is systematically exerted. We learned to act in a political way, before we were not able to do it. The heaviest exertion for CNOAS is not public positioning but avoiding the professionals lag behind compared to where their spokespeople are.' (Former CNOAS President)

Economic crisis and austerity politics have affected CNOAS in so far as 'they have made us raise our voice further' (Former CNOAS President) but they do not drive the design of any extraordinary initiatives. Conversely, there has been a large-scale, innovative and pronounced professional mobilisation against austerity in Spain. Similar to a social movement organisation, Spanish CGTS has mainly mobilised through campaigns, each characterised by an issue, a network, a tactic and initiatives. An example is the Alliance for the Defence of the Public System of Social Services, a network of Spanish organisations (professional actors, trade unions, associations, universities) asking for social dignity and social rights to be placed centre stage in policy making and acting by producing public analyses and proposals for social service reforms.

However, the best known, most original and most widely participated campaign has been the *Marea Naranja* (Orange Tide), launched at the national level in September 2012. Although the loss of jobs and budgets in the social assistance field and the worsening of *trabajadores sociales* work conditions significantly urged professional mobilisation, the campaign has rejected a strict neo-corporative matrix. It has been defined as: 'the citizen's movement that defends the public and qualified system of social services in Spain ... a way to reject the losing of social rights and the reconversion of the social system into a charity one' (www.cgtrabajosocial.es/marea_naranja).

Marea Naranja has had a peculiarly unifying and innovative value. CGTS has coordinated individual discontent and local mobilisations against austerity (first in Valencia and Aragona) under a common 'action frame' (Former CGTS President) in an effort to make the protest clearly visible at the national level and beyond. *Marea Naranja* has joined the other 'professional tides' (white for health realm, green for education, and so on) and the wider Spanish movement against austerity. It has involved social workers, educators and users. The engagement of the latter is considered crucial – albeit very difficult in practice – and clarifies how the political and the professional are specifically intertwined:

> 'we were going to participate to the social movements [...] the principle is "we don't want it is a CGTS initiative" [...] Marea Naranja must not be elitist. It has been a very dispersed movement [...] It has been clearly identified with social work but not only [...] We wanted to go with citizens and not to be their voice ... Trying to involve the users, other organisations, other professionals has been fundamental for us. [...] Mobilising social services users has been difficult because most don't see a social right under the intervention and many feel ashamed to be recognised as users.' (Former CGTS President)

Marea Naranja uses tactics for dramatising the protest and making it as visible as possible. The mobilisation systematically has a scenography (logos, placards, posters), a dress code (the orange and an orange t-shirt with an evocative picture) and choreography in the streets (the *batucada* dance), all mainly brought in non-institutional local and national initiatives.

CGTS and *Marea Naranja* have especially protested against the Spanish National Law on the 'rationalisation and sustainability of local administration' (Ley 27/2013). The protest reached the European Parliament, where a delegation was received by seven parliamentary groups and the European media. As the Former CGTS president stated: 'We wanted to show how the cuts in social services were violating the human rights.' The international echo of *Marea Naranjia* has been strong, contributing to inspire other professional mobilisations in Europe, namely the Social Work Action Network and British Association of Social Workers. The CGTS president who promoted it was recognised for outstanding services to social work by IFSW (International Federation of Social Workers) in 2014, was elected as president of IFSW Europe in 2016 and appointed as Secretary of State in 2018.

According to data gathered by CGTS in 2014, Spanish social workers have widely participated. About 80% agreed with the mobilisation claims and 47% participated in more or less direct ways (such as wearing badges, displaying posters on the bureau wall, demonstrations, and so on) (Lima, 2014: 110–34). The campaign has mainly mobilised practitioners working in municipal social services in both urban and peripheral areas:

> 'They lived with social cuts and injustices in the first person […] the anguish was so strong that rebelling was the only path […] They could channel their own indignation in a protest through the professional structure. We built a space.' (Former CGTS President)

According to the Former CGTS president, *Marea Naranjia* has achieved three main results at the national level: first, the mobilisation has made social services system and social professions publicly visible and social workers united (professional empowerment result); second, it has contributed to slowing down Spanish social assistance cuts (institutional result); and thirdly, it has prompted the regional colleges to co-design all of the political parties' electoral programmes, except the Popular Party. After the elections, several social workers have also been assigned high administrative appointments (political result).

Although the Spanish CGTS and the regional colleges have been placed at centre stage, other professional entities have also developed a significant policy practice against austerity, including the Association of Directors and Managers of Social Services (ADGSS). Established at the national level by expert professionals in 1994 with the aim of contributing to develop Spanish social services, ADGSS has progressively developed an iterative policy practice based on official data and performance indicators about users, social services and policies. From 2008 onwards, the regional-based biannual analyses have had a massive impact on mass media, with more than 200 articles in *El Pais*, a regular presence on TV programmes and a consequent 'terrific influence' on the regional and national political and public agenda (Current AGDSS President). All of this is carried out through a very light organisational structure: ADGSS has never had paid staff or public funds and it acts through a few highly committed people: "researchers, practitioners and anti-austerity activists at the same time. […] We are committed to social services, we defend the public system but our main characteristic is that people are our raison d'etre" (Current AGDSS President).

Another telling case at the local level is Foro Servicios Sociales de Madrid. Established in 2014 based on a manifesto and a dossier, it is an association of professionals and citizens aimed at defending and developing social rights against austerity politics. The re-politicisation of social professions is one of the objectives of Foro.

Discussion: paths of social workers' collective policy practice

Political responsibility lies at the core of the social work profession. Exerting it in a context shaped by neo-managerialism, economic crisis and (permanent) austerity is crucial for the profession, the users and democracy, although it is particularly difficult. Contrary to deactivation hypotheses, since 2008 collective social workers' policy practice has significantly developed in both Italy and Spain through the action of organisations coming from within the profession. Comparative analysis also shows that collective policy practice in the shadow of austerity can follow different paths, even in allegedly similar countries.

Italy seems to follow an institutional and professional mobilisation path, close to the PE model. In this context, the most representative social workers' organisation (CNOAS) has increasingly acted as a conventional professional body by linking efforts from the internal (professional community) and the external (institutions, political forces, public opinion) side. Italian collective policy practice appears to be centred on the need to defend and strengthen professional social work in the institutional and public settings (see also Campanini, 2015: 106). Empowering the profession seems to be the best – albeit an indirect – way to promote social justice. Despite being well-grounded and realistic, this approach risks achieving public advancements as by-products of professional interests' representation activity. Moreover, it seems to encourage an elitist policy practice mainly exerted by delegates. CNOAS has at least partially compensated these risks through the development of official standing activity and a stronger connection with its own members.

By contrast, the Spanish collective policy practice contains many elements of the SM perspective. Here, multiple social workers' organisations have carried out massive mobilisation through different political–professional activities and campaigns. Spanish CGTS has promoted the most visible one (*Marea Naranja*), which has involved a huge number of social workers, tried to engage social service users, joined the wider anti-austerity movement, placed social rights at centre stage, acted through a multi-scale, plural, non-institutional repertoire and inspired further social workers' mobilisations in Europe. Here again, collective policy practice has been used to empower the profession, but this has been done by claiming social rights and public services first. Although 'rights', 'users' and 'justice' are the key terms in Spanish protest vocabulary, the difficulty in actually involving social service users confirms the risk that social workers are representing them in a spurious way.

In line with the arguments of Weiss-Gal and Gal (2013), comparative analysis also invites considering national long-medium term policy models, the political opportunities structure and professional features as key factors to understand the differences of social workers' collective policy practice. In Spain, austerity politics has been shocking and has resulted in popular and original protest, while in Italy austerity has followed the late 1990s welfare policy path and mobilisations have been weak. Spanish social workers have thus found a more favourable political opportunities structure to develop innovative collective policy practice. They have particularly followed the professional mobilisation of the education and health sectors by adapting their form of protest (the *Mareas*) to the social services realm. Nevertheless, beyond the structural conditions, mobilisation has been possible because Spanish professional organisations have played the role of 'political/professional entrepreneurs', of outraged social workers acting for social justice. Collective policy practice paths can thus also diverge because social workers' professional bodies express a specific professional political culture, interpret the role of political entrepreneurs differently and use diverse strategies and tactics.

Conclusion

Social workers' potential in affecting welfare policies emerges as confirmed and enriched in hard times through the mobilisation of collective actors. The consolidation of social work organisations in southern Europe allows social professions' public and institutional legitimation to step forward and social justice to have a further chance.

Beyond one-dimensional visions of social workers' collective policy practice, this study clearly shows the existence of different mobilisation paths in countries belonging to the same welfare model (Ferrera, 1996). The divergence can be explained by the interactions between the political opportunities structure and the characteristics of professional bodies (political culture, resources, skills) in the medium term. These dynamics can push collective policy practice towards particularistic/professional (PE model) or universal/political (SM model) achievements. With the austerity age being such a critical juncture for democracy, SM-oriented strategies seem to have more chance to actually promote social justice, whereas PE-oriented strategies may work better in ordinary times.

Future research on the topic should extend comparative analysis, consider the links between policy practice and the battle for professional empowerment in more depth as well as addressing the crucial question of social services users' involvement in social workers' collective policy practice.

Note

[1] This chapter was produced within the University of Pisa PRA_2017_56 Project. Its preparation was assisted by a research stay at the Department of Social Work and Social Services of Complutense University of Madrid – for which I am grateful – and the invaluable help of Maria Teresa Garcia Giraldez. I am also grateful to the participants of Stream 19 – 15th ESPAnet Europe Conference and Session 22 – 11th ESPAnet Italia Conference, as well as to Annamaria Campanini, Elena Roldan and the editors of this volume for their comments on a previous draft of the chapter.

References

Alberich Nistal, T. (2016) *Desde las asociaciones de vecinos al 15m y las mareas ciudadanas: breve historia de los movimientos sociales*, Madrid: Editorial Dykinson.

Branco, F. and Amaro, M. I. (2011) 'Social work active practices within the new social policy trends: a Portuguese perspective', *Social Work Review*, 4: 7–22.

Campanini, A. (2015) 'Il servizio sociale e le policy practice', in A. Bassi and G. Moro (eds) *Politiche sociali innovative e diritti di cittadinanza*, Milano: Franco Angeli, pp 101–20.

Capano, G. (2009) 'Understanding policy change as an epistemological and theoretical problem', *Journal of Comparative Policy Analysis: Research and Practice*, 11(1): 7–31.

Capano, G. and Howlett, M. (2009) 'The multidimensional world of policy dynamics', in G. Capano and M. Howlett (eds) *European and North American Policy Change: Drivers and Dynamics*, Abingdon, Oxon: Routledge, pp 1–12.

Clarke, J., Gewirtz, S. and McLaughlin, E. (eds) (2000) *New Managerialism, New Welfare?*, London: Sage.

CNOAS (2013) *Documento del Consiglio Nazionale sui punti di criticità delle condizioni sociali del Paese*. Available at: www.cnoas.it

CNOAS (2014) *Il servizio sociale ai tempi della crisi*. Available at: www.cnoas.it

CNOAS (2016) *Manifesto per il Welfare*. Available at: www.cnoas.it

Della Porta, D. and Diani, M. (1999) *Social Movements: An Introduction*, Oxford: Blackwell.

Diani, M. (2000) 'Simmel to Rokkan and beyond: towards a network theory of (new) social movements', *European Journal of Social Theory*, 3(4): 387–406.

Dominelli, L. (2002) *Anti Oppressive Social Work Theory and Practice*, Basingstoke: Palgrave Macmillan.

Ferguson, I. and Lavalette, M. (2013) 'Crisis, austerity and the future(s) of social work in the UK', *Critical and Radical Social Work*, 1(1): 95–110.

Ferrera, M. (1996) 'The "southern model" of welfare in social Europe', *Journal of European Social Policy*, 6: 17–37.

Gal, J. and Weiss-Gal, I. (2013) (eds) *Social Workers Affecting Social Policy. An International Perspective*, Bristol: Policy Press.

Hay, C. (2002) *Political Analysis. A Critical Introduction*, Basingstoke: Palgrave Macmillan.

Harlow, E., Berg, E., Barry, J. and Chandler, J. (2012) 'Neoliberalism, managerialism and the reconfiguring of social work in Sweden and the United Kingdom', *Organization*, 20(4): 534–50.

Healy, K. (2009) 'A case of mistaken identity: the social welfare professions and New Public Management', *Journal of Sociology*, 45(4): 401–18.

Howlett, M. and Ramesh, M. (1995) *Studying Public Policy: Policy Cycles and Policy Subsystems*, Toronto: Oxford University Press.

Ioakimidis, V., Santos, C. C. and Herrero, I. M. (2014) 'Reconceptualizing social work in times of crisis: an examination of the cases of Greece, Spain and Portugal', *International Social Work*, 57(4): 285–300.

Kessl, F. (2009) 'Critical reflexivity, social work, and the emerging European post-welfare states', *European Journal of Social Work*, 12(3): 305–17.

Jordan, B. (2012) 'Making sense of the "Big Society": social work and the moral order', *Journal of Social Work*, 12(6): 630–46.

Jordan, B. and Drakeford, M. (2012) *Social Work and Social Policy under Austerity*, Basingstoke: Palgrave-Macmillan.

Lima, A. (2014) *II Informe sobre los servicios sociales en España*, Madrid: CGTS.

Lavalette, M. (2011) 'Introduction', in M. Lavalette (ed) *Radical Social Work Today: Social Work at the Crossroads*, Bristol: The Policy Press, pp 1–10.

Martínez-Román, M. A. and Mateo-Pérez, M. A. (2015) 'Trabajo social en España. De los recortes sociales a la arena pública', *Visioni LatinoAmericane*, 13: 107–25.

McCarthy, J. D. and Zald, M. Z. (1977) 'Resource mobilization and social movements: a partial theory', *American Journal of Sociology*, 82(6): 1212–41.

Melucci, A. (1996) *Challenging Codes: Collective Action in the Information Age*, Cambridge: Cambridge University Press.

Milbrath, L. W. (1965) *Political Participation*, Chicago: Rand McNal.

Molina, O. and Rhodes, M. (2002) 'Corporatism: the past, present, and future of a concept', *Annual Review of Political Science*, 5: 305–31.

Pavolini E., León, M, Guillén, A. M. and Ascoli, U. (2015) 'From austerity to permanent strain? The EU and welfare state reform in Italy and Spain', *Comparative European Politics*, 13: 1–21.

Pentaraki, M. (2013) 'If we do not cut social spending, we will end up like Greece: challenging consent to austerity through social work action', *Critical Social Policy*, 33(4): 700–11.

Pentaraki, M. (2015) 'The executive committee of the Greek Professional Association of Social Work in an age of austerity: examining its response', *European Journal of Social Work*, 18(1): 140–55.

Pierson, P. (2001) 'Coping with permanent austerity. Welfare state restructuring in affluent democracies', in P. Pierson (ed) *The New Politics of the Welfare State*, New York: Oxford University Press, pp 410–56.

Pizzorno, A. (1978) 'Political exchange and collective identity in industrial conflict', in A. Pizzorno and C. Crouch (eds) *The Resurgence of Class Conflict in Western Europe since 1968*, London: Palgrave Macmillan, pp 277–98.

Rogowski, S. (2011) 'Managers, managerialism and social work with children and families: the deformation of a profession?', *Practice: Social Work in Action*, 23(3): 157–67.

Schmitter, P. C. (1974) 'Still the century of corporatism?', *The Review of Politics*, 36(1): 85–131.

Snow, D. A., Soule, S. A. and Kriesi, H. (2004) 'Mapping the terrain', in D. A. Snow, S. A. Soule and H. Kriesi (eds) *The Blackwell Companion to Social Movements*, Oxford: Blackwell, pp 3–16.

Snow, D., Rochford, Jr., E. B., Worden, S. K. and Benford, R. D. (1986) 'Frame alignment processes, micromobilization and movement participation', *American Sociological Review*, 51(4): 464–81.

Stark, C. (2010) 'The neoliberal ideology and the challenges for social work ethics and practice', *Social Work Review*, 1: 9–19.

Streeck, W. and Schmitter, P. C. (1985) 'Community, market, state-and associations? The prospective contribution of interest governance to social order', *European Sociological Review*, 1(2): 119–38.

Tarrow, S. (2011) *Power in Movement: Social Movements and Contentious Politics*, New York: Cambridge University Press.

Taylor-Gooby, P. (ed) (2004) *New Risks, New Welfare. The Transformation of the European Welfare State*, Oxford: Oxford University Press.

Touraine, A. (1977) *The Self-Production of Society*, Chicago: University of Chicago Press.

Trumbull, G. (2012) *Strength in Numbers: The Political Power of Weak Interests*, Cambridge, MA: Harvard University Press.

Weiss-Gal, I. and Gal, J. (2013) 'An international perspective on policy practice', in J. Gal and I. Weiss-Gal (eds) *Social Workers Affecting Social Policy: An International Perspective*, Bristol: Policy Press.

8

Social policy and welfare movements 'from below': the Social Work Action Network (SWAN) in the UK

Rich Moth and Michael Lavalette

Introduction

The aim of this chapter is to explore the relationship between social movements and social policy with a particular focus on social work activist engagement within the mental health and welfare systems. The primary argument is that while social movements are rarely directly responsible for determining the exact nature and content of particular welfare policies, forms of grassroots mobilisation and intervention can nonetheless play an important role in shaping welfare settlements (Barker & Lavalette, 2015). The first section outlines the theoretical warrant for this perspective on social policy development. We then provide an empirical illustration of this process by offering an account of the Social Work Action Network (SWAN), a social movement organisation (SMO) within the social work field in the UK. This involves a brief history of the emergence of this network and an analysis of its organising methodology. We argue the latter combines ideological, agitational and campaigning elements underpinned by an orientation to cross-sectional alliance building. We then describe the application of these modes of political activity within campaigns to challenge neoliberal mental health and welfare policy reforms. We conclude by acknowledging some limitations of these campaigning interventions but argue nonetheless for their potential to both articulate and embody alternative progressive and democratic welfare futures.

The politics of welfare policy development

Mainstream accounts of social policy formation tend to adopt a pluralist or neo-corporatist approach, which constructs state welfare policy as evolving in an institutional context characterised by interest group competition and/or negotiation (Annetts et al, 2009). The literature commonly treats welfare developments as 'cumulative' and as reflecting the work of resourceful and thoughtful political leaders or civil servants (Fraser, 1984), or, more broadly, as the outcome of political party commitments and interventions (Stephens, 1979). Alternatively 'welfare regimes' may be perceived as the outcome of particular class coalitions within specific cultures (Esping-Anderson, 1990) or as reflections of the economic drives and 'needs' of capitalism (Gough, 1979) or of globalisation (Pierson, 1991).

While such approaches have their strengths, they underplay the significance of protest, collective action and social struggle from below in processes of reproduction and reform of state welfare (Fox-Piven & Cloward, 1979). By contrast, social movement literature acknowledges that movements have been important in establishing key aspects of modern welfare provisions. From regulated working hours to paid annual leave, from housing and rent controls to established rights to health and education, from control over one's fertility to provision for childcare, welfare demands have often been central to movement claims. But exactly how have movements produced welfare developments? To what extent have movement demands and claims been mitigated and refracted through state policy? How successful have movements been at expanding welfare provisions or defending welfare settlements?

Following Saville (1957), we suggest that, historically, the politics of welfare development and change have involved the intersection of three kinds of impulse: the developing requirements of capitalist production, the political calculations of ruling elites and the activities of social movements (Ferguson et al, 2002). Every case for 'welfare improvement' involves arguments about 'economic efficiency'. An educated or healthier workforce should, in principle, be more productive, improved sanitation should cut the impact of endemic disease, better nutrition should improve workers' (and soldiers') performance, and so on. But 'economic efficiency' arguments pose other questions about particular interests: since welfare provision is relatively expensive, who is to pay, and how? Other considerations also shape arguments about welfare provision: ruling elites must find some balance between the needs of continuing accumulation and the need for legitimation (O'Connor, 1973). Popular movements demanding 'reform' must be variously contained, repressed or conceded to, in ways that preserve vital elite interests.

Only occasionally, and in extreme circumstances, have rulers granted 'welfare' measures in a hurry and in ways that seem to directly respond to protest movement activity. In Britain, the 1915 Glasgow rent strikes, backed by the threat of unofficial stoppages in munitions factories, offers the most prominent example: the wartime Parliament rushed through rent control legislation (Damer, 2000). The more typical pattern has been one where welfare reform is 'normalised', made partial, de-fanged in its political impact, contained by the elaboration of administrative controls and always kept subordinate to the imperatives of continued accumulation.

If, on the one hand, behind every significant welfare reform in Britain we can discover a popular movement agitating for improvement, we argue that those movements have rarely succeeded in shaping the actual forms in which what they sought was delivered. Their impacts have been indirect; they increase pressures for change, or challenge policies and their effects in a way that brings pressure upon elites to respond. Social movements create the ground upon which many social policy debates take place, though they are less often the direct architects of policy outcomes (Barker & Lavalette, 2015).

In order to develop this theme we will now examine the work of one particular social movement organisation in the welfare arena: SWAN. Both authors have been active participants in SWAN since its inception.

Social movement organising in social work: SWAN's analysis and strategic orientation

SWAN is a campaigning alliance that has operated in the social work field since its formation in 2006 at a national conference in Liverpool, England called to debate the issues raised in what became known as the 'Social Work Manifesto' (Jones et al, 2004). The Manifesto was written by four activist academics and argued that a rebirth of radical interpretations of social work was possible within the context of the growing global justice (or anti-capitalist) movement and the global anti-war movements of the early twenty-first century. This perspective is based on the notion that radicalism in social work is rarely generated from within the profession itself; rather it develops when social work practitioners and academics engage with new developments, ideas and practices within wider social movements.

The context of the Manifesto was a shift away from the mid-twentieth century role for UK social work in state provision of social care services and support. Instead, under neoliberal reforms at the end of the century, social work was increasingly office-based and focused on assessment, purchasing and management of care delivered through a mixed economy of provider organisations (Harris, 2003). The imposition of these neoliberal modes of welfare provision was accompanied by an increasing role for the practices of 'New Public Management' together with public sector cuts and welfare retrenchment. As a consequence of these changes, the Manifesto argued, social work was in danger of losing sight of its commitment to social justice and meeting the needs of disadvantaged and marginalised people in society. In the face of increasing managerialism and privatised forms of welfare, SWAN asserted that 'Another Social Work Is Possible!'

Nonetheless it should be recognised that social work is itself a site of conflict and contestation that plays out in the following four broad areas. First, such contradictions are rooted in the social work task, with the profession performing both 'care' and 'control' functions within a context set by national and local state regulation. Second, it is shaped by the realities of the social work labour process. Lipsky (1980) suggested social workers were 'street-level bureaucrats', with a 'professional identity' and relevant support from the welfare bureaucracy that enabled them to use a degree of discretion when working with service users. More recent studies of the social work labour process influenced by Braverman (1974) have emphasised that, under conditions of neoliberalism, the social work task has been 'degraded' and subjected to a range of managerialist controls that limit worker autonomy (Harris, 2003). This has led to conflict between frontline social workers and social work managers over work time, caseloads, budget considerations and 'target setting' (Ferguson & Lavalette, 2008). Third, the location of social work activity within the wider social structure (that is, among the poorest and most marginalised) means that social workers are constantly confronted by the realities of poverty, inequality and oppression. Throughout the history of social work there are many examples of social workers who have been radicalised by their direct contact with the victims of an unequal and unjust society (Ferguson & Woodward, 2009). Fourth, at political, ethical and ideological levels social work is, in actuality, a highly contested profession. For instance, the International Federation of Social Work has a global definition of social work that suggests it is committed to promoting both social cohesion and social justice, values between which there may well be significant tensions in practice.

These four areas of contestation mean that social work is not a uniform or unified profession. Historically, there has been a radical current within the profession that advocates for societal change as part of the social work task (Lavalette, 2010). SWAN positions itself within that radical tradition going back to the profession's founding moments (Lavalette & Ferguson, 2007). SWAN's political goals are not simply to secure quantitative improvements in resource allocation to welfare, which it considers a necessary but insufficient condition, but also to realise qualitative transformation in the nature of services towards more radically egalitarian, democratic and inclusive forms of provision, an approach summarised in the demand for 'more and better' (Sedgwick, 2015).

SWAN's founding conference of 2006 formulated a broad definition of membership, open to anyone who agreed with the broad principles of the Manifesto (Jones et al, 2004). However, while SWAN has the conventional attributes of a SMO, it constitutes a form of partial organisation insofar as it has a membership structure but recognises all activists who identify with and participate in its activities regardless of formal membership status (Den Hond et al, 2015). For this reason, while its national membership in the UK is around 500, it has a larger though more fluid base of participants at the local level.

In general terms, we would characterise SWAN's strategic mode of organisation as a 'united front' bringing together those within social work identifying with various strands of left-wing politics (social democratic, green, revolutionary, anarchist, trade unionist, social movement activists) to campaign around common goals (Hallas, 2003). In a more specific sense, SWAN is constituted as a form of cross-sectional alliance involving social work practitioners, service users, carers and trade unionists as well as academics and students. The development and strengthening of these alliances has been integral to SWAN since its inception. By adopting this mode of organisation, SWAN embodies an approach that seeks to integrate diverse demands and interests from across these constitutive networks on an equal footing (Sedgwick, 2015), for instance, the inclusion of representatives from affiliated service user organisations such as Autistic Rights Movement, Shaping Our Lives and Disabled People Against Cuts within SWAN's coordinating structures. Such cross-sectional alliance building has inherent challenges and complexities, not least the need to maintain a fundamentally democratic ethos to ensure that unequal and oppressive social relations, for instance between professionals and service users, are not reproduced within SWAN's structures and initiatives (Moth & McKeown, 2016). Nonetheless, by uniting disparate constituencies around shared goals, this organising strategy has the potential to promote forms of collectivism that enhance strategic capacity through the integration of diverse knowledge and perspectives to inform campaigning (Krinsky, 2009).

As well as being central at the intra-organisational level, *alliance building* is integral to SWAN at the inter-organisational and international levels. SWAN works to develop broader institutional alliances within the labour, welfare and wider social movements. For instance, it is a 'supporting organisation' officially recognised by the trade unions Unison (the main social workers union), Unite (with many social care workers in its ranks) and UCU (the lecturers union). SWAN has also affiliated to the main anti-racist organisations in the UK: Stand Up to Racism and Unite Against Fascism. In addition, SWAN has built alliances with the main professional social work organisation in the UK, the British Association of Social Workers (BASW). Alongside BASW, SWAN set up 'Social Workers and Service Users Against Austerity'. SWAN also organises at the global level with the aim of internationalising the radical social work current. The original social work Manifesto has been translated into Greek, Spanish, Cantonese and Russian and there have been SWAN interventions at each of the last seven (biannual) Global Social Work conferences. Consequently SWAN has become a significant radical current within international social work with groups in Ireland, Greece, Canada and Denmark.

SWAN has adopted three primary modes of political intervention since its formation. The first is *ideological*, strengthening the radical theoretical current within social work via the publication by SWAN activists of critical academic texts and, more recently, establishing the *Critical and Radical Social Work* journal. The second is *agitational* in response to policy and practice developments. For example SWAN has been involved in producing a number of pamphlets on issues such as 'Baby P' (Ferguson & Lavalette, 2008) and reforms to social work education (SWAN, 2014a). The third is *grassroots campaigning/ actions* at local and national levels. In Scotland, the SWAN network made a significant impact in refugee support work. In Bristol, the local group led a successful campaign against a local taxi company, run by a member of the (Nazi) British National Party that had won a subcontract from the local authority to transport disabled children to school. In Merseyside and Norwich SWAN groups were heavily involved in local campaigns against mental health service cuts (Moth et al, 2015). The national Steering Committee also takes up national campaign initiatives. This has included national days of action in support of refugees, establishing a Charter for Mental Health and setting up a support campaign for Hungarian social worker Norbert Ferencz (who faced imprisonment for his work with homeless people in Budapest).

Mental health and welfare policy reforms: SWAN and collective action from below

Having outlined SWAN's analysis of the political context of social work and strategic orientation to activism, in this section we examine the network's contribution to resistance movements challenging recent neoliberal policy reforms. This is presented in two parts, the first examining activism related to mental health policy and the second exploring resistance to welfare reforms and 'psychocompulsion'.

Mental health policy reforms and resistance

Mental health policy in England is a complex and evolving amalgam of legal, professional and institutional strands (Glasby & Tew, 2015). Four dimensions of recent policy are particularly salient in terms of SWAN's interventions: marketisation/managerialism, risk, recovery and austerity. We view these as significant 'moments' (Harris, 2008) in the neoliberal elaboration of UK mental health policy which are sedimented in the present (Moth, 2019). The first policy agenda is marketisation and managerialism, which was embedded in mental health (and other) services through the introduction of mechanisms such as the purchaser–provider split under the National Health Service and Community Care Act 1990 alongside other quasi-market indicators and target regimes (Harris, 2003). The second dimension, emerging in the mid-1990s, was a 'moral panic' regarding the risk and danger to the public purportedly posed by some mental health service users that led to an increasingly coercive focus in policy and, ultimately, led to the imposition of more restrictive measures such as community treatment orders (Holloway, 1996; Glasby & Tew, 2015). A third shift was the promotion of the recovery approach since the early 2000s (DH, 2001). While recovery had initially developed as a (mainly) service user led critique of pathologising biomedical perspectives on mental distress, this has been operationalised in services via highly individualised self-management approaches (SCIE, 2007). As critics note, mainstream recovery approaches have aligned with neoliberal tenets by de-emphasising collective provision of mental health services, inculcating tendencies to reduced service consumption and thereby seeking to minimise purported service/welfare dependency (Harper & Speed, 2012). The fourth and most recent development that has impacted on mental health policy is the post-2008 crisis austerity agenda. As a consequence of this, mental health service delivery has been significantly reconfigured and reduced (Docherty & Thornicroft, 2015; McNicoll, 2015), with swingeing cuts to local authority budgets in England resulting in a 37% reduction in the number of adults with mental health needs accessing adult social care support between 2010 and 2015 (Burchardt et al, 2015). Alongside this, in the National Health Service (NHS), there has been a 15% cut in mental health in-patient beds and reductions in community support (Centre for Mental Health, 2017).

As austerity cuts intensified and exacerbated the negative consequences of earlier policy reforms for service users and social workers, one response developed by activists in SWAN was the Charter for Mental Health (SWAN, 2014b). The charter was conceptualised as a strategic tool for use by campaigners to aid cross-sectional alliance building and mobilisation and thereby enhance political action for progressive policy reform. Its aim was to provide a brief and accessible summary of the harmful impacts of marketisation, risk discourse and cuts to mental health services, and present a series of demands for reform around which diverse activists and campaigns could unite. It did so by drawing out some emergent tendencies in current mental health campaigning, distilling and amplifying their radical possibilities, and making the case for deepening alliances. In this way it sought to enhance the potential for the attainment of social movement goals. The Charter went on to identify potential pitfalls for alliance building, in particular power inequalities between users and practitioners in mental health services, but nonetheless made the case for shared interests across both groups in the defence but also democratic transformation of collective welfare provision. A democratic ethos was also prefigured in the methodology for developing the Charter that sought to involve service user/survivor as well as practitioner and academic participants in an inclusive and egalitarian process. Moreover, consequently, by developing a set of cross-sectional demands that united diverse constituencies around common needs and aspirations the Charter both articulated and reinforced this conception of shared interests representing a form of 'political epistemology' (Moth & McKeown, 2016).

While a modest intervention developed with limited resources, the Charter was circulated nationally to SWAN groups and members, and promoted at SWAN events in a number of parts of the UK. It was circulated in mental health activist circles beyond SWAN and attracted signatories from a wide range of individuals from service user/survivor, carer and practitioner backgrounds as well as campaign groups. However, as well as a means to express dissent regarding the direction of policy, the Charter was conceived as an activist tool to aid intervention. One example of its application was in Liverpool when closure/outsourcing of the last two remaining local authority mental health resource centres was proposed by the council in 2014 as part of a £1 million tranche of austerity cuts to mental health services. A campaign to challenge the council's decision was launched by service users in alliance with activists from SWAN, Liverpool Against the Cuts (local anti-austerity campaign) and the Unite public sector trade union which represented some of the workers in the service. The campaign drew on a 'repertoire of contention' (Tarrow, 1994) that included petitions, demonstrations and lobbying of council meetings (see Moth et al, 2015 for more detail). The constellation of values/principles expressed in and by the campaign reflected, to some degree, those articulated in the Charter and we note three examples here. The first concerns the desired ends of the campaign: the maintenance of non-profit public sector delivery and rejection of further marketisation of services via outsourcing. The second and third reflect strategic and value considerations: the ethos of cross-sectional alliances between users and workers that informed the campaign's organisation, and the critique of stigmatising risk discourse based on an egalitarian and liberatory ethical stance – for instance a proposal by an activist at a meeting to frame the argument for keeping the service open in terms of the risk to public safety was rejected by the campaign. This intervention by campaigners was ultimately successful in keeping the centres open and in the public sector. While the campaign could be considered a 'defensive' mobilisation (Almeida, 2007) to maintain existing provision, as with other local anti-austerity struggles (such as those described in Moth et al, 2015) its outcome also had some transformational elements, for instance greater service user input to service design.

Challenging welfare reforms and psychocompulsion

We will now turn to welfare reform, a second aspect of the austerity policy agenda that has risen to prominence as its detrimental impact on service users and claimants with mental health needs has become increasingly visible. Recent changes to the benefits system in the UK have led to a reduction in eligibility for and levels of social security support and escalating welfare conditionality, where claimant responsibilisation is combined with punitive sanctions for non-compliance (Patrick, 2017). Interventions drawing on behavioural psychology and economics have become an integral feature of coercive conditionality in welfare-to-work regimes. Dubbed 'psychocompulsion' by critics, this policy agenda seeks to impose 'psychological explanations for unemployment, together with mandatory activities intended to modify beliefs, attitude, disposition or personality' in order to activate the unemployed (Friedli & Stearn, 2015: 42). These trends have unfolded in a context of increasing integration of mental health with welfare policy (Moth & McKeown, 2016). A core principle underpinning this convergence is the notion of 'employment as a health outcome'. This thread runs through recent mental health policy initiatives including the Mental Health Taskforce (2016) implementation plans, the expansion of access to time-limited counselling through the Improving Access to Psychological Therapies (IAPT) scheme (NHS England, 2016), and in the Work and Health Programme, a joint initiative between the Departments of Health and Work and Pensions (Department for Work and Pensions and HM Treasury, 2015). These policy convergence trends towards 'work cure' therapies and psychocompulsion have had detrimental impacts on the mental health of claimants and service users (Friedli & Stearn, 2015; Moth & Lavalette, 2017). However, they have also prompted activist responses and the emergence of a new coalition of resistance against psychocompulsion in which SWAN is significantly involved. The next section will detail and explore these new activist alliances.

A significant precursor of the emerging movement against psychocompulsion was the successful campaign led by survivor campaigners Mental Health Resistance Network (MHRN), which established via judicial review that the DWP's medical test, the Work Capability Assessment (WCA), discriminated against claimants with mental health problems (Mental Health Today, 2013). Following this victory, survivor and disabled activists and, increasingly, radical practitioner groups including SWAN began to challenge the rising coercive deployment of psychology in the welfare system. Some progressive mental health workers joined with service users and survivors to question the ethical implications of new DWP policy proposals to pilot aspects of the new Work and Health Programme such as the co-location of mental health and job centres (Walker, 2015) and embedding of job coaches in GP practices (Cotton, 2016). SWAN members participated in protests in London against these policy developments. These included a lobby and brief occupation of the building in Streatham earmarked for a community mental health team office within a Job Centre (Wilson, 2015). Campaigners also demonstrated outside an Islington medical practice to raise concerns about potential conflicts of interest for GPs piloting this embedded job coach scheme (Gayle, 2016; Roberts, 2016). Following these actions, SWAN members who had been involved in developing the Mental Health Charter took part in the 'Mental Health and Welfare Reform' conference co-organised by activists from MHRN and the Alliance for Counselling and Psychotherapy. This event drew together and strengthened the emerging campaigning networks of survivors and mental health workers against psychocompulsion and a new cross-sectional coalition, the Mental Health Activist Alliance (MHAA – formerly the Mental Wealth Alliance) involving 17 organisations, began to coalesce. While the strategic focus during the first phase of campaigning had been the DWP, during the next stage activists also targeted the professional associations for therapy, such as the British Psychological Society (BPS), and mental health charities such as Mind. MHAA activists organised letters to and lobbies of Mind Chief Executive Paul Farmer, and protested at the BPS annual conference in Liverpool in 2017 to demand that both organisations end collaborative working with the DWP on welfare-to-work and shift to a more critical stance towards welfare reforms in order to avoid conflicts of interest, prioritise the needs of service users and (for the BPS) preserve the ethical integrity of the profession it represents (Pring, 2016; MHRN/SWAN, 2017). Another tactical focus during this period has been to utilise the leftward reorientation in the Labour Party since the election of leader Jeremy Corbyn to lobby for a shift in party policy on welfare and mental health. This has involved activists using motions to Labour Conference 2017 and a fringe meeting at the event to challenge the party's current uncritical positions on psychocompulsion and labour market activation.

This analysis of SWAN's contribution to social movement activity in the mental health and welfare arenas has highlighted various dimensions of its organising methodology. These range from agitational elements, such as the development of the Charter, to campaigning, grassroots intervention to save the resource centre in Liverpool, and ideological, for example highlighting emergent critical concepts such as 'psychocompulsion' to a social work audience. An important strategic orientation within these activist engagements is cross-sectional alliance building that brings together groups of workers and service users. This mode of organising was articulated in the Charter and enacted in the local anti-austerity campaigns and wider movement against psychocompulsion. While the campaign in Liverpool achieved a localised victory against service cuts, the wider movement against austerity and psychocompulsion has not (yet) achieved its goal of transforming these policy agendas. Nonetheless, activism in this arena has begun to challenge dominant hegemonic constructions of work as unproblematically positive for mental health and opened up debates within mental health professions concerning the ethics of implementing behaviour change programmes underpinned by coercive welfare measures.

Conclusion

This chapter has argued that SWAN has created an institutional space within which three primary modes of political intervention oriented to policy processes are articulated and enacted. These are ideological intervention through the promotion of radical and critical theoretical perspectives on welfare, the development of agitational resources such as pamphlets and charters and the initiation of and involvement in grassroots campaigning. Operating across these three dimensions is a commitment to cross-sectional alliance building, particularly between service users and practitioners, within a united front framework.

Though there is limited direct evidence that these interventions have led to specific policy shifts or changes, we have suggested they have nonetheless made a significant contribution within social work and wider state institutions by articulating demands for 'more and better' welfare. This formulation advocates the necessity but also insufficiency of simple quantitative improvements in service provision and proposes harnessing emergent political campaigning and mobilisation to secure qualitative transformations of the welfare field. Such practices are enabled by ideological and agitational groundwork that highlights possibilities for more radically inclusive, egalitarian and democratic forms of welfare. Moreover by adopting a strategic orientation to cross-sectional alliance building we argue that elements of these alternative and more socially just welfare futures are prefigured and manifested in the present, thereby strengthening coalitions of resistance.

References

Almeida, P. (2007) 'Defensive mobilization: popular movements against economic adjustment policies in Latin America', *Latin American Perspectives*, 34(3): 127–39.

Annetts, J., Law, A., McNeish, W. and Mooney, G. (2009) *Understanding Social Welfare Movements*, Bristol: Policy Press.

Barker, C. and Lavalette, M. (2015) 'Welfare changes and social movements', in D. della Porta and M. Diani (eds) *The Oxford Handbook of Social Movements*, Oxford: Oxford University Press, pp 711–28.

Braverman, H. (1974) *Labour and Monopoly Capital*, New York: Monthly Review Press.

Burchardt, T., Obolenskaya, P. and Vizard, P. (2015) '*The Coalition's Record on Adult Social Care: Policy, Spending and Outcomes 2010–2015*'. Social Policy in a Cold Climate Working Paper, SPCCWP17, London: CASE/LSE.

Centre for Mental Health (2017) *Briefing 52: Adult and Older Adult Mental Health Services 2012–2016*, London: Centre for Mental Health.

Cotton, E. (2016) 'Job coaches in GP surgeries: another attempt to pathologise the unemployed?', *British Politics and Policy at LSE*, 31 March. Available at: http://blogs.lse.ac.uk/politicsandpolicy/job-coaches-pilot/

Damer, S. (2000) 'The Clyde rent war!', in M. Lavalette and G. Mooney (eds) *Class Struggle and Social Welfare*, London: Routledge, pp 71–95.

Den Hond, F., De Bakker, F. and Smith, N. (2015) 'Social movements and organizational analysis', in D. della Porta and M. Diani (eds) *The Oxford Handbook of Social Movements*, Oxford: Oxford University Press, pp 291–305.

Department for Work and Pensions and HM Treasury (2015) Department for Work and Pensions' Settlement at the Spending Review. *Department for Work and Pensions*, 25 November. Available at: www.gov.uk/government/news/department-for-work-and-pensions-settlement-at-the-spending-review

DH (Department of Health) (2001) *The Journey to Recovery – The Government's Vision for Mental Health Care*, London: Department of Health.

Docherty, M. and Thornicroft, G. (2015) 'Specialist mental health services in England in 2014: overview of funding, access and levels of care', *International Journal of Mental Health Systems*, 9(34): 1–8.

Esping-Anderson, G. (1990) *The Three Worlds of Welfare Capitalism*, London: Sage.

Ferguson, I. and Lavalette, M. (2008) *Social Work After Baby P*, Liverpool: Hope University Press.

Ferguson, I. and Woodward, R. (2009) *Radical Social Work in Practice*, Bristol: The Policy Press.

Ferguson, I., Lavalette, M. and Mooney, G. (2002) *Rethinking Welfare*, London: Sage.

Fox-Piven, F. and Cloward, R. (1979) *Poor People's Movements*, New York: Random House.

Fraser, D. (1984) *The Evolution of the British Welfare State*, London: Longman.

Friedli, L. and Stearn, R. (2015) 'Positive affect as coercive strategy: conditionality, activation and the role of psychology in UK government workfare programmes', *Medical Humanities*, 41(1): 40–47.

Gayle, D. (2016) 'Activists angry at scheme to embed job coaches in GP surgeries', *The Guardian*, 2 March. Available at: www.theguardian.com/politics/2016/mar/02/activists-anger-scheme-embed-job-coaches-in-gp-surgeries

Glasby, J. and Tew, J. (2015) *Mental Health Policy and Practice* (3rd edn), London: Palgrave MacMillan.

Gough, I. (1979) *The Political Economy of the Welfare State*, London: Macmillan.

Hallas, D. (2003) *Trotsky's Marxism and Other Essays*, Chicago: Haymarket Books.

Harper, D. and Speed, E. (2012) 'Uncovering recovery: the resistible rise of recovery and resilience', *Studies in Social Justice*, 6(1): 9–25.

Harris J. (2003) *The Social Work Business*, Routledge: London.

Harris, J. (2008) 'State social work: constructing the present from moments in the past', *British Journal of Social Work*, 38(4): 662–79.

Holloway, F. (1996) 'Community psychiatric care: from libertarianism to coercion. Moral panic and mental health policy in Britain', *Health Care Analysis*, 4(3): 235–43.

Jones, C., Ferguson, I., Lavalette, M. and Penketh, L. (2004) 'Manifesto for a new engaged practice' ['The Social Work Manifesto'], reprinted in M. Lavalette and I. Ferguson (2007) (eds) *International Social Work and the Radical Tradition*, Birmingham: Venture Press.

Krinsky, J. (2009) 'Missing the Marx: toward a dialectical, materialist interpretation of social movements', Unpublished paper from Politics and Protest Workshop, City University New York, 19 February.

Lavalette, M. (2010) (ed) *Radical Social Work Today*, Bristol: The Policy Press.

Lavalette, M. and Ferguson, I. (eds) (2007) *International Social Work and the Radical Tradition*, Birmingham: Venture Press.

Lipsky, M. (1980) *Street-level Bureaucracy: Dilemmas of the Individual in Public Services*, New York: Sage.

McNicoll, A. (2015) 'Mental health trust funding down 8 per cent from 2010 despite coalition's drive for parity of esteem', *Community Care*. Available at: www.communitycare.co.uk/2015/03/20/mental-health-trust-funding-8-since-2010-despite-coalitions-drive-parity-esteem/

Mental Health Taskforce (2016) *Five Year Forward View for Mental Health: An Independent Report of the Mental Health Taskforce*, London: NHS England.

Mental Health Today (2013) 'Government loses appeal against ESA benefit ruling', *Mental Health Today*, 5 December. Available at: www.mentalhealthtoday.co.uk/government-loses-appeal-against-esa-benefit-ruling

MHRN/SWAN (2017) 'United against welfare cuts and reform: report from the lobby of the British Psychological Society conference', 18 January. *MHRN*, 23 January. Available at: http://mentalhealthresistance.org/2017/01/united-against-welfare-cuts-report-from-the-lobby-of-the-bpsociety-conference/

Moth, R. (2019) *Understanding Mental Distress: Knowledge and Practice in Neoliberal Mental Health Services*, Bristol: Policy Press.

Moth, R. and Lavalette, M. (2017) *Social protection and labour market policies for vulnerable groups from a social investment perspective: The case of welfare recipients with mental health needs in England*, Liverpool: Liverpool Hope University/Leuven: HIVA (KU Leuven).

Moth, R. and McKeown, M. (2016) 'Realising Sedgwick's vision: theorising strategies of resistance to neoliberal mental health and welfare policy', *Critical and Radical Social Work*, 4(3) 375–90.

Moth, R., Greener, J. and Stoll, T. (2015) 'Crisis and resistance in mental health services in England', *Critical and Radical Social Work*, 3(1): 89–102.

NHS England (2016) *Implementing the Five Year Forward View for Mental Health*, Redditch: NHS England. Available at: www.england.nhs.uk/wp-content/uploads/2016/07/fyfv-mh.pdf

O'Connor, F. (1973) *The Fiscal Crisis of the State*, New York: St. Martin's Press.

Patrick, R. (2017) *For Whose Benefit? The Everyday Realities of Welfare Reform*, Bristol: Policy Press.

Pierson, C. (1991) *Beyond the welfare state?*, Cambridge: Polity Press.

Pring, J. (2016) 'Mind boss lies to protesters over DWP contracts', *Disability News Service*, 3 November. Available at: www.disabilitynewsservice.com/mind-boss-lies-to-protesters-over-dwp-contracts/

Roberts, N. (2016) 'Protesters criticise scheme that puts job advisors in GP practices', *GP Online*, 8 March 2016. Available at: www.gponline.com/protesters-criticise-scheme-puts-job-advisors-gp-practices/article/1386354

Saville, J. (1957) 'The origins of the welfare state', *The New Reasoner*, No. 3, Winter 1957–58, pp 5–25. Available at: www.marxists.org/archive/saville/1957/xx/welfare.htm

SCIE (Social Care Institute of Excellence) (2007) *A Common Purpose: Recovery in Future Mental Health Services*, London: SCIE.

Sedgwick, P. (2015) *Psycho Politics*, London: Unkant Publishers.

Stephens, J. (1979) *The Transition from Capitalism to Socialism*, London: Macmillan.

SWAN (2014a) *In Defence of Social Work: Why Michael Gove is Wrong*, London: SWAN.

SWAN (Social Work Action Network) (2014b) 'A charter for mental health launched by the Social Work Action Network (SWAN), UK', *Critical and Radical Social Work*, 2(3): 411–12.

Tarrow, S. (1994), *Power in Movement: Social Movements, Collective Action and Politics*, New York: Cambridge University Press.

Walker, C. (2015) 'A dance of destitution – psychology's clash over coercion', *openDemocracy*, 16 June. Available at: 'www.opendemocracy.net/ournhs/carl-walker/dance-of-destitution-psychology%27s-clash-over-coercion

Wilson, B. (2015) Protesters rally against Streatham Jobcentre "forcing unemployed people into mental health treatment"', *SW Londoner*, 26 June. Available at: www.swlondoner.co.uk/protesters-rally-against-streatham-jobcentre-forcing-unemployed-people-into-mental-health-treatment/

Part III
Social work and implementation

9

Policy work and the ethics of obedience and resistance: perspectives from Britain and beyond

Tony Evans

Introduction

Social work, as a profession, is closely associated with social justice and human rights (BASW, 2012). However, in Britain social workers, who overwhelmingly work within welfare agencies, are struggling with increasing policy prescription and welfare retrenchment and austerity – a situation that is likely to continue for decades (Amin-Smith et al, 2018) – and they feel their freedom to act professionally is increasingly restricted by intrusive management control (Munro & Liquid Personnel, 2015).

In the introduction to this book (Chapter 1), the editors highlight the central role of ethics in understanding social work's engagement with policy. Within the policy cycle, practitioner discretion at the point of implementation is a site where the tensions between policy compliance and resistance and challenge to policies are particularly marked (see also other chapters in Part III). In this chapter, I want to explore these tensions, and I will outline the context of the changing relationship between practitioners and public agencies in which they work; arguments that practitioners should put aside their own commitments in implementing policy in light of its democratic legitimacy; and arguments that practitioners have a professional responsibility to resist policy with which they disagree.

The development of social work and the development of the welfare state are closely linked (Evans & Keating, 2015). A continuing theme in this relationship is the role of social workers as practical policy actors, implementing welfare policies.

Policy actors in an increasingly strange land

In Britain, the role of social work crystallised in the late 1960s and early 1970s. Disparate welfare occupations were unified as a distinct profession. The new profession was housed in new dedicated social work (in Scotland) and social services (in England and Wales) departments in local government (Social Work (Scotland) Act 1968; The Local Authority Social Services Act 1970). These departments were infused with a professional social work culture and directed by senior officers with a professional background. They were bureaucracies in which practitioners were given leeway to make decisions about individual cases and develop the range and nature of service provision (Harris, 2003). However, in the last 30 years social work and public policy have fallen out of sorts. Margaret Thatcher's Conservative government tore the fabric of social policy within which the new unified social work profession had been formed (Hadley & Clough, 1996; Harris, 2008; Donovan et al, 2017). The neoliberal ethos – the emphasis on markets and individual responsibility and the demeaning of the role of the state (Springer et al, 2016) – underpinning New Right reforms was echoed in subsequent policy changes in social care. Governments – Conservative and New Labour – have actively eroded funding for social care service and in its place, except in extreme situations of need, have promoted the responsibility of individuals in need, their families and communities to provide their own care (Evans & Hupe, 2019). Alongside this, the organisation of welfare services also changed. Governments, ideologically committed to business ways of working and unsympathetic to 'traditional' public provision, sought to promote private services in a mixed economy of care and deploy business techniques to manage and regulate residual public services. The culture and organisation of public services also changed. In one way there has been a positive move in policy to promote the rights of service users and to recognise their role as co-producers of services (Needham, forthcoming). However, alongside this, and increasingly dominating public service provision, the culture of services has become increasingly economic – focusing on costs, segmenting professional roles and tasks, and promoting entrepreneurial practice (Harris, 2003; Ferguson, 2007; Carey, 2015; Evans, 2016). Professionals and professional judgement are distrusted. They are now managed as 'agents' instructed by 'principals' (their managers) whose task is to control and direct their agents' work to ensure compliance with organisational objectives and corporate goals (Marston & McDonald, 2012; Evans, 2013).

What practitioners can do

The current terrain of social work practice is one in which social workers often feel alienated from organisational goals (see, for instance, Munro & Liquid Personnel, 2015). It is also a context in which social workers' freedom to make judgements and act as professionals is set about by the apparatus of managerial control (Harris & White, 2009).

No one would deny that welfare organisations are increasingly characterised by extensive systems of management control. However, that there are systems of control doesn't mean that the systems are effective. Furthermore, while these systems project external and intrusive control, they continue to rely on extensive (acknowledged and unacknowledged) practitioner discretion.

Welfare agencies are characterised by extensive de facto discretion, which arises from the organisational mess of service to be found in any street-level bureaucracy: gaps in the rhetoric and reality of control, vagueness and confusion in the direction of policy and procedures, mismatch of resources and so on (Lipsky, 2010). For professionals, such as social workers, this de facto discretion is turbo-driven. Applying their expertise to the flexibility and contradictions in procedure and rules and the private nature of key aspects of their work enhances the extent of and their ability to deploy widespread de facto freedom (Evans, 2011, 2013). Scratch the rhetoric of management control and it's possible to identify significant professional discretion – judgement and room to act – which fills in gaps and makes sense of policy on the ground. Practitioners have to use their judgement to interpret procedures and decide how they apply, and to make sense of vague terms such as 'risk' and 'need'. Procedures – criteria, tick-charts and so on – by themselves are meaningless: they require expertise to make sense of them and make them usable (Munro, 1998). The presence of professional discretion is not just the persistence of a substantial substratum of professional judgement; it can also reflect political and managerial strategies to deflect responsibility (and the risk of blame) from policy makers and managers to non-political experts (Hood et al, 2001).

Discretion – space to make judgements and to choose between options – persists as a significant dimension of policy work within welfare agencies (Evans, 2018; Evans & Hupe, 2019). But it's not easy work. It's often about choice and the least worst option, making the situation less difficult and more humane – this is discretion which is burdensome and often frustrating and distressing; and in some situations, discretion that may need to be resisted. Rather than being about freedom to realise professional ideals, discretion is now more about making choices between difficult options.

What should practitioners do? Looking at the question through the lens of ethics

Practitioners' discretion in managerial social services is fraught with ethical challenges. How should practitioners respond to the policies they are employed to implement? Should they put their conscience and professional identity aside, accept the job in hand and implement it? Or, as professionals, should they resist and undermine any policy with which they disagree? Before looking at these ethical questions I want to outline what an ethical perspective entails.

The idea that reason – as careful calculation or objective reflection – provides the foundation for ethics underpins major approaches such as Bentham's utilitarian and Kant's moral law (Driver, 2007). However, Foot (1972), among others, has criticised this narrow focus on reason for failing to recognise that people care for more than just calculations of outcomes or an imposed duty:

> a man may care about the suffering of others, having a sense of identification with them, and wanting to help if he can. Of course, he must want not the reputation of charity, nor even a gratifying role helping others but, quite simply, their good ... a comparison with someone acting from an ulterior motive (even a respectable ulterior motive) is out of place. (Foot, 1972: 313)

Foot's view of ethics as altruistic action combines both a sense of our responsibilities to others and a sense of commitments that make sense of our lives. Wolf (1997: 96) underlines the distinction between these two elements and asks us to consider more carefully their different roles for us. A moral perspective, she argues, entails

> the recognition of the fact that one is just one person among others equally real and deserving of the good things in life as a fact with practical consequences, a fact that demands expression in one's actions and in the form of one's practical deliberations.

However, she continues, we also have other concerns, which are not purely egoistic calculations, that relate to how we understand our own well-being and fundamental commitments, which

> claim for themselves a kind of objectivity or a grounding in a perspective which any rational and perceptive being can take up. Unlike moral judgments, however, the good with which these judgments are concerned is not the good of anyone or any group other than the individual himself … it provides us with reasons that are independent of moral reasons for wanting ourselves and others to develop our characters and live our lives in certain ways. (Wolf, 1997: 95–96)

These are different views of the world – to do with our moral responsibilities and our personal or group commitments – but they do not have to operate in isolation. Williams, for instance, points out that in making an ethical judgement one's identity and commitments must play a role:

> to reach a grounded decision in such a case should not be regarded as a matter of just discounting one's reactions, impulses and deeply held projects in the face of a pattern of utilities, nor yet merely adding them in – but in the first place to understand them. (Smart & Williams, 1973: 118)

When we talk about 'ethics' we elide our responsibilities to others and our responsibilities to ourselves. We seek to justify and defend our position and to explain to others why it's important and compelling. For moral psychologist Jonathan Haidt (2001), this process is theatre; ethics is about asserting intuitions – reason just rationalises and puts the best face on our gut feeling. Recently, Mercier and Sperber (2017: 314) have challenged this view. They point out that people often start from a gut feeling, but they engage in arguments which can sway their feelings and change their perspective. However, they also recognise that this can be an uncomfortable process because 'arguments that challenge the moral values of one's community can be met with disbelief, distrust of motives, even downright hostility. Still, on many moral issues, people have been influenced by good argument'. This account of ethical argument has a strong resonance. It's seen as a process in which intuitions are valued but also explored and challenged – our fundamental hunches are, in effect, ethical hypotheses we test and pull apart. Our own (and others') ethical hunches will be examined in the round (from a range of perspectives), challenged in the light of all the facts (what's relevant now and what we can imagine as being relevant in the future) and assessed with humanity (which rejects the fanatical commitment to an idea at the cost of respecting everyone's interest) (Hare, 1963).

In exploring questions about social work professionals' response to policy with which they disagree, I will look at two ethical hunches that seem to swirl around this issue. First is the idea that professionals – like all other public servants – must follow policies and procedures because they should respect the legitimacy of government policy. The second intuition is that professionals should follow their own commitments, act autonomously and disregard policies with which they disagree.

Following orders: legitimacy

The idea that public officials should follow orders is bound up with the idea of political authority and compliance with legitimate direction: 'it follows that if a law or policy is enacted by a legitimate political authority, those subject to it are afforded good, though not necessarily decisive, reasons to comply with its directions' (Horton, 2012: 130). However, Horton (2012: 143) argues that the idea of political legitimacy cannot just be asserted in abstract; it has to be understood and assessed in terms of 'the concrete context of the culture, political institutions and intellectual and moral traditions within which such reasoning occurs'.

In contemporary Western societies, the idea of political legitimacy interweaves two basic ideas – democracy and rights (for example, European Union, undated). First, modern societies are fractured and diverse, with different and conflicting values. Conflicts are inevitable and resolved in action by compromise and agreement, which characterises democratic political processes. The second idea is that people have rights to be treated fairly and have their substantive rights respected. In the UK, for instance, these ideas are reflected in the sovereignty of parliament, and in the legal constraints on executive decision making that reflect citizens' rights in administrative law (Government Legal Department, 2016).

Democratic authority in policy implementation seems to be contained in the idea of an unbroken chain of command from political decision makers to frontline practice. A subordinate (the agent) carries out the instructions of the superordinate (the principal): ministers instruct civil servants; civil servants instruct local authorities, local authority councillors, senior officers and so on, down the line to frontline staff. However, this principal/agent picture of a well-oiled policy implementation machine is not borne out empirically. The governance literature in politics, for instance, challenges this picture, pointing out that:

> Power appears wherever people interpret and respond to one another ... various actors restrict what others can do in ways that thwart the intentions of policy actors. They show how local actors – Whitehall bureaucrats, doctors and police officers – are able to draw on their different inheritances to resist policies inspired by the narratives of others in the policy chain. (Bevir & Rhodes, 2008: 731)

This is not primarily a problem of bad apples and poor central control; it's an inherent characteristic of any policy control system where the invidious circularity of 'the sour laws of unintended consequences ... [where] command operation code builds failure into the design of the policy. Such centralization will be confounded by fragmentation and interdependence which, in turn, will prompt further bouts of centralization' (Rhodes, 2007: 1258).

The important point here is that there isn't (in fact, there never can be) an unbroken chain conveying policy intention from the centre to the frontline. The ethical significance of this observation is that the democratic authority of policy is likely to be diluted, as policy is continually negotiated and translated in the process of being moved between policy levels. It's like the children's game 'telegraph': the next level down doesn't receive the original policy, but the superordinate's interpretation of it. Local policies and procedures relating to the same legislation can look very different and reflect different interpretations and levels of concordance with original policy intentions (as well as adaptation to local circumstances). Recognising this, the principal/agent argument for frontline obedience on the basis of democratic legitimacy is dubious. It has a homoeopathic quality – a claim that, however diluted or mixed with other policies in the provision of any service, the original policy still retains its original power. The inevitable dilution of the policy in the implementation process suggests that frontline staff have to interrogate the democratic authority of managers' instructions and test them against the relevant laws and the original policy aims. In my research (Evans, 2013, 2014, 2015), for instance, practitioners accepted that they were bound by law, but questioned the authority of local policy interpretations and procedures.

The problem of the principal/agent assumption that political legitimacy is sustained despite the movement of policy through numerous hierarchical layers is particularly stark when we consider services contracted out to the private and voluntary sectors. Carson and colleagues (2015) looked at the implementation of a domestic violence policy where the service had been contracted out to a range of voluntary organisations. They noted that agencies approached the same policy differently, reflecting their different values and priorities. The link between policy intention and local delivery was not strengthened by the supposed clarity of contract, but was, in fact, weakened by the process of contracting out.

The second limitation on the legitimate authority of principals to instruct agents in policy implementation relates to the substance of policy – the extent to which it might contravene the democratic principle of fair treatment and basic human rights. This is a particular version of the argument that it's wrong simply to follow orders (Arendt, 2006): one should retain a sense of ethical propriety and independence of judgement to avoid overstepping ethical red lines. Holding an office does not permit you to ignore ethical requirements (Applbaum, 1999). The uncomfortable point here is that neither orders nor office can absolve one from ethical responsibility. This challenge is illustrated in the starkest terms in the official review of patient deaths in a Hospital Trust in the English Midlands. Families and the community raised concerns about the level of deaths among older patients in the hospital. A public enquiry was set up, and it found that there was a disproportionate level of patient death, related to organisational priorities of cutting corners in clinical care to achieve management goals, and the bullying of staff to comply with management goals. Among other things, the enquiry reiterated what it took as a basic moral imperative: that professionals should not simply follow instructions, but should air ethical concerns or challenge organisational priorities (Francis, 2013).

Of course, a problem here is that one is often faced with unpalatable alternatives. What, ethically, should one do? This was a situation described to me by some practitioners in a study where their employing authority (the council) issued informal instructions – word of mouth from managers – that the current policy on rationing was suspended and would be replaced by a more punitive policy to bring down council spending. The instructions – which were informal, to avoid political embarrassment about a new and contentious policy – were that, before a new service could be provided to one person, two people currently receiving that service should stop receiving it (Evans, 2016). Practitioners were given the freedom to choose between alternatives (who should not receive the service, to enable others to receive it), but within an architecture of decision making that contravened their sense of justice. Bernard Williams (1973) identifies this as a common problem in many ethical dilemmas. This is not a situation of your own making, and you are not bound to accept it. It's not your responsibility to solve – in fact, it may be your ethical responsibility to call it out and challenge it. You can choose to reject or accept this. It's an ethical decision in itself. The practitioners in the study, in fact, refused to implement this new informal policy, and pushed the issue back to the councillors and senior officers.

Not following orders: autonomy

The idea of political legitimacy, in theory, has a strong claim to obedience but, in practice, this authority seems to be diluted as it passes through layers of management and contracting and commissioning. Furthermore, there's also a strong brake on simply following orders when basic democratic rights are at stake. The other intuition we need to consider, underpinning ethical responses to policy with which one disagrees, is the idea of professional autonomy. Does professional autonomy provide a stronger basis for understanding the relationship between social work practitioners and policy instructions?

Professions often set out their values in codes. Social workers in England, for instance, are required to register with an official body which publishes a set of professional standards, and may also choose to join a professional association – the British Association of Social Workers (BASW, 2012: 11) – which publishes its own 'Code of Ethics for Social Work'. Interestingly, given the point at issue here, the code specifically states that 'Social workers should strive to carry out the stated aims of their employers or commissioners, provided they are consistent with the Code of Ethics'.

However, is there an ethical obligation to prefer a professional code when it conflicts with public policy? To answer this question, we need to look at the nature of these codes and how they relate to ethical decisions in practice. It's possible to find at least three broad forms of imperative – rights ethics, consequentialist ethics and virtue ethics – running through most professional codes (Evans & Hardy, 2017). Here, though, I want to focus on the form and authority of ethical codes, rather than examine their substance.

To critics of professions, codes are smoke-screens, cloaking self-interest in the language of altruism. Codes mark out professional territory to deter competitors and discipline individual practitioners by the threat of sanction. However, even if we accept that an aspect of a professional code is to advance and police an occupation's professional project, this doesn't exclude the possibility that professional codes also reflect positive concerns. Friedson (2001), for instance, having previously been a critical analyst of professionalism, came to argue that professions embody a socially valuable set of commitments – a third logic in contrast to the logics of managerialism and consumerism.

In drawing out these imperatives, it's helpful to revisit Wolf's (1997) distinction between moral concerns with our responsibilities to others, and commitments and projects that embody our sense of purpose. Codes mix these two concerns. However, codes can elide expectations of good and admirable practice (professional commitments) and ethical responsibilities in a way that confuses professional commitments with ethical imperatives.

The BASW (2012: 11) code, for instance, emphasises two ethical principles: 'social justice' and 'human rights'. The code acknowledges it can't prescribe these principles in detail for all four countries in the UK – it directs practitioners to legislation, local codes of practice standards and so on to fill in the gaps – but it also emphasises professionals' responsibility to apply the code's standard.

However, it's difficult to see how a code has authority to supersede the moral agency of practitioners. Insofar as the code is concerned with moral responsibilities, it cannot prescribe practice. Moral responsibilities apply to everyone, not any particular occupation. They are a function of our moral agency (Applbaum, 1999). A code may mention or interpret moral responsibilities, but it can only guide or direct attention to a potentially significant issue. It cannot replace the individual's responsibility to make a judgement about the right thing to do in the situation. (Here we are returning to the argument that it isn't good enough to say 'I was following orders'. Morality, in the end, is a matter for moral agency, taking responsibility to work out what you should do for yourself.) Because a code may focus on particular issues, this doesn't take away the individual practitioner's responsibility to consider all relevant moral issues, even if they are not mentioned in the code.

The second aspect of the code is that it expresses the profession's commitments: what it is to be a good professional. Joining that profession involves committing to these characteristics. These commitments set out what can be expected of a member of that profession by the world outside. In the BASW (2012) code, the major part is taken up with explicating commitments such as 'professional integrity', 'objectivity and self-awareness in professional practice', 'assessing and managing risk' and 'developing professional relationships'. Anyone joining takes on these commitments: practitioners who have signed up to the profession accept the benefit and limitation of this and being accountable as a professional. If you want the advantages of being in the club you have to accept the rules. You can't have your cake and eat it!

While, strictly speaking, professional commitments are not moral imperatives, they have ethical implications. In considering ethical questions, 'I must deliberate from what I am' (Williams, 1993: 200). Professional commitments can sensitise (or desensitise) one to ethically relevant material – such as the oppression and disadvantage experienced by particular groups and communities – and they reflect professional attributes that can contribute to achieving morally valuable goals. Furthermore, setting out the profession's commitments to the outside world in a code, provides a backcloth for the relationship between principal and agent – between an employer and a social worker. The code tells potential principals: 'this is the mind-set of someone from this profession'. A principal employing a 'social worker' can't be surprised that their agent acts in line with their professional expertise and commitments. Montaigne tells the story of Crassus, a Roman general, who told an engineer to bring him a specific mast to act as a battering ram. The engineer brought a different mast, which was better suited as a battering ram. The general punished the engineer for disobeying orders, but Montaigne concludes 'did not Crassus, when he wrote to an expert and advised him of the use for which that mast was destined, seem to consult his judgement and invite him to interpose his opinion?' (Montaigne, 1958: 51).

Is there an ethical obligation to prefer a professional code when it conflicts with public policy? As a professional social worker, you can reasonably assume that your 'principal' understands that your role, including in the area of policy implementation, involves exercising your judgement and expertise and drawing on your commitments to good professionalism. If your 'principal' says this not the case, then you can require them to explain to you and to others why they are stepping in and interfering in areas where the assumption is that decisions are based on professional judgement and commitment.

Conclusion

So where have we got to now? We identified two strong ethical intuitions that are often at the core of questions of obedience and resistance in policy implementation. They pull in different directions. We have a strong sense that public agents should comply with the policy based on political legitimacy. However, the connection between policy and the frontline experience of local policies and management instructions is problematic, and frontline practitioners – and managers, and citizens more generally – also have to be aware of the backdrop of rights and be continuously troubled by moral questions: is what I'm doing fair? Is it just? Is it right?

Recognising a practitioner's responsibility to test and question, rather than just follow orders, points to the importance of the second intuition – professional autonomy. This is the idea that, faced with a policy with which they disagree, practitioners should follow their professional judgement, not the policy. In relation to understanding moral responsibility, including the requirements of a professional code adds an unnecessary additional layer to consider. If it's wrong to follow orders, it's wrong, whether you're a professional or not. Professionals have no fewer and no more moral responsibilities than anyone else. Codes may note moral responsibilities but, in the same way that policy can't supersede one's moral responsibility and judgement, neither can following a professional code become a proxy for moral thinking. However, professional codes also set out professional commitments that underline what it means to practise that particular profession. These commitments are compelling for members of that profession – they signed up to them, and they are the promises they make to the public about how they will go about their work. They provide non-moral but ethically relevant reasons that should be given weight in considering whether to comply with management instruction. Furthermore, professionals can assume that in the absence of clear instructions otherwise, their commitments should fill in policy gaps, resolve contradictions or clarify imprecisions.

Both intuitions have something important to say, but neither alone provides a satisfactory account. The answer seems to lie in the relationship between the two. This relationship – a fundamental tension – can be captured in recognising social work practice in policy work as a 'recourse role'. Kadish and Kadish's (1973) idea of recourse roles arises from the recognition that it's not possible to organise rules in any policy system so that they don't conflict, or can deal with every situation. Recourse roles provide room for flexibility and responsiveness in policy systems. They provide the space within which practitioners can think on their feet and adapt policy to people's circumstances, rather than officiously follow rules; there's also a recognition that 'any role we're in has its obligations – and if we don't take them seriously the role doesn't make sense' (Kadish & Kadish, 1973: 62). However, there's also the recognition that discretion isn't simply to be deployed because it's convenient or preferable against the democratic mandate; it has to be necessary: 'In departing from rules, we need to have a damn good reason' (Kadish & Kadish, 1973: 62).

In considering the ethics of discretion in policy work there is a need to move beyond knee-jerk assumptions of either compliance or resistance, to consider not only one's own preference, perspective and ethical agency but also the ethical agency and views of others, particularly of those with whom one disagrees, recognising that 'discretion in itself is neither "good" nor "bad". In some circumstances, it may be an important professional attribute, in others it may be a cloak for political decision-makers to hide behind or it may be an opportunity for professional abuse of power' (Evans & Harris, 2004: 871).

References
Amin-Smith, N., Phillips, D. and Simpson, P. (2018) *Adult Social Care Funding: A Local or National Responsibility?*, London: Institute for Fiscal Studies. Available at: www.ifs.org.uk/uploads/BN227.pdf
Applbaum, A. (1999) *Ethics for Adversaries*, Princeton, NJ: Princeton University Press.
Arendt, H. (2006) *Eichmann in Jerusalem: A Report on the Banality of Evil*, London: Penguin.
BASW (British Association of Social Workers) (2012) *Code of Ethics for Social Work*, Birmingham: The British Association of Social Workers.
Bevir, M. and Rhodes, R. (2008) 'The differentiated polity as narrative', *British Journal of Politics and International Relations*, 10(4): 729–34.
Carey, M. (2015) The fragmentation of social work and social care: some ramifications and a critique', *British Journal of Social Work*, 45(8): 2406–22.
Carson, E., Chung, D. and Evans, T. (2015) 'Complexities of discretion in human services in the third sector', *European Journal of Social Work*, 18(2): 167–84.
Donovan, J., Rose, D. and Connolly, M. (2017) 'A crisis of identity: social work theorising at a time of change', *British Journal of Social Work*, 47(8): 2291–307.
Driver, J. (2007) *Ethics: The Fundamentals*. Oxford. Blackwell.
European Union (undated) 'Human rights and democratic governance'. Available at: https://ec.europa.eu/europeaid/sectors/human-rights-and-governance_en
Evans, T. (2011) 'Professionals, managers and discretion: critiquing street-level bureaucracy', *British Journal of Social Work*, 41(2): 368–86.
Evans, T. (2013) 'Organisational rules and discretion in adult social work', *British Journal of Social Work*, 43(1): 739–58.

Evans, T. (2014) 'The moral economy of street-level policy work', *Croatian and Comparative Public Administration*, 14(2): 381–99.

Evans, T. (2015) 'Professionals and discretion in street-level bureaucracy', in P. Hupe, M. Hill & A. Buffat (eds) *Understanding Street-level Bureaucracy*, Bristol: Policy Press, pp 279–93.

Evans, T. (2016) 'Street-level bureaucracy, management and the corrupted world of service', *European Journal of Social Work*, 19(5): 602–15.

Evans, T. (2018) 'Orientations of Professional Discretion in the Welfare Service State'. Paper presented at: Ambivalences of the Rising Welfare Service State – Hopes and Hazards of fundamentally realigning the Architecture of Welfare Modernity. Universitat Bielefeld & Université de Genève. Volkswagen Stiftung, Hannover 28–30 May.

Evans, T. and Hardy, M. (2017) 'The ethics of practical reasoning – exploring the terrain', *European Journal of Social Work*, 20(6): 947–57.

Evans, T. and Harris, J. (2004) 'Street-level bureaucracy, social work and the (exaggerated) death of discretion', *British Journal of Social Work*, 34: 871–96.

Evans, T. and Hupe, P. (2019) *Palgrave Handbook on Discretion: The Quest for Controlled Freedom*, London: Palgrave Macmillan.

Evans, T. and Keating, F. (2015) *Policy and Social Work Practice*, London: Sage.

Ferguson I. (2007) 'Increasing user choice or privatizing risk? The antimonies of personalisation', *British Journal of Social Work*, 37(3): 387–403.

Foot, P. (1972) 'Morality as a system of hypothetical imperatives', *The Philosophical Review*, 81(3): 305–16.

Francis, R. (2013) *Independent Inquiry into Care Provided by Mid Staffordshire NHS Foundation Trust January 2005–March 2009*, London: The Stationery Office.

Friedson, E. (2001) *Professionalism*, Cambridge: Polity Press.

Government Legal Department (2016) *Judge Over Your Shoulder*, London: Government Legal Department.

Hadley, R. and Clough, R. (1996) *Care in Chaos: Frustration and Challenge in Community Care*, London: Cassell.

Haidt, J. (2001) 'The emotional dog and its rational tail: a social intuitionist approach to moral judgment', *Psychological Review*, 108(4): 814–34.

Hare, R. M. (1963) *Freedom and Reason*, Clarendon Press: Oxford.

Harris, J. (2003) *The Social Work Business*, Routledge: London.

Harris, J. (2008) 'State social work: constructing the present from moments in the past', *The British Journal of Social Work*, 38(4): 662–79.

Harris, J. and White, V. (eds.) (2009) *Modernising Social Work: Critical Considerations*, Bristol: Policy Press.

Hood, C., Rothstein, H. and Baldwin, R. (2001) *The Government of Risk: Understanding Risk Regulation Regimes*, Oxford: Oxford University Press.

Horton, J. (2012) 'Political legitimacy, justice and consent', *Critical Review of International Social and Political Philosophy*, 15(2): 129–48.

Kadish, M. and Kadish, S. (1973) *Discretion to Disobey*, Stanford, CA: Stanford University Press.

Lipsky, M. (2010) *Street-Level Bureaucracy: Dilemmas of the Individual in Public Services* (2nd edn), New York: Russell Sage Foundation.

Marston, G. and McDonald, C. (2012) 'Getting beyond "heroic agency" in conceptualising social workers as policy actors in the twenty-first century', *British Journal of Social Work*, 42(6): 1022–38.

Mercier, H. and Sperber, D. (2017) *The Enigma of Reason: A New Theory of Human Understanding*, London: Allen Lane.

Montaigne, M. (1958) *The Complete Essays of Montaigne* (trans D. M. Frame), Stanford, CA: Stanford University Press.

Munro, E. (1998) 'Improving social workers' knowledge base in child protection', *British Journal of Social Work*, 28(1): 101–2.

Munro, E. and Liquid Personnel (2015) *The Social Work Survey 2014–15*, Manchester: Liquid Personnel. Available at: http://cdn.basw.co.uk/upload/basw_40843-5.pdf

Needham, C. (forthcoming) 'Managerial discretion', in T. Evans and P. Hupe (eds) *Palgrave Handbook on Discretion: The Quest for Controlled Freedom*, London: Palgrave.

Rhodes, R. (2007) 'Understanding governance: ten years on', *Organisational Studies*, 28(8): 1243–64.

Smart, J. and Williams, B. (1973) *Utilitarianism: For and Against*, Cambridge: Cambridge University Press.

Social Work (Scotland) Act 1968. United Kingdom. Available at: www.legislation.gov.uk/ukpga/1968/49/contents

Springer, S., Birch, K. and MacLeavy, J. (2016) 'An introduction of neoliberalism', in S. Springer, K. Birch and J. MacLeavy (eds) *The Handbook of Neoliberalism*, London: Routledge, pp 1–14.

The Local Authority Social Services Act 1970, United Kingdom. Available at: www.legislation.gov.uk/ukpga/1970/42

Williams, B. (1993) *Ethics and the Limits of Philosophy*, London: Fontana.

Wolf, S. (1997) 'Moral saints', in R. Crisp and M. Slote (eds) *Virtue Ethics*, Oxford: Oxford University Press, pp 79–98.

10

Systemic barriers to effective implementation of child protection reform in Israel

Ravit Alfandari

Introduction

This chapter is positioned at the implementation stage of the policy cycle and focuses on the role and organisation of social workers in the process. The subject of policy implementation – or unsuccessful implementation in this case – is investigated in the context of the recent reform introduced into the child protection work of the social service system in Israel. The qualitative study discussed here is part of a global debate about the competence of reformative actions to improve social workers' care-plan decisions regarding the help offered to children to improve their safety and well-being. The priority given to the issue by governments around the world is driven, among other things, by harsh public condemnation and outcry over ineffective practice when maltreatment ends in the tragic event of death or serious harm to a child (Munro, 2010; Israel Ministry of Social Services and Social Affairs [IMSSSA], 2014).

This chapter aims to enhance the understanding of the reasons why welcome, well-informed and generously resourced policy initiatives by governments to promote high quality service for children in need do not fully achieve their goals. As an example, Munro's (2011) review of the English child protection system demonstrates how inquiries into child abuse tragedies that conclude on the impact of human error, in conjunction with extreme public outcry over defective practice along with political pressures, consistently produce policy countermeasures to safeguard children. Unfortunately, these solutions have often been ineffective in preventing the next tragic death and, in effect, had cumulative, unexpected and unwarranted consequences. Rapid growth in the bureaucratisation of childcare work has gradually diverted the workforce from opportunities to exercise professional judgement and invest time in direct work with service users.

The originality of the analysis presented in this chapter is that it directs attention to the context, that is, the working environment where social workers meet children and families. Since empirical studies have not focused sufficiently on the impact of working conditions on child protection practices and policy outcomes (López et al, 2015; Shlonsky, 2015), this study could explain trends that have been overlooked by previous research.

Child protection reform

For over two decades, the government of Israel has invested considerable efforts in formulating policy on child protection practices that will improve decision making in formal committees called Planning, Intervention and Evaluation Committees (PIECs). These committees operate within the social services departments (SSDs) in all municipalities throughout the country. They are multidisciplinary forums comprising representatives of the welfare, education and health systems, as well as family members, and serve as the key framework for consultation, assessment and decision making concerning care plans for children who are suffering, or likely to suffer, from significant harm from abuse or neglect. The government's intensive endeavours have yielded a well-resourced reform that reflects policymakers' conceptions of the core practice principles that underpin sound decision making and effective service delivery, including working together with various professionals, partnership with parents, children's participation, systematic documentation of practice, and follow-up and review of the outcomes of the decisions. The reform introduces new regulations and procedures designed as purposeful directives towards an advanced routine way of working through all stages of the child protection process. It is now obligatory for parents to participate in the discussion and the working procedures make it mandatory for children's views to be heard and for children over 12 to participate in the committee meetings. Changes have also been introduced to the composition of the forum and a new follow-up scheme has been put in place (IMSSSA, 2004a; 2004b). At the heart of the reform is a new standardised tools package that organises practices according to scheduled tasks. The package includes four tools: a tool for collecting information designed to support the family assessment processes; a checklist to confirm that all new preparation measures have been carried out; a tool for managing and documenting the discussion and its outcomes; and a follow-up tool to report on the level of implementation of the intervention plan (Alfandari, 2017).

The reform has been gradually implemented in the field nationally since 2008 and to date is still evolving. At the beginning of that year, the government allocated IMSSSA a budget for professional training, development of technological infrastructures and additional staff at the SSDs (mostly social workers and committee chairs, the remainder administrative workers). Over the following two years, the ministry initiated an extensive nationwide training programme for SSD managers, PIEC chairs and team leaders, who function as both team leaders and professional supervisors (State of Israel Comptroller [SIC], 2013). It should be mentioned that the ministry has not developed or provided any designated programme or training for frontline social workers, although tasks such as referral to the committee, case preparation and the implementation of the decided interventions are among their responsibilities. Instead, chairs and team leaders have been assigned the duty of disseminating the principles of the reform through departmental and supervision meetings and helping staff apply them in their daily work.

As mentioned, the reform continues to evolve through a vigorous process. In January 2017, the ministry's ordinance regarding the PIECs was updated to reflect the new practices. The key problem in monitoring the reform's progress remains the lack of a central data collection system. Once the process of implementing the reform was underway at national level, the ministry began working on a dedicated information and communication technology [ICT] system for collecting data on the PIECs' operation at local, regional and national levels. This task is still in progress. Thus the current study provides the first in-depth insight into implementation of the reform in the field.

Besides the contribution to local knowledge, the key merit of this study, which can be projected to other contexts, relates to the utilisation of the 'systems approach' as a conceptual framework. The systems thinking was clearly proven in this study to elevate the depth, creativity and originality of the insights it produced.

The systems approach

There is extensive and ever-expanding literature on the systems approach or the 'new view', which has its origin in safety engineering in industries such as aviation and nuclear power, which is beyond the scope of this chapter. It should be mentioned here that the starting point of the systems way of thinking was inquiry into causation of accidents and disasters. It was later adopted to study the normal activities or everyday practice of actors on the frontline of service provision in various fields (Reason, 2000; Dekker, 2002). Recently, the systems approach has been utilised by pioneering child protection researchers to explore contributory factors to practice and to policy implementation (Fish et al, 2008; Munro, 2008, 2011).

Principally, the systems approach is a holistic perspective that 'places individuals within the wider system of which they are part' (Munro, 2008: 17) when it comes to studying their performance. Its basic premise is that employees' work is inherently connected to the multiple features of the organisational context (Dekker, 2002). Following the same lines, the SSDs in which the child protection service is conducted may present a variety of systemic factors that might interconnect with performance to sufficient depth, including workloads and time, training and qualification, professional and administrative support and so on. Hence, the conditions under which social workers operate were also investigated in the study in order to obtain a whole-organisation knowledge about what is happening in everyday practice under the reform and why.

The current study

The current study set out to meet three key targets: to examine the extent to which the changes prescribed by the reform are being implemented in the field; identify underlying systemic factors of the work environment that act as barriers or facilitators to implementation; and evaluate whether the reform is having the desired impact on improving outcomes for children.

A case study design was employed to explore these questions. It was conducted in seven SSDs of five local municipalities across the country, which were selected using convenience sampling. The cases of 21 families (45 children in total) brought before PIECs were rigorously investigated and followed up after six months. Data was collected through field observations of the committee meetings; semi-structured interviews with social workers and parents conducted immediately, or as soon as possible, after the discussion; semi-structured interviews with the responsible social worker conducted six months after the PIECs; and document review. Conversations with the committee chairs prior to data collection were also included in the data analysed. The methodology, research design and research methods adopted in the study made it possible to obtain a system-wide perspective of the events.

The study findings are presented in the following three sections of this chapter. The next section describes the characteristics of the 22 social workers who participated in the study (four were responsible for two cases, and there was a turnover of staff between interviews) and the organisational context of their professional activity, including roles in the department, professional experience and qualifications, caseloads, professional support and so on. Note that the findings show that the study sample reflects well-known features of the Israeli SSDs' working arrangements (Ofek, 2009).

Social workers and their organization

On average, interviewees had 10.4 years (SD = 6.2; Median = 9) of social work experience. Length of service varied greatly from 1.25 to 26 years, with only 4 workers having less than 6 years' experience. The majority of workers (16/22) were employed as generalist social workers; among them, just over half had dual roles in the SSDs. Six workers were specialists (for example, specialising in rehabilitation or the population of people with disabilities) or had other roles in the department. Overall, workers had been in their position long enough (mean = 6 years; SD = 6.3; median = 4.2 years) to develop context-based knowledge and skills.

Fitting with the legal entry route to the profession, all the social workers in the study had undergraduate degrees in social work; five also held graduate degrees in social work; and six had participated in post-qualification programmes on child therapy and/or child protection. Regular weekly meetings with supervisors were exceptional and reported by only five participants. Most met every 2–3 weeks, once a month, or only occasionally. Six respondents did not receive any supervision in the department. In regard to the reform's new ways of working, most of the workers recalled participating in departmental or supervision meetings where the new procedures were first introduced. However, apart from that, the involvement of the chairs and team leaders in workers' implementation of the new regulations in the cases examined was very limited and usually concerned the initial decision whether to refer the case to the PIECs (reported in 18 cases). In only five cases did social workers report consulting with their team leaders and/or the PIEC chair in the process of preparing the case for discussion following the new regulations.

Social workers have heavy caseloads. The majority of respondents (13/21) were responsible for 120 to 200 families, 3 for over 200 families and 5 for up to 60 families (most worked full-time or close to full-time). There was consensus among practitioners that the most important requirement for improving child protection practice in general and in the PIECs in particular, was to reduce their caseloads. Otherwise, the quality of service they offer is compromised. Finally, organisations should provide their staff with administrative support so they can concentrate on the professionally demanding aspects of their work. The departments included in the study had designated administrative staff responsible for the general bureaucratic demands of the department, but no support staff were formally assigned to assist the social workers.

To sum up, the reform was implemented within a social services system that suffers from some critical weakness. The respondents were working under immense daily pressure with heavy caseloads and multiple roles, and with only limited organisational support to deliver high quality service. The next section describes how social workers adapted to the reform.

Implementation of the reform

With regard to practice in the field, the study found little indication of implementation of the reform in everyday practice. The tendency was to maintain the conventional practice, which consumed less time and energy. The most straightforward example of this is the actual use of the new tools package introduced by the reform. Out of 21 cases, only 5 workers completed the tools designed for collecting information about family life and documenting case preparation, and this was done only partially and inaccurately. None of the workers used the tools package user guide for writing the family assessment report according to the instructions and there was no evidence of use of the new follow-up tool. In addition, observations revealed that the chairs were not using the tool designated to manage and document the committee's deliberations systematically throughout the hearings (Alfandari, 2017).

Another example relates to the guidelines for an innovative participatory model for working with children. Only 7 children, out of 45, participated with their social workers in a pre-committee meeting intended to provide them with information about the PIEC, elicit their views or prepare them for participating in the discussion. Two children attended the committee without any preparation. Only 7 of the 14 children who were eligible to participate in the committee under the new regulations were indeed invited to do so and only 4 met with their social worker after the discussion in order to be briefed about its outcomes and implications – a new mandatory procedure in all cases (Alfandari, 2015).

Findings revealed that, all too often, team leaders and chairs did not perform the tasks prescribed to them by the new regulations, in particular neglecting their responsibilities to ensure the quality of case materials presented to the committee; to include children's voices in decision making; and to follow up the implementation and outcomes of the intervention plans. Consequently, some of the tasks for which the chairs are responsible, such as inviting participants and distributing case materials in advance, were delegated to overburdened frontline social workers, while others, such as conducting follow-up discussions, were occasionally ignored.

Nor did the leaders of the reform take steps to ensure staff compliance with new procedures. Apparently they accepted, or at least overlooked, the situation of workers neglecting to adopt the reform's regulations. Another pattern found was an organisational culture that encourages employees to engage in shortcuts that become routinised within the work. A prevalent trend among the SSDs investigated was to adapt and abridge the mandatory tools package. Another common example of shortcuts was social workers' strong reliance on the accounts of others (such as school staff) through the family assessment instead of striving to obtain first-hand impressions of family life through home visits and conversations with all family members.

Evidence also showed that attempts to implement the reform's new practice standards, for example to engage with children and fathers and to cooperate with professionals external to the SSDs, were demonstrated to be one-off events. The alarming portrayal of the children's condition that was generated through discussions raised expectations that the social workers' engagement with them would be subsequently strengthened. Yet findings revealed that during a six-month period 20 children had no contact with their social workers (this was due to staff turnover in only 6 of the cases). The expected increased engagement of the children also applies to their fathers. This is in view of the fact that in eight cases fathers participated in the PIEC and were assigned responsibilities in the intervention plan, and in three other cases it was decided to actively reach out to the fathers and get them more involved. However, it was found that when good cooperative relationships with the fathers had already been established prior to the PIEC, as was evident in two cases, they endured after the discussion, whereas when the relationships had to be developed, the social workers all too easily abandoned the task. Furthermore, the PIECs usually remain isolated episodes of multidisciplinary collaboration that fail to produce further efforts to sustain permanent cooperation among the various professionals. In regard to collaboration with educational system professionals, for example, only six social workers reported maintaining regular communication with the school staffs; in only two cases were they routinely in contact every month.

In summary, the study found clear evidence that the reform's expectations of a high standard of enhanced professional performance were not met in practice. Overall, there were no noteworthy differences in the routine work, which remained rushed, superficial and fractional. Problems with the committees' functioning prior to the reform – and identified as obstructions to sound decision making, such as a lack of sufficient information about family circumstances; partial participation of children; an unsystematic deliberation process; and very limited follow-up on the committees' outcomes (Dolev et al, 2001) – were also evident in the current study. Notwithstanding, the problems are arguably not due to the shortcomings of individual workers.

The next section follows the 21 case studies sampled six months after the PIECs convened (around three to four years after the reform was first launched). Follow-up interviews were designed to examine how the intervention plans were implemented and evaluate their effectiveness in improving the children's situation.

The reform outcomes for children

The assessment of the reform's outcomes for children was based on two key criteria: the degree to which the PIECs' intervention decisions were actually carried out; and the degree to which realisation of the PIECs' intervention decisions enhanced children's safety and well-being. Assessing the ability of the reform to achieve its goals on the basis of these two criteria was designed to prevent confusion between the means and the end, which is often the outcome of child protection reformation actions that focus on procedurally based improvements (Munro, 2011). The overall goal of the reform was to achieve on-the-ground improvement in children's safety and welfare; implementation of the PIECs' decisions is a means to that end, a step on the way, not the end in itself.

Starting with the first criterion, the implementation rate of the PIECs' intervention plans was noticeably low: in 13 cases, it was partly implemented; in 6 cases it was not carried out at all; and in only 2 cases was it fully implemented. Another way to report these findings is to note that out of the 44 children who had been recognised as in need of help and for whom it was decided to provide one or more services (the condition of one child, a six-year-old girl, was deemed not to require intervention), just under half (19 children) were provided with all the services decided on. Over a quarter (13 children) were provided with some of the services only, while none of the decisions was implemented at all for almost a quarter of them (10 children). These included three children who were waiting (at home!) for a suitable out-of-home arrangement and three who were on the waiting list for individual therapy. (The social workers of two of the children had no up-to-date information.) In addition, when the services were provided, it was very frequently a considerable time after the PIEC, in some cases even four or five months after the decisions had been made.

In interview, the respondents voiced their frustration and disappointment at not being able to provide the help that was so urgently needed. They noted that the lack of resources and services was one of the predominant obstacles to implementing the interventions and a key reason for substantial and frequent delays in service provision. The chronic gap between growing needs and available resources is an enduring detrimental characteristic of the social services in general, which results in SSDs being able to provide only limited service to only a fraction of the population in need (Horev & Kop, 2009; Weiss, 2016). The PIECs' intervention plans were no exception.

Moving to the status of the children, there were reports of positive changes in the condition or life circumstances of only a third (15/45) of them. In most of these cases it was attributed to the help they had received. In a few cases, the improvements indicated were not the direct outcome of a specific service, but nevertheless occurred following the PIEC. (For instance, three children were better protected physically after moving to live with their father, away from their mother, a change that was advocated by the committee.) Nine children were reported to have adjusted well to the service, yet there was still no evidence of meaningful progress in their condition. A troubling finding was that some of the PIECs' decisions had unfavourable and even damaging effects on the children's condition; the functional and/or emotional state of nine children declined following the interventions. Most were children who had been involuntarily removed from home for the first time. In a few cases, it was the reverse decision, that is, their return home from out-of-home placements had negative results. It seems that in both situations not enough support had been provided to the child and family to secure the adjustment to such a drastic change in family life. In the rest of the cases, where the recommended interventions for the children were not, or were only partly, carried out, their condition either remained stable or worsened. Among them were six children whose behavioural and emotional condition severely and persistently deteriorated without meaningful intervention.

To conclude, very disappointing findings show that, overall, the intervention plans decided on in the PIECs were ineffective. Whether the decisions were not implemented, delayed for considerable time, or did not lead to a positive improvement, the general picture after six months was that there was improvement in the condition of only a third of the children discussed in the committees. It can therefore be stated that the reform did not meet its end.

The lesson of the reform

Before presenting the conclusive arguments about the reform's lack of success in accomplishing its valuable ambitions, it is important to emphasise it is well recognised that there is much commitment and good intention within the Israeli social services system. Professionals spoken to during this study, from senior ministry policymakers, through SSD leaders, to frontline workers, showed great dedication, passion and commitment to do better for the benefit of children and families. Unfortunately, this study could find only limited evidence of improved outcomes for children. Using the systems approach in this study, the search for explanations for the very limited realisation of the reform's aims for strengthening practice and improving the safety and well-being of vulnerable children went beyond individual workers' performances to reveal systemic barriers to implementation of the reform in practice.

On a positive note, the reform in the PIECs' work is an important step forward towards improving the provision of effective help for children in need and their families. It does not aspire to provide a 'quick fix' for the problems identified in the committees, but rather to be a milestone for the Israeli child protection services and to generate a new uniform code of good practice (IMSSSA, 2004a). The tasks assigned to the social workers under the new regulations are complex and require intellectual competence, significant professional judgement, communication skills and confident proficiency to establish constructive working relationships with the families and other professionals. However, the workforce is not equipped to take on these challenges and meet them successfully. Their work environment has not supported, encouraged or enabled the anticipated change in practice.

The analysis identified factors of the organisational environment and culture that interacted together and led to particular patterns of outcomes for children. These factors included: (1) heavy workloads and an organisational culture that seeks opportunities to shortcut procedures and processes; (2) inadequate professional supervision and support; (3) insufficient training and qualifications; and (4) lack of strong organisational leadership.

The pressures of an overburdened workplace were experienced by professionals at all levels of the organisation – team leaders, chairs and frontline social workers – and had negative impacts on their performance and ability to comply with the reform's increased demands. Due to workload pressure, the new procedures and guidelines were systematically disregarded, delegated to others or carried out in an overly superficial and patchy way. Frontline workers lacked some essential skills and knowledge as well as professional support and guidance. The training programme offered to SSDs' leaders through the reform's implementation process was proven ineffective in setting the practice on the right track. The nature and complexity of the tasks assigned to generalist social workers required their qualification to be given precedence over senior professionals. While not always having the right knowledge and skills to be effective, generalist social workers could not depend on SSD leaders who in effect offered only little support and guidance and tended to become uninvolved after the decision to refer a case to the PIEC had been made. The study identified several communication, interpersonal and analytical skills known to contribute to sound decision making, effective service delivery and successful outcomes, where frontline workers required more qualification and proficiency. Moreover, without sufficient administrative support, the professionals' limited time was erroneously invested in bureaucratic or procedural aspects of the work. Finally, with team leaders and chairs not fulfilling their own responsibilities and overlooking failure to comply with the new regulations, it is difficult to expect a strong ownership of the new way of working in their organisation.

Nevertheless, the most serious impediment to achieving the reform's overall target was unsatisfactory availability of help options both in the community and out-of-home residential care. It is therefore suspected that even if the PIECs operated in complete accordance with the guidelines, their decisions would not have improved the available selection of interventions.

The significance and pertinence of the Israeli case described in this chapter derives from efforts to raise awareness of the organisational conditions required to prescribe changes of top-down reformative actions to meet expectations. Social service users rely on confident and effective social workers. Such professionals are found in organisations that provide them with the appropriate conditions, qualifications, resources and support. It can thus be argued that the systems' underlying problems need to be resolved and the quality of the work environment needs to be raised significantly if effective delivery of services for children and families is to be achieved. Policymakers are called upon to consider how time and workloads are allocated at all levels of the system in order to create opportunities for workers to increase the depth of their practice and judgement; to promise the provision of high quality continuous professional supervision to help frontline workers respond better to the challenges thrown up by practice; to invest in improving social workers' key skills to enable them to manage complexities in their practice; and to establish strong organisational leadership committed to professional progress.

To conclude, the key message of this chapter, using Reason's (2000) very straightforward analogy, is that reformative actions that merely tell workers what to do are as effective as swatting mosquitoes one by one, as they keep on coming. A more useful solution would be to drain the swamps in which they breed – that is, to introduce changes throughout the system.

References

Alfandari, R. (2015) 'Evaluation of a national reform in the Israeli child protection practice designed to improve children's participation in decision-making', *Child & Family Social Work*, 22: 54–62.

Alfandari, R. (2017) 'Systemic barriers to effective utilisation of decision making tools in child protection practice', *Child Abuse & Neglect*, 67C: 207–15.

Dekker, S. (2002) 'Reconstructing human contributions to accidents: the new view on error and performance', *Journal of Safety Research*, 33: 371–85.

Dolev, T., Benbenishty, R. and Timer, A. (2001) *Decision Committees in Israel: Their Organization, Work Processes and Outcomes*, Jerusalem: Myers-JDC-Brookdale Institute.

Fish, S., Munro, E. and Bairstow, S. (2008) *Learning Together to Safeguard Children: Developing a Multi-agency Systems Approach for Case Reviews*, London: SCIE.

Horev, T. and Kop, Y. (2009) *Israel's Social Services 2008*, Jerusalem: The Taub Center for Social Policy Studies in Israel.

Israel Ministry of Social Services and Social Affairs (IMSSA) (2004a) *Planning, Intervention, and Evaluation Committee: Final Principles Paper*, Jerusalem: Israel Ministry of Social Services and Social Affairs.

Israel Ministry of Social Services and Social Affairs (IMSSA) (2004b) *Planning, Intervention, and Evaluation Committee: The Implementation Team's Decisions*, Jerusalem: Israel Ministry of Social Services and Social Affairs.

Israel Ministry of Social Services and Social Affairs (IMSSA) (2014) *The Commission to Examine the Ministry's Policy in Relations to Children's Removal to Out-of-Home Placement and Custody Arrangements*, Jerusalem: Israel Ministry of Social Services and Social Affairs.

López, M., Fluke, J. D., Benbenishty, R. and Knorth, E. J. (2015) 'Commentary on decision-making and judgments in child maltreatment prevention and response: an overview', *Child Abuse and Neglect*, 49: 1–11.

Munro, E. (2008) *A Review of Safety Management Literature*, London: London School of Economics.

Munro, E. (2010) 'Learning to reduce risk in child protection', *British Journal of Social Work*, 40: 1135–51.

Munro, E. (2011) *The Munro Review of Child Protection Final Report: A Child-centred System*, London: The Stationery Office.

Ofek, A. (2009) *Preparations for the Reform in Social Services Departments*, Jerusalem: Israel Ministry of Welfare and Social Services.

Reason, J. (2000) 'Human error: models and management', *British Medical Journal*, 320(7237): 768–70.

Shlonsky, A. (2015) 'Current status and prospects for improving decision making research in child protection: a commentary', *Child Abuse & Neglect*, 49: 154–62.

State of Israel Comptroller (2013) *The Working Procedures of Planning, Intervention and Evaluation Committees Regarding Children at Risk: Annual Report 63c of the Year 2012*. Available at: www.mevaker.gov.il

Weiss, A. (2016) *State of the Nation Report: Society, Economy and Policy in Israel*, Jerusalem: The Taub Center for Social Policy Studies in Israel.

11

Social workers implementing social assistance in Spain: reshaping poverty in a familialistic welfare state

Sergio Sánchez Castiñeira

Introduction

This chapter shows the active role of social workers in trying to turn a passive public programme of public social assistance into an effective social policy. In the familistic Spanish welfare context (Flaquer, 2004), these professionals alleviate the desperation and deprivation of the newly poor through a normative, cognitive and emotional approach that helps them to adapt to their new circumstances. The crisis impacted mostly the population that tends to depend on wages, such as families with children. In Spain, the rate of severe material deprivation increased from 5.5% in 2008 to 8.3% in 2013, and the at-risk-of-poverty gap rose from 26.2% to 35.4% (Social Protection Committee, 2015). A considerable share of middle-income families with children were also hit by the recession: 22.5% of households with children that were in 2008 in the fourth, fifth and sixth income percentiles had already plummeted to the first and second percentile in 2011 (Marí-Klose & Martínez, 2016). On the other hand, family networks, which palliated some of the most exclusionary effects of the crisis, were showing some signs of saturation (Marí-Klose, 2016). In turn, the public social protection system became more residual because of cuts in public social assistance, and the responsibility of being in charge of the most vulnerable population was transferred to non-governmental organisations (NGOs) (Lorenzo, 2014). In this context, NGO agencies went through a process of internal restructuration, networking, searching for new funding and implementing new strategies for lobbying, which led to an extension of the charity sector (Fresno, 2015).

The lack of comprehensive anti-poverty policies at the national and regional level leaves the highly residual local social assistance system as the main response of the state to the rise and diversification of social needs. Yet the resources of this system seem insufficient to help the newly poor clients, a sector of the population that has seen their social world fall apart and who are now feeling powerless. Yet in between the state and the newly poor clients are the social workers who directly bring the policy to the newly poor. Working in a constraining context, those practitioners are nonetheless a highly skilled and vocational workforce that can reframe people's lives.

This chapter analyses social workers' practice to show how those professionals utilise, manipulate and improvise available socioeconomic, institutional, professional and personal resources in order to combat desperation and helplessness. More specifically, it analyses the emotional and cognitive labour required for the client to come to terms with their new social standing. In addition, the study shows how social workers try to provide clients with a new social lens through which they can perceive and then maximise external resources (family, informal work and charity). Finally, some potential social consequences of this intervention are presented.

(Passive) familialism of anti-poverty policies in Spain

The southern European social protection system posits that families should sacrifice by pooling scarce resources to protect their members (García & Kazepov, 2002). This familistic and communitarian assumption is also present in the market and the state, which are partly framed by informal practices and social and affective ties (Mingione, 1991; Camargo, 2016). Access to benefits depends mostly on local public agencies, which offer a residual social assistance that is managed discretionarily (Aguilar et al, 2012). What is a scarce and fragmented public support integrates with family transfers and aid from the community and 'third sector' organisations to form safety nets for families in need (Arriba & Moreno, 2005). However, the fact that those resources are often rather insufficient means that families must resort to some forms of informal work and debt, which could render them even more vulnerable (García & de Schampheleire, 2002). Focusing on how social assistance is played out at the local level by social workers and clients helps to understand how this familistic system is produced (and challenged?) on a daily basis.

The institutional construction of poverty

The analysis of welfare practices sheds light on the way that social policies may reframe previous social inequalities and economic needs: 'They offer, in fact – to different degrees and with different outcomes depending on the institutional framework, local culture and circumstances – social definitions as well as resources, opportunities as well as constraints' (Saraceno, 2002: 3). The implementation process becomes especially decisive because the relationship between the state and the client involves complex interactions with professionals that deeply affect the final outcome (Lipsky, 1980). Those street-level bureaucrats must deploy discretion and generate coping strategies to deal with ambiguous goals and scarce resources (Lipsky, 1980). Public officers are in part the final producers of policies, and they play a political role as 'formal law derives its substantive meaning from the ways in which it is routinely translated into practice' (Brodkin, 2007: 3). In the case of Spain, public social assistance is implemented by a highly qualified vocational workforce of social workers. Most of those professionals embrace the goals of social justice and of empowering the vulnerable (IFSW, IASSW and ICSW, 2012). Nevertheless, organisational and ideological conditions often divert the professional stance of poverty towards personal attitudes and behaviours and away from the systemic reproduction of inequalities (Jones, 2002).

Context

This study is set in Tarragona, a north-eastern Spanish city on the Mediterranean Sea. Tarragona is the capital of a province from the autonomous region of Catalonia and has a population of 131,255 (2015). In 2013, the rate of unemployment in the whole province of Tarragona was 26%. About half of those unemployed people did not receive any unemployment benefits from the regional or central administrations (INE, 2014).

According to the Catalan Law,[1] local authorities must organise and manage basic social services to cover the essential socioeconomic and personal needs of the population. Basic services in Tarragona are organised in seven offices in the city, which are formed by teams of qualified frontline social workers. Individuals who resort to social services usually demand economic or in-kind support to access basic needs, such as housing, food or school supplies. In a context of constrained human and economic resources, social workers assess the needs of the basic family unit to process the most suitable benefit.

They also provide the users with basic competences to promote their labour and social inclusion. In 2013, 33 social workers in Tarragona were directly dealing with economically vulnerable families. In the same year, those social workers carried out at least one intervention with 5,523 individuals (4.2% of the total population), affecting 3,375 households (6.2% of total households in the city).

Methods

The study is based on 17 semi-structured individual interviews and eight focus groups with frontline social workers, which were carried out, recorded and transcribed by the researcher.[2] Individual interviews, which were 80 minutes long on average, took place in the summer of 2015. These interviews did not aim to predict behaviour accurately but 'to gain insight into the participants' interpretative processes and the multifaceted nature of their stock of knowledge' (Jenkins et al, 2010, 3). The use of an inductive approach using Atlas.ti7 generated new concepts in interaction with a thematic list that had previously been made. The analysis was oriented to identify and explain instances about the situational types of economic hardship that social workers experience and the strategies they pursued to help clients. Subsequently, eight focus groups lasting an average of 75 minutes were carried out. Each of the 28 social workers participated in two focus groups. The first focus group discussed the existing resources within the organisation to deal with newly poor clients. The second explored the use of external welfare sources to work with those clients (family and community ties, the labour market and other welfare agencies).

Overall, 23 out of the 33 social workers that are directly attending families in material hardship in public local social assistance in Tarragona participated in an individual interview and/or a focus group. Eight supervisors, who had previously been frontline social workers, also participated in the focus groups.[3] The selection of professionals was based on availability and the willingness to participate. On the other hand, fieldwork was influenced by the fact that I had been a project officer (not a 'social worker') in the institution from 2009 to 2014. This working and relational experience provided me with the initial ideas that I could further develop. Interviewing my former colleagues might have helped communication by breaking some trust barriers. However, by talking to a former workmate, some social workers might have tended to enhance their professional competence.

Results

The social workers' goal is the socioeconomic inclusion and well-being of the clients, which results from obtaining suitable material, relational and symbolic resources. From the *ideal social work*, clients access those resources through inclusive labour and housing markets, cohesive family and community systems and supportive public services. Yet from the *real social work of public social assistance in Tarragona*, clients access those resources when they perceive and then seize the scarce and unreliable opportunities offered by the extended family and the community, through the least protected sector of the labour market and the increasing array of private and public agencies providing basic relief. The following results show how social workers try to modify the relationships the client has with these resource providers by yielding new information and interpretations, changing values and expectations, promoting new skills and interventions. Public social assistance, by reshaping the characteristics and functions that this welfare system has for the new clients, actively participates in the social construction of the local welfare context.

Learning how to be a client

Poverty means a lack of economic means and embarrassment, diminished citizenship and powerlessness (Lister, 2004). The link between material deprivation and the psychological costs caused by being unable to keep up with society expectations is a constant in every national and cultural context (Chase & Bantebya-Kyomuhendo, 2015). People's economic downward spiral is often accompanied by a process of social disqualification that crystallises when they resort to social assistance (Paugam, 1991). Social workers face the challenge of accommodating the newly poor clients to their new reality of having to resort to (and trust) public social assistance.

New clients are often paralysed by feelings of shame and frustration when they initially resort to social services. In order to counterbalance the emotional block, social workers sometimes present the clients' reliance on social assistance as temporary so that the new situation is progressively accepted. They also manage the timing of the relationship to make clients increasingly receptive towards a more engaged social intervention. In addition, laws from the last decade have proclaimed that basic social services are 'universal'. Social workers may use this rhetoric to introduce benefits as a right and to try to break the stigmatising link between social assistance and marginality.

> 'You can see their pain because they are reluctant to open up, you work very slowly, you play it by ear until they trust you [...] I tell clients that people from all walks of life come here, not just drunks.' (Leticia, individual interview)[4]

Relational skills can be masterfully deployed to separate the intrinsic value of the person from the situation they are living in and, therefore, to protect them from the social devaluation associated with their new status.

> 'I try to dignify the person, I respect her [...]. I'm never in a hurry to finish an interview, it can take an hour and a half, I don't care. I value people's time. I value the good things without being superficial. I am not saying it's OK. Visual contact. I shake hands [...]. If I bump into them on the street, I sit and speak with them for a while.' (Júlia, individual interview)

Despite widespread recession, some new clients still blame themselves for their precarious situation. Social workers may give the clients credit for trying not to become a beneficiary of social assistance and, at the same time, shift the responsibility of the situation onto external causes or use the example of other people also in hard times. Once the clients internalise the inevitability of their new situation, they might be ready to accept the social services' help and readapt their survival strategies to obtain 'small improvements', leaving the search for the 'great solution' behind. An evolving identity also means that social workers could suggest morally dubious but essential coping strategies: "And we told him: 'look, stop paying the rent, and once you start receiving the minimum income, we'll see if you can afford it or not'" (Raquel, individual interview). These social workers' interventions promote the newly poor clients adopting the institutional definition of 'users' ('*usuarios*'). This change of identity predisposes the newly poor to engage with the new welfare resources that may be actually available for them.

Maximising external resources

Once the newly poor clients are fully aware they no longer have access to the formal labour and housing market, or to the most inclusive forms of public social protection, some social workers skilfully introduce (and make feasible) alternative means for survival. This section shows how those professionals mobilise the family and communitarian ties, the mostly unprotected jobs and activities, and the new and varied forms of charity in order to help those clients to make ends meet.

(Re)turning to family and communities

Family and community ties are considered to be the main source of social protection in southern Mediterranean regimes (Paugam, 2005). In effect, social workers' statements openly prioritise the extended family or even the 'community' as the main source of economic support for the poor:

> 'There is always someone, there's always family, and if it's not the family, there's the community. People have a network and they're survivors, they know how to make a living. I try to avoid always providing [economic] aid.' (Alba, individual interview)

When clients are reluctant to resort to the extended family, social workers can change such attitudes through their experience and expertise. In that case, family support is not the institutional intervention's initial premise, but its goal.

> 'I had a case of a family with a baby that was going to be evicted. They had relatives in Extremadura but did not want to contact them. I didn't want to be pushy but I told them "It's normal for the relationship to deteriorate, but if they knew you were going through hardship, they might help you out". In fact, when they finally called their extended family, they were told that they could live in the grandparents' home, which was empty.' (Leticia, individual interview)

However, current newly poor clients find it harder to resort to the extended family. In the last decades, interwoven processes of socioeconomic prosperity and individualisation could have excluded intense economic support from kinship commitments (Meil, 2011). "The family might not be ready to give this support [pay the electricity bill]" (Ariadna, individual interview).

Informal occupations

Public social assistance must deal with the unbalances between the goals promoted by central bureaucratic institutions and the means that are available for people who are being pushed to the margins of society. While public employment and social security agencies penalise activities in the underground economy, public social assistance frames those jobs as basic resources not to be missed. This organisational strategy is facilitated both by the social workers' principles of prioritising the needs and the welfare of the clients, as the professionals widely express the belief that the newly poor clients need to gain new abilities and attitudes so they do not end up 'depending' on public benefits.

> 'Maybe the woman starts working part time without a contract, but they still cannot afford to pay rent. Then they get by thanks to what they make and social assistance [...] Some people say: "I'm not paying the rent" and "What's going to happen if I occupy a flat?" Some people fear their children will be taken away by social services. They talk to me about it before anyone brings it up. I tell them that it is not sufficient reason to have your children taken away. It's taken into consideration whether the children are dirty, whether they skip school, whether they're deprived of food.' (Laura, individual interview)

As the above quotation shows, a lack of alternative welfare sources could lead social workers to condone the behaviour of clients who also engage in mildly illegal actions. The attitudes, skills and acquaintances that clients develop when carrying out those activities might prove useful when more inclusive labour opportunities turn up. Social workers sometimes play by the rules, but sometimes they confine clients' coping strategies to those perceived as less socially harmful.

> 'Some people stop by a public restroom to take a toilet paper roll [...] Some people have been caught dissembling a toilet in a coffee shop because they needed rubber because theirs was leaking. [...] They are just making their ends meet with their own resources. Yes, it's morally reprehensible, but I'm not a priest, nor the police, nor the coffee shop owner. I'm an educator, you know? I'm not going to judge them, but those children will have toilet paper at home because dad and mom found their feet [...] It's a way of making a living, of making your ends meet in the least harmful possible way. It's not a felony, they are not hurting anyone. But they are making their ends meet.' (Fina, individual interview)

On the other hand, social workers protect themselves from the legal and reputational risks of using those extreme resources. The following discussion shows how they can skilfully define their professional borders in dealing with the informal economy:

> GUADALUPE: '[Using informal economy] as any other resource is not appropriate. However, when you realise there is no other chance, you say to clients: "Look, try to find some private flats to clean". I definitively have done that.'
> ÀNDREA: 'Yes.'
> EVA: 'That is true, Guadalupe. But I would be concerned if I say: "this client needs someone to clean her house", and then give her private telephone number to another private person.'
> GUADALUPE: 'No, not that, but as a rule of thumb…'
> EVA: 'For example, in one of the social service offices, social workers hang a notice board, so people could put their announcements up.'
> SUSANA: 'Yes, they also included housing ads…'
> EVA: '… I think that's a way to inform, but you do not inform directly. It's simply displayed there.'

Benefiting from extended assistance arrangements

Social workers tend to consider that resorting to the family and the informal market is more empowering than charity. However, sometimes professionals have to refer clients to the new and diverse forms of public and private charity that have emerged out of the economic and human crisis. The attachment of the newly poor clients to their middle-class values and expectations makes them try to avoid more stigmatising organisations. However, social workers could progressively familiarise clients with what is going to become 'their reality':

> 'At the end of the day, it's all about accepting they are poor, which they are accepting internally, and they dare say it openly here, because they know it's confidential […] I try to help them apply for Red Cross economic and material support. My job is to help them accept that it's their reality.' (Leticia, individual interview)

Economic vulnerability in the current context involves navigating in an increasingly complex world of social benefits and other kinds of institutional support. Most experienced social workers have the informational and relational assets to take advantage of the opportunities of the system. In the context of scarce resources, part of the job might require transmitting this knowledge and mindset to the inexperienced clients. The following quote shows that role of *financial advisers*:

> 'Clients need little tricks to get by. I say to her [a single mother at risk of eviction and without family support]: "I'll give you emergency aid for other basic expenses, but you won't use it to pay the rent. Once you start working in Port Aventura, we'll apply for the benefit aimed to pay the debts that you'll have accumulated".' (Julia, individual interview)

Social workers usually associate this streetwise approach to long-term and marginal clients of social services. These professionals often reprimand such behaviour but only because it is deemed to be carried out abusively. The approach itself is understood to be part of the rules of the game, and social workers may consider they have to impart it gently to inexperienced newly poor clients.

On the other hand, in their daily activities, social workers give information and orientation, as well as refer and sometimes advocate for clients to access some mainstream services and benefits (social security, employment services, education, housing, and so on). They act as a bridge between an increasing and heterogeneous array of services and organisations that are assuming charity tasks and the new low-income families.[5] As those organisations are not ready to assess necessity by themselves, they endow social assistance professionals with the function of validating the social situation of vulnerable families. Therefore, it's becoming more usual for social workers to combat hardship through a social certification role: housing services demand a 'social report' in order not to evict a family, the regional welfare office asks social services to verify the number of members in a household, or the public water provider requires from social services a list of the poor people whose water bills should be subsidised. These new interventions may help clients' material existence, but the resulting reinforcement of social control could also entail clients' defencelessness and humiliation. The following quote shows the reluctance of some social workers to be defined by such a monitoring role:

> 'There are several institutions that have discovered social services as a great source of information. And sometimes that's not "coordination". It bothers me when they say something like: "since you're on the frontline and have access to an important part of people's life, which is their private life, even their family life…".' (Dolors, focus group)

Together with approaching and making viable the resources from other peripheral welfare spheres, a lot of social workers try to fill with sense and content their role in public social assistance. However, the following section shows the limits of this intervention for the social inclusion of new clients but also for the well-being and self-respect of the social workers themselves.

The social consequences of social worker's (constrained) intervention

In some way, the social workers' mission of reducing social desperation and deprivation is being accomplished. The following quote shows that both the newly poor and the professionals may actually adjust to a context of higher deprivation:

> 'The new clients coming right now don't experience it [shame and desperation] like before, since their neighbours have been already there. Those people are adjusting happily to their new situation, well, I shouldn't have said "happily". It's not pleasant to ask for food, but they don't feel shame anymore, they see it as normal, and that's their new reality […] I've also been relativising, because, now, when a family comes because they're being evicted, I tell them, "I got it, I know how it works, don't worry, you won't be homeless".' (Claudia, focus group)

However, some social workers remain highly uneasy because they realise that the current organisational context prevents them from living up to their professional goals of promoting opportunities and fighting inequality.

> 'When we see injustice, or that we can provide information, we should have a platform to speak from, so that we can create projects or decide changes. The problem is that we keep it to ourselves, individually.' (Leticia, focus group)

A few of them express impotence and preoccupation because they feel they are part of wider societal arrangements that are constraining the lives of part of the population.

> 'Some families don't even receive the minimum income; they live off from meagre benefits. They squat and don't pay electricity and water bills because they can't afford them. What are we supposed to tell them? Well, we can urge them to take their children to school. However, they clearly attend school without the most basic items, so they find themselves on an uneven playing field. And the inequality gap is growing.' (Raquel, focus group)

In the case of a more mature social worker, who had been professionally socialised in a more communitarian and critical approach to social work (Bailey & Brake, 1975), she exposes lucidly the social function that the emergent regime of poverty assigns to social workers:

> ANDREA: 'Are one-off benefits good for anything?'
> ÚRSULA: 'They have an appeasing effect.'
> ANDREA: 'It might be better if those people, instead of keeping quiet, revolt against the local authorities [...] What can we do? At the end of the day, we are elements of the system, we promote destitution.'
> LUZ: 'They could revolt even if you paid their electricity bill, but you can't push a family to their limit [by not giving basic assistance].'
> ANDREA: 'I disagree with that, because the minute you are solving some of their problems, or you are giving them money, you are establishing a bond and a barrier they'll never cross. Besides, you are educating them to earn their livelihood by begging. And they'll keep living in destitution having their mouth shut.'

This quotation shows that not all social workers share the same opinion and attitudes. Personal and professional trajectories may provide them with different levels of normative, cognitive and relational resources to creatively deal with the immediate needs of the newly poor. On the other hand, those more resourceful professionals could certainly empower citizens in an alternative context of more opportunities for social change.

Conclusion

Institutional and socioeconomic conditions have put social workers' action well in the centre of a network of resources that are riddled with constrictions and infused with disparate commitments, which eventually leads to ambivalent social consequences. Social assistance laws, organisations and professionals widely proclaim the official goal of social inclusion. Since resources are insufficient to complete the task, there are frontline workers, that is, social workers, who accomplish the latent political function of balancing promise and practice (Brodkin, 2007).

These professionals try to fill those institutional gaps by mobilising available material, symbolic and relational resources while struggling to help their clients and to protect the dignity of both the clients and themselves. Some professionals skilfully attempt to minimise the devastating effects of hardship by engaging the newly poor client in a social intervention process of social adjustment more attuned to the current economic circumstances. In brief, they try to offer a pragmatic response to the deprivation and desperation of helpless families that have seen their social world fade away. The other side of the coin is that, in the institutional and socioeconomic context of a lack of resources, social workers' agency could eventually contribute to confining clients within the material and symbolic limits of an expanding grey zone with scarce opportunities and diminished wellbeing between inclusion and exclusion.

Data also shows that the social workers, under certain circumstances, are constrained to give in to an instilled bureaucratic logic that is deemed to undermine the goal of involving the newly poor clients in more proactive behaviour. A high caseload, work isolation, a lack of complementary services, or a predisposition for administrative rule over the informal practices may prevent those professionals from carrying out those wearing and sometimes insufficient interventions. Therefore, the way and the extent to which social workers actually make public social assistance a key institution in the management of poverty in Spanish local contexts remain open to further research. How social class, ethnicity, gender, type of family and age frame those institutional processes must also be studied.

What this study proves is that public social assistance in southern European countries is not (at least potentially) just a residual and irrelevant institution clearly overshadowed by the family and the community in dealing with poverty. On one side, the social workers' constrained actions reinvigorate familism by promoting a continuum of new 'affective relationships', which range across different welfare resources, from the most disinterested and integrative to the most exploitative and consuming, including the more caring but patronising ones. But, on the other hand, by suggesting and imposing new knowledge, attitudes and behaviours, social workers in public social assistance agencies in Spain might redefine the relationship that the newly poor establish with family, the market and the *state*. Therefore, those professionals can frame a new structure of opportunities and, hence, actively participate in the social construction of poverty.

Notes

1. *Ley 12/2007 de Servicios Sociales del Parlamento Catalán.*
2. Six out of the eight focus groups were carried out by other researchers. It included two previous team meetings to get familiar with and revise the interview guides (for example, by sharing the initial results from the individual interviews).
3. Participants' quotations only include a feminine pseudonym in order to keep anonymity.
4. Social workers' quotations have been translated by the author.
5. In the last years of the crisis, central welfare institutions have been subjected to an increasing social pressure to become more socially responsible (Navarro, 2012).

References

Aguilar, M., Llobet, M. and Pérez, B. (2012) 'Los servicios sociales frente a la exclusión', *Zerbitzuan*, 51: 9–26.

Arriba, A. and Moreno, L. (2005) 'Spain. Poverty, social exclusion and "safety nets"', in M. Ferrera (ed) *Welfare State Reform in Southern Europe: Fighting Poverty and Social Exclusion in Italy, Spain, Portugal and Greece*. London: Routledge, pp 141–203.

Bailey, R. and Brake, M. (1975) *Radical Social Work*, London: Pantheon Books.

Brodkin, E. Z. (2007) 'Bureaucracy Redux: "Management Reformism and the Welfare State"', *Journal of Public Administration Research Theory*, 17(1): 1–17.

Camargo, S. (2016) *The Relative Success of Individual Job-Seeking Practices: Young University Graduates in Spain, the Netherlands, and the United Kingdom*. PhD Thesis, Universitat de Barcelona.

Chase, E. and Bantebya-Kyomuhendo, G. (2015) *Poverty and Shame. Global Experiences*, Oxford: Oxford University Press.

Flaquer, L. (2004) 'La articulación entre familia y el Estado de bienestar en los países de la Europa del sur', *Papers. Revista de Sociología*, 73: 27–58.

Fresno, J.-M. (ed) (2015) *El Tercer sector de Acción social en 2015. Impacto de la crisis*, Madrid: Plataforma de ONG de Acción Social (POAS).

García, M. and de Schampheleire, J. (2002) 'The inclusive power of standard and not-standard work', in R. van Berkel and I. Moller (eds) *Active Social Policies in the EU. Inclusion through Participation?*, Bristol: Policy Press, pp 73–102.

García, M. and Kazepov, Y. (2002) 'Why some people are more likely to be on social assistance than others', in C. Saraceno (ed) *Social Assistance Dynamics in Europe. National and Local Poverty Regimes*, Bristol: The Policy Press, pp 127–72.

Instituto Nacional de Estadísitica (INE) (2014) *Encuesta de Población Activa. Cuarto trimestre de 2013. Nota de prensa.*

International Federation of Social Workers (IFSW), International Association of Schools of Social Work (IASSW) and International Council on Social Welfare (ICSW) (2012) *The Global Agenda for Social Work and Social Development Commitment to Action*. Available at: http://cdn.ifsw.org/assets/globalagenda2012.pdf

Jenkins, N., Bloor, M., Fischer, M., Berney, L. and Neale, J. (2010) 'Putting it in context: the use of vignettes in qualitative interviewing', *Qualitative Research*, 10(2): 175–98.

Jones, C. (2002) 'Poverty', in M. Davies (ed) *The Black Companion to Social Work*, Oxford: Blackwell, pp 118–25.

Lister, R. (2004) *Poverty*, Bristol: Policy Press.

Lipsky, M. (1980) *Street-level Bureaucracy: Dilemmas of the Individual in Public Services*, New York: Russell Sage Foundation.

Lorenzo, F. J. (2014) 'Pobreza y exclusión social en España: consecuencias estructurales de nuestro modelo de crecimiento', *Ehquidad*, 1: 91–114.

Marí-Klose, M. (2016) 'Solidaridad intergeneracional en época de crisis: ¿mito o realidad?', *Panorama social*, 22: 61–78.

Marí-Klose, P. and Martínez, A. (2016) 'Empobrecimiento en tiempos de crisis: vulnerabilidad y (des)protección social en un contexto de adversidad', *Panorama social*, 22: 11–26.

Meil, G. (2011) *Individualización y solidaridad familiar*, Barcelona: Obra social La Caixa.

Mingione, E. (1991) *Fragmented Societies: A Sociology of Economic Life beyond the Market Paradigm*, London: Blackwell.

Navarro, F. (2012) *Responsabilidad social corporativa: teoría y práctica*, Madrid: Esic.

Paugam, S. (1991) *La disqualification sociale*, Paris: La decouverta.
Paugam, S. (2005) *Les formes élémentaires de la pauvreté*, Paris: Le lien social.
Lorenzo, F. (ed) (2014) *VII Informe sobre exclusión y desarrollo social en España*, Madrid: Fundación Foessa.
Saraceno, C. (ed) (2002) *Social Assistance Dynamics in Europe. National and Local Poverty Regimes*, Bristol: Policy Press.
Social Protection Commitee (2015) *Annual Report of the Social Protection Committee on the Social Situation in the European Union, 2014*, Luxemburg: European Union.

12

Layering, social risks and manufactured uncertainties in social work in Poland[1]

Paweł Poławski

Introduction

In recent decades, active labour market reforms within the European Union have reshaped the landscape of the welfare state. The transformation has involved policy and governance reorientation. The retrenchment is understood as both cost cuts and recalibration of social support aimed at improving its economic efficiency (Pierson, 2001), limiting universal social entitlements (Taylor-Gooby, 2009), placing pressure on work-based remuneration and establishing individual providences as the main sources of financial security. Governance reforms have also strengthened decentralisation and the autonomy of local institutions in shaping social policy. The findings of the Organisation for Economic Co-operation and Development (Venn, 2012), for example, prove that eligibility criteria are indeed flexible. Numerous case studies show differentiation in responding to social needs in various local contexts (for example, Jewell, 2007; Liwiński et al, 2008). Regardless of how these transformations are assessed, the literature on the welfare state seems to be dominated (Van Berkel, 2013) by analyses focusing on governance and the formal dimension of reforms. In the first mainly case-legislative efforts, historical aspects and systemic path-dependency are discussed, usually in a comparative approach (for example Palier, 2010). The emphasis on governance means studying the structure of dependencies between different levels of government, and the relations between public administration and other actors (Halvorsen & Hvinden, 2016). The third significant dimension of reform – the functioning of street-level activation policy – is usually overlooked, and research on this subject is rather limited.

This chapter is an attempt to address that deficit; it shows which features of the locally implemented social assistance reforms enhance the adverse effects and latent functions of activation policy. The chapter focuses on the consequences of layering of social support institutions from social workers' point of view, on their experiences in the implementation of governance and activation measures that have been modified and adjusted to local realities. The analysis focuses on the effects and organisational factors related to how social workers perform as implementers, how local social assistance centres operate, and the effects of social work.

The case of Poland seems interesting here for several reasons. First, Poland is a 'high social risk' country, which sets the context for activation policy in general and social work in particular. Although both income poverty and unemployment rates have been declining, the stabilisation of in-work poverty and precariousness remains problematic for Poland (Nolan et al, 2011; Employment and Social Developments in Europe, 2016). Second, underfunded social assistance – the basic organisational structure for social work – is still an *in statu nascendi* institution. It has been operating in its present form since 1991, or since the Social Assistance Act was passed as an element of transformation after the collapse of the socialist system. Thus, contrary to other EU countries, social assistance seems to be relatively 'young' in terms of time needed to adapt to the market economy and related risks. Before 1991, social assistance was an element of a centralised health protection system, targeted mainly at needs related to age, disability or illness. A distinctive aspect of the 'old' system was its highly discretionary and paternalistic character, later replaced with 'objectivised' support, means testing, subsidiarity and empowerment. Nevertheless, active and work-oriented measures were only incrementally introduced to social work after Poland joined the European Union in 2004. These measures were introduced mostly in a top-down fashion, imitating solutions and methods (such as individual action plans or community social work) that were popular elsewhere. Despite the gradual change, the statutory definition of social work is still basically a copy of the IFSW definition from 1957 (see introduction to this volume). Both practice and professional training of social workers still concentrate more on clients' individual deficiencies and casework than on communities, social change or cohesion. There is still a lack of political consensus on the key aspects of social assistance; for example, what general model of social policy should be implemented and what role social assistance and social work play in this model are still under discussion. This ambiguity causes incoherence in appropriate regulations (Kaźmierczak, 2016). Even the strongly declared linkage between social assistance, social work and labour market policy has not necessarily been regulated in a consistent manner (Rymsza, 2012). Although conditionality – the basic feature of workfare – has been included in the relevant laws, it is also discretionary: work requirements need not be enforced by social workers, and non-cooperation usually does not affect entitlements and support. Third, the new public management and governance concepts are also relatively new in social assistance – managerialism and orientation toward efficiency and cost-effectiveness are not necessarily the subject of professional training for social workers, but related bureaucratic requirements are another source of tension in social work (Rymsza, 2012).

This chapter uses the data collected within the research project 'Conditionality and Contractualism in Social Assistance' conducted in 2015–17. The qualitative part involves 29 in-depth interviews with social workers in six locations (both rural and urban) in Poland. The main goal of the project was to analyse efficiency factors of so-called social contracts (a variant of individual action plans). However, the collected data has a wider scope and is useful in characterising regularities of social support at the local level and social work in general.

Layering and social work

The text argues that one of major sources of tension within reformed social assistance and the shaping of how social work is carried out is the process that Streeck and Thelen (2005) referred to as 'layering' – a politically safe incremental strategy of implementing institutional change:

> New dynamics are set in motion ... by introducing amendments that can initially be 'sold' as refinements of or correctives to existing institutions. Since the new layers created in this way do not directly undermine existing institutions, they typically do not provoke counter mobilization by defenders of the status quo. ... Over time they may fundamentally alter the overall trajectory of development as the old institutions stagnate or lose their grip and the new ones assume an ever more prominent role in governing individual behaviour. (Streeck & Thelen, 2005: 23)

This strategy has consequences; it leads to pressure on creating functional 'pillars' inside existing systems that are oriented toward modified logic, use different legal provision and grant different kinds of benefits or service particular segments of the population.

Managerialisation, understood as introducing quasi-market arrangements for social work, (Harris, 2003) followed by changes in the employment structure in social assistance shall be treated as a variant of layering. Risk analysis, implemented as an obligatory element of social work management in Poland, needs assessment, performance monitoring or evidence-based planning shall be interpreted as other consequences of rationalisation efforts, and also as technical expressions of quasi-market orientation in social assistance. These are efforts that have pillarised social assistance itself.

The obvious example of such pillarisation is the specialisation of social workers forced by reporting systems. The problem is that IT solutions implemented in local assistance centres are not necessarily compatible with each other, as they were designed to handle separate types of services or benefits (family benefits, housing allowances, rehabilitation and so on) even if the customer is the same. The multitude of parallel reporting systems translates into either increasing bureaucratic obligations for social workers in smaller centres or creating units in larger centres specialised in servicing databases and reporting:

> 'Last year a small unit was created to do analyses, because so many of us are currently swamped with work that we have never done before. [...] Resource assessment, strategies, the violence programme, the family support programme... [...] And who'll do it in the end? A field social worker doesn't have the time to do it. The manager? Well, no... Hiring someone who was not a social worker before to make him sit down and analyse it? Maybe a sociologist, but for this, in turn, there are no financial resources.' (Social worker; all quotations translated by the author)

What's more, the multiplication of reporting systems is somewhat beyond the casework needs of social workers. Lack of system compatibility translates to the fact that the reconstruction of family welfare history is hampered, as is tracking the effects of the support. It is still rational to keep notes and paper files which, unlike reporting systems, contain complete information about cases and build the 'environmental memory' of an institution.

This kind of pillarisation is also visible in the dynamics and structure of employment in Polish social assistance. The change over the past decades covers gradual altering of the ratio of social workers (43.8%

of all employed in 2001, compared to 34.4% in 2016) and personal care workers (respectively 22.4% and 10.8%). At the same time, the percentage of 'other staff' – those responsible for benefit application processing, reporting, accounting, IT specialists, lawyers and so on – has increased from 25.9% to 43.0%. In other words, the need for monitoring, control and planning determines the organisational structure of social assistance, which increasingly reflects the logic of statutory reporting rather than the logic of social needs. It also increases the sense of alienation among social workers, their declared distance towards reforms, and significantly limits the time for fieldwork:

> 'These organisational solutions are wrong, because the centre, instead of being a social assistance centre, slowly becomes another institution, dealing completely with other affairs. […] All social workers have additional responsibilities […] my deputy is a personnel and family assistance manager. She has a lot of things that have nothing to do with social work at all, right? […] Other employees – the same. Well, who will run the archive? A social worker. A social worker conducts public procurement, deals with an EU project and so forth.' (Manager)

> 'So, this bureaucracy… the social worker has already flown out of me, I'm not working anymore, I'm mostly an office worker.' (Social worker)

Complaints concerning bureaucratisation and excessive involvement in formal duties were common in the declarations of social workers, regardless of their position in the organisational structure. They also confirmed the existence of what Harris called a 'social work business' which is a direct consequence of recent governance reforms. Harris (2003: 66) points out that 'the direction in which managerialism took social work … was away from approaches that were therapeutic, or which stressed the importance of casework, let alone anything more radical or progressive. Turning professionals into managers involved making them responsible for running the business, showing also that traditional social work skills are – as a result – valued less than management and information processing skills (Harris, 2003: 68). In social assistance centres this tendency has been institutionalised by the clear distinction between social workers and family assistants, who constitute the new 'pillar' of field workers, supposedly balancing the deficiencies caused by extensive bureaucratic duties. In fact, family assistants do what was formerly part of social work. They work directly with families to help them overcome everyday problems, performing simple pedagogical tasks and controlling the progress of activation. The difference lies in the number of families under supervision (significantly higher in the case of social workers), time spent with families and the frequency of contact, personal relations, limited authorisation to perform formal tasks (related to benefit granting), but also in the different employment situation of family assistants, who are usually on fixed-term contracts and earn less than social workers – often the minimum statutory wage. In other words, layering in social assistance has resulted in the creation of a less esteemed and valued caste of field workers supplementary to 'professional' social workers.

'Care management' or social work?

Factors in how the activation is addressed can be found in social workers' interpretations of the needs and situations of clients, and how they pursue their objectives in the context of activation goals. The interpretations can be shown in relation to the problem of reporting data consistency and missing information – a common question when analysing administrative datasets. The Ministry of Labour datasets show for example, that 30% of client cases have unidentified education, 12% have no income and 23% have missing data for employment status.

The amount of missing data may indicate the number of persons whose status on the labour market is truly hard to define, or the fact that social workers do not classify those who work in the grey zone as active in the labour market. If this is the case, the data also serves as indirect proof that the problem of the working poor is being addressed by social workers to an increasing degree and that when they determine the form of support, they consider level of income and family problems first and are less interested in the source of money.

The 'missing data' issue seems to illustrate one of the tensions in social work: the dilemma between professional values and formal rules. In this case, it is strengthened by knowledge of the local labour market limitations and by a shared interpretation of the basic function of social assistance. When asked about the assessment of the amount of benefits, one of our respondents said:

> 'The allowance is only for basic needs. [...] This is the minimum for now to meet the needs, and that's why we are here and for this is social work, to make them use [...] their resources as soon as possible, to find other sources,

some money, and then, later, we are talking about taking up employment.' (Social worker)

This kind of interpretation of the professional role positions social workers in opposition to the employment goals and general logic of activation policy. In fact, focusing on satisfying minimum needs entails a departure from the conditionality principle, regardless of the requirements related to labour market activation. More precisely, it establishes the order of support, in which activation turns out to be secondary to social integration, and the social worker's role is to deal with needs and education in this regard, not employment. Social integration efforts take priority, even if they are outside the structure of the legal labour market and its institutions. Further interpretations of this principle indicate the integrational function of paid help in housework, small repairs and garden work, but also allow for unregistered seasonal and occasional jobs as an 'activation measure', even if this activation is not exactly legal (in a sense that any remuneration shall be declared and counted as income for the means-testing procedure):

'I must admit that there have been cases when someone took work on the side. So what? […] So we tried not to put obstacles in his way. […] When there are chances that the employer will notice him and offer employment.' (Family assistant)

Often, illegal work is justified if it ensures the well-being of all household members. There is also a shared belief that enforced poorly paid work, even when legal, is not necessarily compatible with social integration and family welfare:

'Many clients work in the shadow economy […] We are trying to eliminate that and limit the support […]. Well, we are trying to, but we deal with it individually, because if a client says he works illegally and has – for example – four dependants in his household, well, we cannot say "look, man, you've got to stop right now" […] We assume that if someone doesn't take up legal work for purely financial reasons, it's because he should earn more than the minimum wage in that work.' (Social worker)

In other words, social workers compensate for the risk of partial loss of household income, giving it a greater priority than the risks associated with undeclared work. The priority is given easily because most families, including those in which someone works in the grey economy, do not exceed the income threshold anyway. The income threshold and means-testing procedure itself is also questioned, because the need to apply formal rules to granting benefits is often perceived as a threat to the autonomy of social workers and to their competence in identifying problems and assessing household living conditions. The doubts of social workers in this regard are, moreover, related to the processing and credibility of claimants' data:

> 'For me, those rigid income criteria are absurd, because it's me who is responsible for who gets help. And it should be flexible in such situations when the social worker can help [...] Well, there is always the possibility of writing "other causes" [...] You can always extend the description of the family situation to these other causes.' (Social worker)

The issue is important not only because it illustrates the mechanism that generates limitations on the accuracy of official data and professional dilemmas of social work. Classifying a beneficiary as unemployed implies that they failed to register at the employment office and to follow the activation regime, which does not have to improve the person's and family situation. This is why social workers treat reporting and related classifications rather arbitrarily. It is important also because of the kind of relationship involved, one that is based on trust and mutual accountability between social workers and beneficiaries: "It just depends on the customer. Because if they are fair to me [...] if they see that I am there in good faith and I want to help them and not harm them, they really cooperate" (Social worker).

Violation of trust may result, among other things, in an investigation of true incomes, pursuing legal action related to submitting a false income statement, a charge of fraud and the need to return illicitly collected benefits. However, accountability in this case is not formal; it introduces elements of discretion and thus, to some extent, violates the structure of entitlements, even if the balance of well-being is positive. The mechanism itself is typical of 'street-level bureaucracy' (Lipsky, 1980). It also leads to different treatment of beneficiaries, depending on whether they are accountable. Additionally, most of our respondents have repeatedly stressed that investigations are rarely conducted, and clients' statements about the lack of income written under criminal liability are in fact difficult to challenge. Building on trust and reliability seems to be a rational solution, because building an integration-oriented assistance relationship is, in principle, difficult to reconcile with the bureaucratic rules of labour market activation. Workfare contractual arrangements assume a departure from supportive and therapeutic relations with clients (Ruch, 2010), which are valued by Polish social workers and considered more effective, flexible and based on professional skills and positive discretion, not on purely managerial, procedure-oriented competences. This regularity confirms findings on work-related values in social work (Bieńko, 2012). The emphasis is clearly on values that are the reference for shaping relations in social work (responsibility, reliability, righteousness, dignity, and so on). Disregarding formal rules can be, in some cases, interpreted as an attempt to maintain coherence between shared values and acting in an increasingly bureaucratic environment. However, the emphasis on integration and disregarding some of the activation rules shows the reaction to tensions between market- and relation-oriented modes of social work.

Trust, social contract and the EU pillar of social work

Trust also plays a role in the case of the flagship solution for Polish active social policy – the 'social contract', a written agreement specifying family resources, measurable goals and ways to achieve them, compliance rules, sanctions and client and social worker responsibilities. The unified form of the contract was introduced in 2010, and since then we talk about the systemic character of this tool. However, the scope of contracting is still relatively small. In 2016, a total of 55,258 contracts were signed covering 69,235 persons – only 4.1% of all social assistance beneficiaries, despite intense promotion and pressure to use them.

As the author has pointed out elsewhere (Poławski, 2017), one of the reasons for the small number of contracts is the financing structure for activation programmes. Over the last decade, the European Social Fund has enabled the testing and implementation of activation instruments. With EU funding, social assistance centres have received instructions and extra resources to finance activation measures. This is important as social assistance budgets are shrinking systematically. The share of spending on social assistance in total commune budgets between 2004 and 2015 decreased by around 3%. The extra resources from EU projects have been used willingly, yet the mechanics and the 'project' type of the support have had consequences. Research findings imply that a common element of those projects was 'creaming', which involved targeting credible and 'easy to serve' clients who were more likely to reach the planned project goals. After completing the project, the logic of implementing the same activities in the 'project mode' and 'regular mode' seems different, as the former is more often oriented toward achieving activation objectives, while the latter focuses more on discipline and control of beneficiaries.

The problem faced by social workers trying to use 'regular' contracts in their work is the lack of capabilities and proper rewards. Even if a social contract addresses the active search for a job, the condition is often treated as empty, by both claimants and social workers, who are perfectly aware of the very limited chances of finding any employment if the unemployment rate is high and the labour market is limited. On the other hand, activation by finding a precarious job does not seem to be a reasonable choice. Deficiencies in local institutional resources (psychological counselling, therapies, vocational training) and lack of funds necessary to contract services are especially severe in smaller towns, which frequently lack funds to meet all diagnosed needs. The difficulties in planning also result from the financing mechanisms – delays in budget subsidy delivery usually imply lack of funds or accumulation during certain periods of the year. Consequently, 'regular' contracts work as disciplinary measures – they are used as a penalty for disobedient clients or to gather evidence to be used against the troublemakers.

The 'project' logic implies a clear timeline, measurable objectives, defined outcome measurement indicators, systematic reporting and its own (usually appropriately high) budget. A reasonable strategy to increase the likelihood of achieving the planned objectives means limiting the dropout rate. The following statement is typical in this matter:

> 'We do not wish to work with someone who will not carry out the contract. Because if it is not settled, you need to get the money back. This is a serious matter. I always have two or three back-up people.' (Social worker)

Having 'back-up' is a specific strategy used for dealing with the risk of failure to achieve the indicators assumed in projects. It has little to do with activation efforts, since the selection of participants is almost always based on previous experiences with a family, or knowledge and trust of persons with a 'good history' in social assistance. Paradoxically, it also builds on dependency and the softened version of clientelism, which turns out to be a safeguard against rigid criteria for financial settlements. This strategy was usually effective in the sense, as our respondents reported, that not only were the formal goals of the programmes achieved, but the labour market situation, competences and skills of beneficiaries were also improved. In this case, the signing of a contract is treated primarily as a formal condition of joining a project and obtaining a relatively attractive (in financial terms as well) form of support and activation:

> 'For them [...] they do not know what a contract is. For them it is a document that they signed somewhere there, and for them [...] there is no obligation that an agreement has been made [...]. This is a paper that needs to be signed, as they see it, and as we see it either, [...] because they will be in the project then.' (Social worker)

The problem is that the strategy, however effective it seems regarding the safe achievement of project goals, is to some extent an illustration of the Matthew effect in social assistance. 'Project' type of contracts are in a sense a reward for those who not only meet the terms and conditions but are also sufficiently trustworthy and responsive to the imposed cooperation rules. In this way, at least a part of the activation bypasses 'difficult' clients, those with more severe social deficits. However, if we can speak about risk management, in this case at least an attempt has been made to follow 'defensible decision' standards (Kemshall & Wilkinson, 2011: 15). Based on the professional judgement of social workers, these standards uphold that the decisions are informed and grounded in available evidence, they are appropriately communicated, the plan delivered with integrity, appropriate steps are taken, and so forth. Despite this, the choice of programme participants and type of support are still determined by organisational factors rather than diagnosed needs. To put it differently, in certain circumstances (pressure to achieve goals, imposition of rigid procedures, time pressure and satisfactory financial resources), social workers rationally choose to 'manage poverty' rather than offer help.

Conclusion

Prevailing explanations of social work and social assistance deficiencies in post-communist countries point to the unfinished professionalisation and modernisation processes. These are understood as a persistent attachment to paternalism, emphasis on protective measures, limited rationalisation and lack of adaptation of appropriate action patterns related to activation. For example, Kaźmierczak (2012) writes about path dependency dating back to the nineteenth century. He claims that inherited institutional patterns, including common interpretations of social problems as well as definitions of professional roles and identities, mean that social workers are still oriented more towards serving as agents between families, value themselves as available institutional resources rather than valuing the principle of cooperation, and work towards the sorting and classification of claimants than the efficiency of their support. They are also supposed to focus more on basic needs, consequently favouring financial support, emphasising common knowledge and personal experience, while rejecting more consistent models of social work. Other studies mention tendencies towards mechanical use of rules and procedures imposed by default in a top-down fashion (Granosik, 2012; Racław, 2012). The latter would actually be a good omen for current trends toward standardisation in social work and social assistance in general.

The above text, in part, confirms these conclusions. Social assistance proves to be moderately effective. Bureaucratic tendencies and orientation toward 'poverty management' are strengthened by 'pillarisation' of organisational structures and financial mechanisms, the 'project-like' nature of innovations and reforms. Moreover, the reforms generate various dysfunctions such as the deepening of differentiation and segmentation of predominating entitlements. These dysfunctions themselves generate additional areas of uncertainty for both beneficiaries and social workers. Beck (2009) clearly distinguished two types of threats: risk and manufactured uncertainties, which turn out to derive from various decisions as a 'product' of policies and not necessarily an effect of external processes and powers. It is quite likely that risk-oriented, pillarised management may generate such uncertainties in social work.

Reactions to reforms and to changes in the social work model are, however, mediated by values and locally rooted practice, as well as by important elements of context, such as the depth of the local labour market. Rationality here is clearly 'situated'. Social workers are prioritising various risks, efficiently navigating through the local contexts and interpreting requirements, negotiating the meaning and importance of formal rules with beneficiaries, modifying procedures imposed by the new public management regime, and adjusting the scope of institutional and personal responsibilities. An important element of these modifications, typical of the street-level bureaucracy (Lipsky, 1980), is rather loose treatment of reporting and formal categorisations, for which available datasets only partially reflect the realities. In other words, the embedded reactions of social workers make the informational basis for risk management less accurate than we would expect. Imposed procedures (as in the case of a social contract) are subject to various modifications and, in some cases, seem to overlap with more traditional and secure 'trust and reciprocity management' for all parties involved.

Note

[1] Work supported by National Science Centre (grant UMO-2014/13/B/HS5/03615).

References

Beck, U. (2009) 'World risk society and manufactured uncertainties', *Iris* 1(2): 291–99.

Bieńko, M. (2012) 'Dylematy profesji i roli w refleksyjnym projekcie tożsamości współczesnego pracownika socjalnego' ['Dilemmas of profession and roles in the reflective identity project of a modern social worker'], in M. Rymsza (ed) *Pracownicy socjalni i praca socjalna w Polsce. Między służbą społeczną a urzędem*, Warszawa: Instytut Spraw Publicznych, pp 93–120.

Employment and Social Developments in Europe. Annual Review (2016) Luxembourg: Publications Office of the European Union.

Granosik, M. (2012) '"Mówię, jak jest, robię, co mi każą" – o interpretacyjnym rozdarciu współczesnego pracownika socjalnego' ['"I say how it is, I do what they tell" – the interpretive problems of a modern social worker'], in M. Rymsza (ed) *Pracownicy socjalni i praca socjalna w Polsce. Między służbą społeczną a urzędem*, Warszawa: Instytut Spraw Publicznych, pp 187–202.

Halvorsen, R. and Hvinden, B. (eds) (2016) *Combating Poverty in Europe: Active Inclusion in a Multi-level and Multi-actor Context*, Cheltenham: Edward Elgar.

Harris, J. (2003) *The Social Work Business*, London: Routledge.

Jewell, C. J. (2007) *Agents of the Welfare State. How Caseworkers Respond to Need in the United States, Germany, and Sweden*, New York: Palgrave Macmillan.

Kaźmierczak, T. (2012) 'W cieniu prawa o ubogich: o źródłach i rozwoju (praktykowanej w OPS) pracy socjalnej' ['In the Poor Law shadow: about sources and development of (practiced in OPS) social work'], in T. Kaźmierczak and M. Rymsza (eds) *W stronę aktywnych służb społecznych*, Warszawa: Instytut Spraw Publicznych, pp 109–32.

Kaźmierczak, T. (2016) 'O kontrakcie socjalnym i reformie aktywnej integracji, czyli jak pomoc społeczna (znów) obroniła się przed zmianą' ['The social contract and active integration, or how social assistance (again) defended itself against changes'], *Problemy Polityki Społecznej. Studia i Dyskusje*, 35(4): 75–92.

Kemshall, H. and Wilkinson, B. (2011) *Good Practice in Assessing Risk: Current Knowledge, Issues and Approaches*, London: Jessica Kingsley Publishers.

Lipsky, M. (1980) *Street-level Bureaucracy. Dilemmas of the Individual in Public Services*, New York: Russell Sage Foundation.

Liwiński, J., Sztanderska, U. and Giza-Poleszczuk, A. (2008) *Rynki pracy na obszarach popegeerowskich. Raport z badań* ['Labour markets in former state farms. Research report'], Warszawa: Ministerstwo Pracy i Polityki Społecznej.

Nolan, B., Maître, B. and Whelan, C. T. (2011) 'Low pay, in-work poverty and economic vulnerability. A comparative analysis using EU-SILC', *Dublin Discussion Paper Series*, WP 10 28.

Palier, B. (2010) 'The long Conservative corporatist road to welfare reforms', in B. Palier (ed) *A Long Goodbye to Bismarck? The Politics of Welfare Reform in Continental Europe*, Amsterdam: Amsterdam University Press, pp 333–88.

Pierson, P. (2001) 'Investigating the welfare state at century's end', in P. Pierson (ed) *The New Politics of the Welfare State*, Oxford: Oxford University Press, pp 1–14.

Poławski, P. (2017) 'Warunkowość, sankcje socjalne i aktywizacja w pomocy społecznej' ['Conditionality, sanctions and activation in social assistance'], in P. Poławski and D. Zalewski (eds) *Problemy społeczne. Między socjologia demaskatorską a polityką społeczną*, Warszawa: Oficyna Naukowa, pp 329–53.

Racław, M. (2012) 'Zmiany w pracy socjalnej z rodziną – w stronę kontroli stylu życia i zarządzania marginalizacją' ['Changes in social work with family – towards lifestyle control and marginality management'], in Rymsza, M. (ed) *Pracownicy socjalni i praca socjalna w Polsce. Między służbą społeczną a urzędem*, Warszawa: Instytut Spraw Publicznych, pp 227–44.

Ruch, G. (2010) 'The contemporary context of relationship-based practice', in G. Ruch, D. Turney and A. Ward (eds) *Relationship-based Social Work: Getting to the Heart of Practice*, Philadelphia: Jessica Kingsley Publishers, pp 13–28.

Rymsza, M. (ed) (2012) *Pracownicy socjalni i praca socjalna w Polsce. Między służbą społeczną a urzędem* ['Social workers and social work in Poland. Between the social service and the office'], Warszawa: Instytut Spraw Publicznych.

Streeck, W. and Thelen, K. (2005) 'Introduction: institutional change in advanced political economies', in W. Streeck and K. Thelen (eds) *Beyond Continuity. Institutional Change in Advanced Political Economies*, Oxford: Oxford University Press, pp 1–39.

Taylor-Gooby, P. (2009) *Reframing Social Citizenship*, Oxford: Oxford University Press.

Van Berkel, R. (2013) 'Triple activation: introducing welfare-to-work into Dutch social assistance', in E. Z. Brodkin and G. Marston (eds) *Work and the Welfare State: Street-level Organizations and Workfare Politics*, Washington, DC: Georgetown University Press, pp 87–102.

Venn, D. (2012) 'Eligibility criteria for unemployment benefits. Quantitative indicators for OECD and EU countries', *OECD Social, Employment and Migration Working Papers*, No. 131.

13

'A little more humanity': placement officers in Germany between social work and social policy

Markus Gottwald and Frank Sowa

Introduction

With the so-called Hartz reforms[1] introduced in 2003, German social and labour market policy was geared towards the welfare-to-work principle. The merging of unemployment assistance and social welfare benefits into 'unemployment benefit II' (*Arbeitslosengeld II*) and the shortening of the periods of entitlement to 'unemployment benefit I' (*Arbeitslosengeld I*) resulted in people who had lost their jobs being in danger of sliding more rapidly into the sphere of means-tested basic social security.[2] Unemployed persons claiming 'unemployment benefit II' become de-facto social work clients.[3] Not least in order to prevent this, the public employment service (PES) was restructured in organisational terms with the aim of creating a more efficient and effective method of finding work for unemployed persons who were drawing 'unemployment benefit I' pursuant to insurance law. This was supported by three measures taken from New Public Management: increasing the number of placement staff; improving the quality of the employment service by separating the functions of employer and employee consulting and by creating more time for consultation including more frequent interviews; and ultimately developing a comprehensive target and management system. The idea behind management by objectives was to bring about decentralisation which would afford the placement officers and senior management at the local agencies more freedom when making necessary task-specific decisions. Moreover, by means of target indicators, the placement performance of the agencies and their placement teams could also be measured and compared, and then optimised with the aid of analysis indicators that map the operative processes. In addition, a few years before the Hartz reforms, the German Federal Employment Agency

(*Bundesagentur für Arbeit*; BA) had already begun to refer to unemployed people as 'customers'. These semantics indicate that the concerns of the unemployed are of core importance.

The question addressed in this chapter may initially seem to be unimportant: what about the 'social work' performed by the placement officers in the context of the reformed PES? In the second section of the chapter, we take classical research studies as a basis to illustrate that this question is anything but irrelevant. Although clearly defined institutional boundaries between PES and social work exist, some aspects of job placement work do require that the placement officers at least adopt a 'social worker's perspective', which is what they express when they describe their work as social work. However, what exactly does social work mean with regard to PES and how does it relate to the organisational reforms mentioned? The reforms could give rise to the expectation that, like social workers, the placement officers now have greater discretionary authority for a case-specific approach and are in a better position to prevent unemployed people from having to draw unemployment benefit II. If this is not the case, however, then why? What does the use of the term 'social work' indicate with regard to the implementation of social policy in PES. We address these questions in the third section of the chapter, based on our own empirical research. One of the conclusions is as follows: in the context of PES, 'social work' can be understood as polyvalent semantics whose essential function, however, is to indicate the dysfunctional effects of a *means of implementing social policy*.

The 'social worker's perspective' in the context of the job placement

By definition, placement officers do not perform social work in the employment agencies. Their task consists of implementing and enforcing the legal guidelines with regard to unemployment insurance. Their clients are not 'people in need of help' de jure, but are insurance holders who have a claim to insurance benefits in the event of unemployment based on contributions paid. Unemployment can result in a need for help, and unemployment insurance benefits are aimed precisely at averting this by means of compensatory wage replacement payments on the one hand and advisory and job placement services on the other. In contrast, social workers assume the '*responsibility for such cases and aspects of the need for help ... that are not seen as being sufficiently supported by the instruments of the generalised containment mechanisms of the security systems*' or which '*are not recorded*' (Bommes & Scherr,

2012: 182; italics in the original). They focus primarily on the causes and negative consequences of unemployment. In order to identify, process or attenuate these, they must regard their clients as 'complete individuals' in the context of their respective lives. Furthermore, the focus is not on placement but on maintaining their clients' capacity to work and restoring their employability. Social workers deal with the organisation of life *in unemployment* (for example, clarifying legal claims). They try to stabilise the clients and help them to develop new perspectives. They may already help simply be being available for day-to-day communication and acting as an attachment figure. Therefore, social workers cannot avoid developing a closer social relationship with their clients – a circumstance that is beyond the placement officers' task, which is first and foremost to help their 'customers' to find work.

Placement officers and social workers are therefore subject to completely different institutional framework conditions and imperatives, which is manifested most clearly in the respective administrative, bureaucratic integration. Although social workers perform their work within organisations that follow instructions based in social law and make certain demands of their staff, these organisations must grant their staff the greatest possible autonomy so that they can provide effective help, as this is the only way that allows a case-specific approach that accommodates the clients' personal needs. The social worker/client relationship is characterised by openness, intense negotiation, unpredictability and sometimes strong dynamics. The formulation of work goals thus tends to come 'from below' rather than as centrally determined specifications which are passed down the hierarchy. 'Welfare bureaucracies' like the BA treat their clients in a manner that 'is bound by rules, file-focused and highly standardised' (Bode, 2012: 156). In their work, the placement officers are bound by a multitude of programme specifications and procedural regulations; they are part of the executive authority, which allows them to decide whether applications are to be approved or refused, to check whether the legal obligation to cooperate has been met and, where applicable, to impose sanctions if this is not the case. The structure of their relationship with the clients is more formally defined and asymmetrical.

Against this background, there is basically nothing to indicate a connection between job placement work and social work. Nevertheless, the consultation and placement work conducted at the agencies still involves certain elements of social work. As early as the 1980s, a study by Eberwein and Tholen (1987: 107–24) presented a typology of placement officers which includes 'social worker' as a type, in addition to 'broker', 'bureaucrat' and 'advisor'. According to the authors, what was characteristic of this type of placement officers was that they appeared to be particularly open to the problems of the unemployed: they listened and responded to their clients' worries and hardships, encouraged and motivated them, investigated employment opportunities and provided help by calling in specialised third parties. In a way, the 'social worker' contrasted sharply with the 'bureaucrat' and 'broker' types. While the 'bureaucrat' dealt with clients in a more reserved manner and was intent on complying with the specified rules of procedure, the 'broker' aspired to the success of speedy placements where the unemployed person's vocational qualifications and needs were regarded as less important; the 'broker's' professional pride was largely fed by the service provided for employers. Eberwein and Tholen far from idealise the 'social worker' type, however. In fact, they draw attention to the structural working conditions that are conducive to its occurrence. In this regard, they discover that the placement officers did not actively aspire to take on the social worker role; it was a role forced upon them by their clients. It is simply a fact of life that unemployed individuals, who frequently experience their situation as an existential crisis, expect the placement officers to be empathetic listeners who provide comfort and help with their lives. The majority of the placement officers interviewed by Eberwein and Tholen perceived this role as too much of a strain, reporting that they had neither the time resources nor the professional skills to fulfil this role adequately. Moreover, they were well aware that this type of (psychological) support was not part of their remit. Furthermore, it is also observed that placement officers of the 'social worker' type were frequently those whose clientele predominantly consisted of hard-to-place individuals. Here, providing support compensated for the lack of success with regard to placement; in other words, the 'social work' label gave meaning to the placement officer's actions.

However, a study by Cramer (1979) revealed that placement officers who seriously regarded their task as social work ran the risk of rapidly losing faith in the benefit of what they were doing, as a marked social work ethos conflicts with the administrative requirements. Cramer cites the case of a woman with a degree in education who worked as an intern in the PES labour administration. This woman constantly became involved in arguments with her superiors by giving the clients tips 'to help them get by'; she cried a great deal and exhibited psychosomatic symptoms because she was of the opinion that people were being treated 'like animals' (Cramer, 1979: 139). At the same time, Cramer sees this case as an example showing that the placement officers' professional background is not insignificant with regard to dealing with clients – a fact that also emerges from a study by Ludwig-Mayerhofer, Behrend and Sondermann (2009), who examined the implementation of labour market policy soon after the Hartz reforms. What is even more interesting, however, is that the 'social worker's perspective' appears in this study in the guise of 'overbearing' social pedagogy. The majority of the placement officers interviewed were found to have internalised the activation paradigm. Meanwhile, the idea that the receipt of unemployment benefits presupposed that the clients would have the will to look for work on their own initiative and that starting gainful employment of whatever kind was preferable to not working at all formed the naturally accepted core reference for the placement officers' activities. Thus, the well-meaning intention to help the clients merges with the slogan associated with the Hartz reforms: 'If it creates jobs, it's social'. This accordingly makes educating and pedagogising the dominant action strategies, particularly with regard to clients considered 'unwilling'. The unemployed must be brought to reason so that they want what the placement officers want in the name of the law – if necessary by employing sanctions. However, this does not mean that the placement officers did not commiserate with their clients' fates. The opposite is often the case: the 'activators' portrayed by Ludwig-Mayerhofer and colleagues (2009: 113–48) sometimes even stood out due to their particularly empathetic and understanding approach: they listened, comforted, raised hopes, perceived their clients as complete individuals and tried to put themselves in their clients' position. They exhibited all the characteristics of the 'social worker' type defined by Eberwein and Tholen (1987). Nevertheless, it is essential that the clients are encouraged to cooperate in precisely this way, using gentle force, which consequently implies that they forget their own needs and requirements, possibly taking economic and social decline into account by accepting jobs that are not suited to their training or professional status. Hence, in their study, Ludwig-Mayerhofer and colleagues (2009) expose a placement practice which is to be judged as problematic.

Placement officers are faced by conflicting priorities: legal and political specifications, administrative demands, client expectations and professional requirements. The Ludwig-Meyerhofer study discerns an intensification of these contradictions. However, that is not only associated with the readjustment of labour market policy targets (welfare-to-work; activation) but also with the changes in *administration management and organisation*. As we mentioned at the beginning of the chapter, the organisational reforms at the BA were aimed at creating opportunities for more intensive, high quality placement services. Due to the functional separation between the services for employers and those for jobseekers, some of the staff deal solely with the needs of the unemployed. Thus, it may be inevitable that placement officers get to know their clients as complete individuals, perhaps developing closer relationships with them and acting in a more personalised manner. At the same time, the formal aspect of placement work is very structured. This specifically manifests itself in management by objectives. Even if the principle of this is purely to bring about decentralisation, the placement officers are confronted by numerous formal, bureaucratic requirements: in line with specified criteria, so-called customer profiles have to be created which stand for defined customer segments which, in turn, are associated with standardised strategies for dealing with the unemployed. Furthermore, the placement team's performance is measured and compared on the basis of target and process indicators. It is well known from the literature (for example Sowa & Staples, 2016) that this results in an area of conflict for the placement officers – what the 'world of figures' frequently demands does not correspond with the concrete problems and needs of the unemployed. This brings us to the starting point for the empirical analysis presented in the following: we ask how the placement officers relate to the social work aspect of their activity today in view of the conditions concerning the organisational context described. Does social work still function as semantics that lend meaning, as described by Eberwein and Tholen (1987), or is something else or more meant by it? What do we learn about the placement officers' work situation when they speak of social work, and what does this imply for the implementation of social policy?

Empirical findings

To answer the questions raised, we draw upon qualitative data that was collected from 2007 to 2012 in the project 'Practice of the Placement Process: Qualitative evaluation of the pilot project. Increased Capacity of Job Placement Officers in Selected Regional Types' (Sowa & Staples, 2016) and from 2014 to 2018 in the project 'Placement Officers' Action in the Refined Target System of the German Federal Employment Agency: An Organisational Ethnography' (Gottwald et al, 2018). Narrative interviews were conducted in both projects. In our secondary data analysis, we noticed that interviewees repeatedly referred to themselves as social workers. For this chapter, we analysed examples of passages from the interview corpus using hermeneutic sequence analysis (Overmann et al, 1979).

We start our analysis with a quote which reveals that jobseeker-oriented placement officers today actually have difficulty continuing to see themselves as *job placement officers* in the true sense:

> 'I always say, the classical placement officer, we call ourselves placement officers, we're, well, I don't regard myself as just a placement officer. Well, I'm a coach, I'm a motivation trainer, sometimes I'm a social worker, I'm a listener, now and then I'm even a fashion advisor as well [...] So then I'm more likely to focus on having an elaborate profile, giving the customer a personal ID if he's got an Internet connection. And he can do a search based on his profile. Or the employer service has a really good profile on hand and can work with that.' (trans Z_05-05: 563-575)

The unemployed are supposed to find a job either themselves or with the help of the employer service (Arbeitgeber-Service – AGS). Although jobseeker-oriented placement officers carry out job searches based on the database, this task is regarded as secondary to others. It is primarily a question of preparing the unemployed for a successful placement. In this sense, the placement officers are many things, including 'coach', 'motivation trainer', 'fashion advisor' or 'social worker'. In the end, the important thing is that the 'customer profile' to be created in the database system and the classification in the 'customer segment' match so that AGS placement officers can successfully perform computer-based matching. Jobseeker-oriented placement officers frequently regard themselves as doing no more than the legwork for the AGS, which is expressed in complaints about the work becoming devoid of content and about the loss of status. The placement service for unemployed persons is abstract; it is generally only discernible as a deregistration from the customer base. We therefore see, as described by Eberwein and Tholen, that the established wording 'social work' still functions as *compensatory semantics that lend meaning* and is unlikely to have become less important in view of the organisational reforms. The following quote by another placement officer also draws attention to this, extending the range of meanings of placement-style 'social work' even further, however:

> 'We were told quite clearly [...], we're not social workers – we're not actually supposed to go into the customers' personal concerns. And I think – that can't be right. First of all, I have to build a relationship based on trust so that

the customer will tell me anything at all, perhaps even sometimes telling me things that are important for my work. If I don't find out for weeks that he's in debt or that he hasn't got anyone to look after his child after all [...] I have to control that, of course, and say, that's enough now [...] the important thing now is for us to get to the point.' (trans_Z_06_03: 437-458)

It is not possible to reconstruct the interpretation of 'social work' which was passed on to the placement officer. However, when the message is not to address the customers' personal concerns, it may simply be that the classical sense of ethics or duty, *sine ira et studio*, was insisted upon. In this respect, 'social work' would stand for client treatment that was saturated with personal sensitivities, lacked the necessary objective distance and therefore represented a *foreign element from the standpoint of the authorities*. The decisive factor is how the placement officer interprets the instruction. The officer sees it as an inappropriate adjustment to the counselling interviews to be conducted, which fails to recognise the purpose of these sessions: to obtain information from the unemployed person in order to categorise them and at the same time to decide how the case will subsequently be processed. The 'social work' called into play therefore contains a manifest and latent significance: manifestly, 'social work' stands for a *conversation technique* which uses the fact that the unemployed are allowed to talk about their lives to elicit information which goes beyond what is covered merely by the records. 'Social work' constitutes the minimum amount of skill required to understand the case that the placement officer is to address. At a latent level, the insistence on 'social work' is interesting. It reveals the placement officer rejecting what they perceive as *being dictated to*: first, that they do not want to be robbed of their understanding of placement work as 'social work', and second, that they nevertheless know what it is about: to 'get to the point' with the client.

'Getting to the point' not only means that by the end of the first interview the placement officer should have determined the 'customer group' to which the unemployed individual is to be assigned in the database system behind the scenes, but also that during the actual conversation the placement officer should have discussed with the individual how the placement process works, in other words informing the individual about their rights and obligations, which are generally set down in a 'integration agreement'. It is important to see that the customer categorisation, including any specifications concerning placement strategy, also has consequences for the assessment of the placement officer's performance in the context of target management and performance monitoring. This is because cost forecasts are based on statements regarding the estimated duration of unemployment, the likelihood of integration and measures implemented, which are ultimately entered as dates in the monthly team-accumulated evaluations regarding the planned target achievements. If purchased measures are not utilised, expected durations of unemployment are exceeded and prescribed integration quotas not met, there must be reasons for it, especially if better values would have been expected of the segmented client base. This may mean that the placement officers have to justify what has not been achieved to their team management:

> 'And if you then say, "Now let's be straight! Why have you been here for three months now?! What's going on?' And that's when they first start to talk about the fact that he's just got divorced, that he doesn't know what to do with his children and all kinds of things, you know. So it's always like that. In this job you're also/partly a social worker, you know? The other day, for example: some customer or other – she was emotionally at rock bottom [...] she'd been working for her employer for 29 years and the boss had just sacked her. – Now you're 59, and all at once your world explodes, you know? The word "work" was enough to make her burst into tears.' (AA3_AV1: 1293-1344)

Here, the placement officer first broaches the issue of the main requirement in the counselling interview, which was already mentioned in the previous quote: obtaining information that permits a realistic categorisation, integration strategy and integration prognosis. The problem he points out is that the knowledge required is often not mentioned in the first conversation, but only emerges in subsequent sessions after detailed enquiry: 'Now let's be straight!' The time to be straight comes at the latest when the manager takes the controlling data as a basis for a reminder about achieving targets. This is precisely the moment when the placement officers find themselves caught in a situation in which they have to justify themselves. One possible justification at that moment is to say that they did not yet have the necessary facts when they categorised the customer. Let us think back to the previous quote: there, 'social work' was used to describe the eliciting of such facts. Likewise, the term 'social work' also appears in the quote above, although it has more nuances and is framed differently: the nuancing is such that the placement officers are obviously not automatically allowed to question the unemployed person about their life in the first interview (inappropriate intrusiveness) and/or it may not be technically possible for them to do so (there is only enough time for them to record the basic data). Accordingly, placement officers only become 'social workers' in the sense mentioned above if the figures do not meet the targets. However, it is the framing that is of greater interest. In the quote, a situation requiring justification is re-enacted performatively and the fascinating aspect of it is that this re-enactment ends in a highly dramatic account which shows the placement officer in a social worker's role par excellence. '*Social work*' appears as the *semantics* of *justification* here: the imperatives of the world of figures are countered with the day-to-day 'madness' of the world of placement.

In the following quote, the imperatives of the world of figures are characterised even more precisely. Here, a further function of social work is illustrated. In the interview, a team manager answers a question about the changes he would like to see with respect to the prevailing working conditions:

> 'A little more humanity […] That it's really not just target achievement that you see, but that you can pay it a bit more attention […] that you have the time now and then to pay more attention to this or that case that's gone a bit off track as well […] and we come from a generation, of course, where we've sometimes been social workers as well as placement officers or whatever. That's necessary sometimes too. And there are enough cases where you just say, damn it. That won't be any help to him now if his benefits are cut for a while.' (tans_05_12: 1617-1644)

The desire for 'more humanity' stands for a treatment of clients that is not bound by standardised customer formats and the action programmes behind them; in the best sense, it signifies an individual approach to each case. This individual approach is described as a luxury; it draws attention to the virtually all-encompassing claim of target management and a Tayloristic production logic which is implicitly ascribed to it, which identifies the individual approach to a case as something akin to a 'muse' and which must be justified. At first glance, social work in this context refers to placement officers' altered understanding of their role: they say that as placement officers they have been 'social workers' at times. This is a role that is actually inappropriate under the present conditions but would still be justified in view of clients' requirements for action. Here, social work not only legitimises a placement practice which is uncoupled from the standard specifications of the management regime but also the existence of a professional ethos which sustains this practice. A closer look reveals something else as well. In fact, the team manager struggles with the term 'social worker', implicitly questioning whether that has ever been the case. This shows that 'social work' actually only functions as a *placeholder*: it is used to broach the issue of discretionary authority, which is of functional necessity in the placement officers' day-to-day operations. The placement officers believe that they once possessed this discretion but, confronted with the imperatives of target management, they clearly regard it today as being increasingly obstructed by bureaucracy. We now present an example of how this bureaucratic restriction is reflected in the interaction between the placement officers and their clients. These examples do not illustrate any further levels of meaning with regard to social work in the context of job placement, but reveal certain competencies that are obviously required of placement officers more than ever today and which confirm the functions of 'social work' which were last elaborated.

The example shows a placement officer who had worked in a typical caring profession before being employed at the BA; a background which can be perceived in the way she understands placement. Thus, for the placement officer it is a matter of providing 'holistic' support for her 'customers'; she would like to 'take them by the hand', look behind 'the curtain' and work out a solution with them that fits perfectly. Therefore she tried to keep her 'customer base' as small as possible. Furthermore she specified the following:

> 'If you're clever and know your customer base a little, you can also swap one for the other a bit occasionally [...] So you simply have to somehow identify customers creatively.' (AA1-AV2: 1422-1433)

This statement refers to two demands made of the placement officer as a result of target management: on the one hand, purchased employment and training measures have to be utilised. The placement officer is therefore often confronted with the problem of having to send clients to measures despite having doubts as to their suitability. On the other hand, she and her team are expected to achieve the highest possible integration rate. The higher the number of outflows from the customer base, the higher this rate is. The knowledge about her customer base now helps her to 'identify customers creatively', whereby she attempts to meet both target requirements. Creatively identified customers are those she selects to take part in a purchased measure in order to save other unemployed persons from having to participate. In such cases, selected customers may perceive their allocation to the measure to be patronising and choose to leave the jobseeker register. This has a positive impact on the integration rate. We thus see here that when confronted with the requirements of target management logic, a customer selection is needed which must be referred to as problematic. The selection of the creatively identified customers is justified by the fact that they do not want to accept help in a way that corresponds to the placement officers' perception of an ideal placement. However, the case holds a further matter of contention: in the interview, the placement officer scrutinises her selection practice self-reflectively. This means that she scans her rationalisations and, in this sense, the foundations for her actions, and, with regard to the requirements of the management regime, finally realises: "*Well, it affects you*" (AA1-AV2: 1914). This case is reminiscent of that described by Cramer (1979); the search for meaning is apparent – not simply because an excessive social work ethos conflicts with the harshness of bureaucratic structures, however, but because it becomes clear to the placement officer that the conflict cannot be resolved and that she has adjusted to the demands of the system. Admittedly, this example cannot simply be generalised, but it nonetheless stands for a structural constellation in which the problem of cognitive dissonance observed in many fields of social work arises more intensely. Therefore, it would be entirely legitimate to ask whether the placement officers might be in demand precisely in the implicitly practical development of coping strategies.

Conclusion

With our analysis, we addressed the question of how placement officers relate to the social work aspect of their work in view of the radical organisational reforms, and what can be learned from it with regard to their work situation and the implementation of the objectives of social policy. An important point of connection here was the observation made by Eberwein and Tholen (1987) that the placement officers were often unable to be what they should be, namely job finders, which is why in social work they find compensatory semantics which lend meaning to their work. Our analysis showed that this still applies. While the effects of social work entailed in job placement services are to be assessed as rather ambivalent – it does not exclude 'harsh' activation – it appears as semantics in an organisational, functional manner, as this is capable of cushioning the dissatisfaction felt by placement staff as a result of the market situation or reforms. However, we also saw that the spectrum of meanings with regard to the semantics of social work is richer. What was noticeable was that this richness primarily arises from references to the target management regime prevailing in the PES. Again one could speak of a kind of functionalisation of the semantics of social work by the placement officers, as on the one hand it is used to justify the placement officers' performance and on the other to defend discretionary authority. If it was a question of the latter, it seemed to us that 'social work' served as a placeholder. It is actually used to designate discretion that is of functional necessity for administrative action (see Blau, 1973) and which is bureaucratically blocked by an indicator system of Tayloristic design whose implementation is also relatively rigid. Thus, the organisational functionality of the social work semantic evidently lies in calling attention to organisational dysfunctionalities. If one also takes into account the competencies enumerated at the end of our analysis which are required of the placement officers in this connection (handling cognitive dissonance), the insistence on 'social work' could even point to a harmless form of protest with which the placement officers oppose the unreasonable demands that are made of them and that they have to endure in their interactions with the clients. In the analysis it must therefore also be taken into consideration that for the placement officers the interview with researchers can serve as a mouthpiece to communicate with the organisational elite and/or the political public sphere (see Gottwald et al, 2018). It is precisely in this sense that the placement officers also appear as actors in socio-political *agenda setting*, in so far as they identify flaws in *instruments of policy implementation*. Responsible administrative action is not only measured by formal rules of accountability, the hierarchy or financial control but also by professional ethics. It seems that these come into play when placement officers describe themselves as 'social workers'; in other words, it has obviously been noticed that the Hartz laws, which follow the welfare-to-work principle and are to be implemented to that end, are made unnecessarily more stringent by organisational structures and that the necessary pragmatism for attenuating legal, bureaucratic rigidities is ailing. Placement officers are not social workers, but they are quite aware that their cases could rapidly become cases for genuine social workers. Even the most confirmed activator knows that it is not their task to do the groundwork for such a development. Based loosely on Selznick (1984: 7): 'the crucial question for' social policy 'is not what to strive for, but by what means to strive'. Perhaps that is the real message delivered by placement officers when they utter the word 'social work' today.

Notes

[1] The reforms were named after the former automotive manager (Volkswagen, VW) Peter Hartz, who headed the reform commission (Hartz Commission).

[2] Until the implementation of the Hartz reforms, unemployed people continued to be protected from becoming welfare recipients even after their entitlement to unemployment benefit had expired as they were then entitled to unemployment assistance, an insurance benefit of indefinite duration that was higher than the social welfare benefit rate.

[3] By law recipients of 'unemployment benefit II' were still listed as 'employable persons in need of assistance' until 2011. Furthermore, the support approach envisages *individual and holistic case management* including classical social work measures.

References

Blau, P. M. (1973) *The Dynamics of Bureaucracy. A Study of Interpersonal Relationships in Two Government Agencies*, Chicago: University of Chicago Press.

Bode, I. (2012) 'Organisationen der Hilfe', in M. Apelt and V. Tacke (eds) *Handbuch Organisationstypen*, Wiesbaden: Springer VS, pp 149–64.

Bommes, M. and Scherr, A. (2012) *Soziologie der Sozialen Arbeit. Eine Einführung in Formen und Funktionen organisierter Hilfe, 2* (revised edn), Weinheim: Beltz Juventa.

Cramer, M. (1979) 'Verwaltete Arbeitslosigkeit – Zu den Bewältigungsstrategien von Arbeitsvermittlern', in S. Wolf, T. Lau, S. Kundera, M. Cramer and W. Bonß (eds) *Arbeitssituation in der öffentlichen Verwaltung*, Frankfurt: Campus, pp 115–59.

Eberwein, W. and Tholen, J. (1987) *Die öffentliche Arbeitsvermittlung als politisch-sozialer Prozeß*, Frankfurt: Campus Verlag.

Gottwald, M., Sowa, F. and Staples, R. (2018) '"Walking the line". An at-home ethnography of bureaucracy', *Journal of Organisational Ethnography*, 7(1): 87–102.

Ludwig-Mayerhofer, W., Behrend, O. and Sondermann, A. (2009) *Auf der Suche nach der verlorenen Arbeit. Arbeitslose und Arbeitsvermittler im neuen Arbeitsmarktregime*, Konstanz: UVK Verlag.

Overmann, U., Allert, T., Konau, E. and Krambeck, J. (1979) 'Die Methodologie der objektiven Hermeneutik und ihre allgemeine forschungslogische Bedeutung in den Sozialwissenschaften', in H. G. Soeffner (eds) *Interpretative Verfahren in den Sozial- und Textwissenschaften*, Stuttgart: Metzler, pp 352–434.

Selznick, P (1984 [1949]) *TVA and the Grass Roots. A Study of Politics and Organization*, Berkeley: University of California Press.

Sowa, F. and Staples, R. (2016) 'Public administration in the era of late neo-liberalism: placement professionals and the NPM regime', in A. Ferreira, G. Azevedo, J. Oliveira and R. Marques (eds) *Global Perspectives on Risk Management and Accounting in the Public Sector*, Hershey: IGI Global, pp 25–48.

14

Conclusion: social work and the making of social policy – lessons learned

Ute Klammer, Simone Leiber and Sigrid Leitner

The aim of this book has been to link comparative welfare state and social work research from an atypical, 'reversed' perspective, by using a bottom-up instead of a top-down approach: because social work constitutes an integral part of the welfare state, and social policy has such important structural effects on the lives of social work clients, social work – at different political and actor levels – is considered a 'political actor' with an ethical duty as well as the potential to actively engage in the making of social policy. This is also the message of the global definition of social work: 'social work engages people and structures to address life challenges and enhance wellbeing'.[1] As welfare states across industrialised countries have been transformed significantly since the turn of the century, it is all the more important to gather systematic knowledge on how the profession and discipline of social work, which is very close to the most vulnerable groups of society, is involved in these important changes. Analytically, we have used the concept of the policy cycle in order to structure and connect the analyses.

Social work, problem definition and agenda setting

What can we learn from the analyses presented on social work(er) s' role at the stages of problem definition and agenda setting of the policy cycle? A key question at these stages seems to be: who is regarded as being responsible for perceived social problems? And what is the role of social work in this – either by contradicting or even reinforcing mainstream perceptions? Are we talking about an issue of child neglect or about poor families in need of support (see Chapter 2)? Are sexually exploited youngsters treated as criminals or as victims (see Chapter 3)?

By exploring developments in the UK during the last few decades, Roger Smith (Chapter 2) has identified a number of inhibiting factors in terms of the profession's capacity to act as a 'policy innovator'. According to these observations, individualising tendencies in social work practice are often linked with a 'partly self-imposed limitation' of social work which focuses on individuals, families and 'private' issues. Therefore, in social work there are also tendencies to expound the problems of individuals who are in need of support, rather than (primarily) the societal environment or structural problems around them. In particular, in the discourse on poverty in the UK, the author criticises how social work itself tends to underplay structural causes of poverty. Thus, social work does not always appear as a 'natural ally' of vulnerable people; it can also become 'part of the problem'. This should be considered against the backdrop of difficult structural conditions for social workers themselves. Under circumstances of cost reduction, unfavourable working conditions or managerial preoccupations of employers, the capacities for social workers in everyday work to broaden their perspectives on structural issues, and engage in policy practice (which frequently is not considered a regular part of the job, and where social workers therefore do not have much experience and expertise), are limited.

When looking at examples where social work – despite these constraints – has nevertheless been successful in influencing policy making, the following furthering factors seem to be important: as Roger Smith highlights, it is a particular challenge for social work to legitimise interventions in the political sphere and establish its own authority to comment on societal developments. He expects that social work is more successful when policy issues are concerned where social work's role is perceived more legitimate, and where the claims for expertise appear particularly credible. The US case study (Chapter 3) underlines this as well. Thus, we should expect differences in success between policy fields, depending on the extent to which these areas are considered as social work's core business, such as, for example, child protection, or whether they instead fall outside its recognised fields of expertise. It would be interesting for future research to systematically test this explorative assumption in a broader comparative study. In addition, processes of 'making' such perceptions of 'legitimate fields of competence' in terms of social work in an interplay between professional discourse and public perceptions would be an interesting field for further research. Some additional factors that may increase the profession's ability to 'speak out for their clients' have been identified, in particular: the importance of support by academic research (see also the results of Chapter 5 by Francisco Branco, and Chapter 6 by Idit Weiss-Gal and John Gal), network building and the existence of bodies of collective representation, such as the British Association of Social Work (BASW) or the Social Work Actions Network (SWAN) (see also Chapter 8 by Rich Moth and Michael Lavalette). A recent example of collective agenda setting is the position paper of the German Association for Social Work (DGSA) entitled 'Appeal for Global Solidarity and the Right to Asylum', which has also been launched by the International Association of Schools of Social Work.[2]

In Chapter 3, by Lisa Werkmeister Rozas, Megan Feely and Jason Ostrander, the attribution of responsibility for social problems is of utmost importance. Their US case study on legislative improvements for young victims of sexual exploitation in the state of Connecticut is a success story for social work policy practice. After a series of legal reforms, the victims – sex-trafficked youth – were no longer equated with criminals, and the buyers of sex with youngsters faced heavier criminal charges. In the case study, the following general aspects seem to be central to the explanation of this success. First, the role of critical theories of social work: in this case structural social work and critical consciousness theory, in social work education, can assist in raising the awareness of structural social problems and of a 'false' attribution of responsibility to individuals (in this case the exploited youngsters, who had been criminalised) among social workers themselves. Second, once awareness of the problems of exploited youth had been raised among the social workers involved, having social workers in decisive political office positions meant that a new problem perception could be transferred to the broader political sphere, thus shaping a political reform agenda. In this case a political committee, the 'Trafficking in Persons Council', was led by a social worker, and many positions on the Council were held by social workers as well.

The study by Matteo D'Emilione and colleagues (Chapter 4) underlines how important it is that social workers are closely involved in the policy process. In this case, social workers took part in the evaluation of an experimental local policy measure that targeted poverty. The authors show that due to constant engagement of social workers in political committees throughout the evaluation process, the social workers' voices were taken into account to an extent when the national poverty measure was defined. Thus, in analytical terms, social workers have been part of the problem of redefining the policy cycle, where the ends meet between evaluation and the start of a new policy process. Further research is needed in order to explain why some of the social workers' positions were taken up, while others have been neglected.

Social work interests in policy formulation and decision making

The contributions of the book focus on different types of actors in the field of social work. Some have shown that individual social workers can influence social policy at different stages of the policy cycle. While the most prominent point of influence emerges at the street-level, that is the implementation stage (see below), there is also the opportunity for individual social workers to make a difference during the policy formulation and decision-making process. Francisco Branco (Chapter 5) has shown the importance of single political actors among the pioneers of social work such as Jane Addams, Mary Richmond, Florence Kelly and Lillian Wald, who cooperated with other key actors and advocacy organisations in order to create the Children's Bureau in the US Federal Department of Labor in 1912. Only through their intense networking was it possible to build up the pressure needed for social reform. Undeniably, those pioneers were outstanding and independent activists who knew how to build advocacy coalitions and to campaign in order to transfer their interests into public policy. However, the case of the Children's Bureau also illustrates that one individual social worker could not have changed social policy: co-combatants seem to be a necessity for success.

Interestingly, the social work pioneers promoted social reform as a research-based political action. They collected data from their practical work with clients in order to challenge the system of social support. They also translated this idea of research-based political action into their teaching to form the next generation of social workers.

This close connection between empirical evidence and political action can be seen in many of the book's contributions: the laws to protect sexually exploited youth were challenged by social workers dealing with sex-trafficked minors in the US (Chapter 3); conditional anti-poverty cash transfer schemes were reformed due to the feedback of social workers working with poor families in Italy (Chapter 4); activation policy was modified by social workers as implementers in Spain (Chapter 11), Poland (Chapter 12) and Germany (Chapter 13). While the evidence-based political action of social workers does not usually include full academic research, there is one group of social work professionals that is especially devoted to research: social work academics. Their status as experts in their field of research may open a window of opportunity to influence policy making by consulting politicians. Idit Weiss-Gal and John Gal (Chapter 6) have identified various areas of involvement for social work academics in Israel. These included developing, reforming and advancing social policy and were closely related to the academics' fields of expertise in research and/or teaching. As well as motivational factors like ideology, personality and values, faculty members were able to pool resources for their policy involvement by combining teaching, research and policy consultancy. Thus, their activity profile resembles very much that of the pioneers of social work, although their networking and campaigning is more limited. Nevertheless, social work academics can be a part of the policy network and they should make their expertise available on a regular base.

Moreover, Weiss-Gal and Gal's Israeli case study points out the importance of opportunity structures for policy practice: the Israeli policy formulation process allows a high degree of access by unofficial actors to policy-making arenas, and policymakers often ask academic experts for assistance with policy formulation, which builds upon a longstanding tradition dating from the early 1960s. It seems that personal contact with politicians as well as the small size of the country give social work academics a voice in policy making. Building on work by Weiss-Gal and Gal (2014), it would be interesting to systematically compare social work's and social work academia's influence on policy making against the background of different polities since the relationship between the two is still an academic void. We can only speculate on the importance of lobbying in more competitive political systems like the United States (Chapters 3 and 5) or the UK (Chapters 2 and 8) where policy practice is also more prominently part of the education of social workers than in other (European) countries. On the other hand, neo-corporatist polities that provide institutionalised access to social policy making for collective actors and academic experts seem to differ regarding the possibilities of exerting political influence (Chapters 4, 6 and 7).

However, social work academics might be in a special position for policy practice. In the Israeli example, they experience autonomy and a high degree of job security. Even if universities do not usually acknowledge and value policy involvement in the same way as achievements in research, it is nevertheless legitimate and faculty members are free to become politically involved. Whether social work academics benefit from similar working conditions in other countries is an open question. Certainly this is not the case for most social workers in ordinary frontline settings, such as the German labour market activation service (Chapter 13), as well as, interestingly, in Israel, as Ravit Alfandari shows in her case study on child protection (Chapter 10). As she points out, sometimes social workers' working conditions don't even leave room for a satisfactory implementation of a 'good' reform (see below). Often social workers have to strictly adhere to the intentions of lawmakers and employers, or at least they feel obliged to do so (see Tony Evans in Chapter 9). Thus their space for policy engagement is limited and their opportunities for discretion are narrowed to a minimum. In these cases, collective actors are all the more important in translating social work interests into the making of social policy. The book includes two contributions on collective actors from the field of social work, one dealing with national associations of social work and the other describing the functioning of a social work movement.

The national associations of social work are central collective actors for agenda setting and policy formulation, though their strategies for political action can be very different. Riccardo Guidi (Chapter 7) describes two distinctive paths of professional mobilisation: an institutionalised political exchange perspective and a social movement perspective. Whereas the Italian *Consiglio Nazionale Ordine Assistenti Sociali* operates in a neo-corporatist manner as an organised and legitimated collective actor that promotes and defends the interests of the profession within the realm of institutionalised negotiations with the state agencies, the Spanish *Consejo General del Trabajo Social* performs non-institutional collective action and mobilises episodically based on the networking between different actors that share a common goal and identity. Both social work organisations resisted austerity policies, although by different means. While in Italy, news releases, open letters and pamphlets (like the Manifesto for Welfare) were produced to build up pressure against cuts in social policy, Spanish social workers mainly mobilised through campaigns and mass demonstrations (like *Marea Naranja*/Orange Tide). Also in this case, specific features of national contexts help to explain this difference. In Spain austerity politics went along with a 'shock' and triggered powerful protests. This provided what Kingdon (1984) would have called a 'policy window' or political opportunity structure to pursue 'collective policy practice'. In addition, the policy practice paths also diverged, because social workers' national professional bodies had different views of their role as 'political entrepreneur', depending on different political cultures. More comparative research will be necessary to assess various mobilisation strategies of national associations of social work and their impact on the making of social policy.

Rich Moth and Michael Lavalette (Chapter 8) give an example of the political involvement of individual social workers as well as social work organisations within a broader social movement that also comprises service users, carers, trade unionists, academics and students as well as their interest organisations: the Social Work Action Network. SWAN was very successful in cross-sectional alliance building by promoting more inclusive, egalitarian and democratic forms of welfare. The network also developed pamphlets and charters and it initiated grassroots campaigning in order to strengthen the coalition of resistance against cuts in social welfare. Though the direct impact of SWAN on policy making cannot be quantified, it surely had a voice in the public discourse.

Social work and implementation

Resisting welfare state retrenchment and enhancing social work's resilience are recurrent motives not only for collective actors but also for the involvement of individual social workers in policy practice, especially in the implementation stage of social policy. Five chapters of this book are therefore dedicated to issues of the role of social work(ers) in the implementation of social policy, contributing insight into implementation practices in Britain, Israel, Spain, Poland and Germany.

Tony Evans in his opening chapter of Part III (Chapter 9) sketches some of the core tensions social workers have to face in their role as policy implementers in today's reformed welfare states: social workers frequently find themselves in the conflict between their duties as professionals who should respect the legitimacy of government policy on the one hand and the intuition that they should oppose and follow their own commitment, act autonomously and disregard policies with which they disagree. As Evans shows, this conflict often cannot be solved easily – 'the answer seems to lie in the relationship between the two in an area where one is often faced with choosing the least worst option'. This conflict can be stressful, but also energising, Evans claims.

As Evans points out, behind the rhetoric of management control in social services there is often space for significant professional discretion and room to act. Practitioners have to use their judgement to interpret procedures and decide how they apply, and to make sense of vague terms such as 'risk' and 'need'. The 'freedom' social workers have when implementing social policies is therefore somehow ambivalent: the presence of professional discretion is not just the persistence of a substantial substratum of professional judgement; it can also reflect political and managerial strategies to deflect responsibility (and the risk of blame) from policymakers and managers towards non-political experts.

We also have to be aware that there might not always be a direct link between policies and social workers as street-level bureaucrats. As Evans found in his research, local agencies approached the same policy differently and practitioners accepted that they were bound by law, but questioned the authority of local policy interpretations and procedures. Codes and ethical standards (such as the 'Code of Ethics for Social Work' formulated by the British Association of Social Workers in 2012) can be helpful in navigating through such a dilemma and to realise professional autonomy.

As the following chapters reveal, Evans' analysis not only reflects the situation in Britain, but also characterises the experiences and practices of social workers in other countries. All authors reveal conflicts and problems that social workers have to face when implementing social protection systems. Ravit Alfandari in her case study on the child protection reform in Israel (Chapter 10) shows that these conflicts even occur where reforms aim at the improvement of the situation of the group under scrutiny. In this case, the reform's aims of strengthening practice and improving the safety and well-being of vulnerable children have not been achieved due to organisational as well as cultural barriers. Heavy workloads of social workers, a lack of strong leadership (inadequate support by superiors) as well as an organisational culture that seeks opportunities to take shortcuts in procedures and processes hinder the realisation of the reform and the desired positive outcome. Alfandari doesn't blame the social workers for this, however, underlining that they receive inadequate professional supervision and often insufficient training and qualifications. The main problem seems to be the missing dialogue between political leaders and social work: as the chapter shows, top-down policies that do not recognise and solve the underlying problems (of social work) are most likely to fail, even in a country like Israel where the overall conditions for professional social work are better than in many other countries. It would be an interesting future research task – in line with the bottom-up school of implementation theory (see for example Elmore 1982; Majone & Wildavsky 1978) – to systematically study whether ex ante involvement of relevant social work actors in policy formulation improves actual implementation.

Spain, the country Sergio Sanchez Castiñeira focuses on (Chapter 11), is certainly a country where social workers face particularly hard conditions due to the enduring financial and social crisis. Interestingly, Sanchez's findings are more or less in opposition to the findings of Alfandari: whereas Alfandari focuses on the failure of a reform with positive intentions, because social workers were not able to 'translate' this into practice, Sanchez shows us how social workers in Spain have developed an inefficient public programme into an active social policy through a cognitive, normative and emotional approach. Both authors, however, stress the role of professional qualifications: while insufficient training and qualifications is identified by Alfandari as one reason for social workers' inability to satisfactorily implement the political reform in Israel, Sanchez presents us with professional and motivated social workers doing their best to help their clients in times of scarcity. These professionals try to fill those institutional gaps (see also Evans in Chapter 9) by mobilising available material, symbolic and relational resources while struggling to help their clients and to protect the dignity of both the clients and themselves. They develop their own strategy, trying to prepare their clients for a life in poverty. Within the context of the book, however, this strategy evokes mixed feelings: obviously the Spanish social workers Sanchez describes have accepted the social situation of their clients – they seem not to mobilise their energy to influence the political process, but instead focus on the 'street level' and their clients.

Paweł Poławski in his case study on Poland (Chapter 12) takes a more systemic view. Like authors of many other studies in the social work literature, he discusses the 'perverse effects of activation policy', but with a particular focus: he draws our attention to governance problems, in particular the institutional layering and pillarisation of organisational structures and financial mechanisms in the reformed, activating welfare state. These structures generate various dysfunctions. As he shows, the layering of responsibilities in Poland (and presumably also in other countries) creates additional uncertainties for both beneficiaries and social workers and increasing bureaucratic obligations, for example due to reporting tasks. Similar to the Spanish social workers Sanchez describes in Chapter 11, the Polish social work professionals try their best to modify and to adjust their behaviour and strategies to local realities. They disregard formal rules in order to comply with their work-related values that are the reference for shaping relations in social work (responsibility, reliability, righteousness, dignity, and so on).

As mentioned earlier, Lipsky (1980) suggested that social workers are 'street-level bureaucrats' with a professional identity that enables them to use a degree of discretion when working with service users. The case studies in Part III of the book – focusing on various countries such as Britain, Israel, Spain and Poland – support and enrich this debate with their findings. They provide up-to-date insight into different modes and strategies of implementation under difficult framework conditions: the implementation modes range from the structural inability and unwillingness to implement reforms (Israel) through a pragmatic adaptation to regional circumstances (Poland) to an independent interpretation and realisation of one's own professional tasks (Spain).

Whereas social workers in various countries seem to struggle increasingly with the conflict between their professional duties and their personal commitment, Markus Gottwald and Frank Sowa in the final case study of the book (Chapter 13) make us aware that 'social work' is still widely associated with the idea of compassion, empathy and advocacy for the clients. In their study on the strategies and behaviour of placement officers in Germany, who are expected to implement activation policy when dealing with their unemployed clients, the assumed typical attitude or habitus of a social worker is practised by some of the placement officers (who usually are not social workers by training). These officers interestingly suffer from the post-liberal efficiency targets in the German labour agency that has increasingly turned into a company-like institution. Since they neither can nor want to act as expected, they imitate the ideal of a social worker to comply better with their own humanitarian ideals. Similar to Sanchez and Poławski, Gottwald and Sowa thereby confirm Evans' thesis that the professional self-concept and ethical beliefs of social workers are crucial for the way they implement policies.

To sum up the main findings of this volume, we want to stress furthering and inhibiting factors for social work(er)'s influence in the making of social policy. Table 14.1 builds on the individual book chapters and their evaluation in this conclusion. The logic of presentation follows the policy cycle of social policy making, and the list of furthering and inhibiting factors is of course not complete but rather selective according to the contents of this volume. Some of these factors seem to be specific for a distinct phase of the policy cycle. Others, marked with a star in the table, have a potential relevance across several stages of the policy cycle (but are listed here at the respective stage that the case studies of this book referred to it). At the stage of implementation it is important to distinguish between furthering and inhibiting factors for successful policy implementation, in the sense that the policy was intended by the political decision makers, and strategies of discretion (opposition and/or reinterpretation) carried out by social workers against or beyond state intentions in the process of implementation.

Across the findings of many contributions in this volume, one point becomes quite obvious, and underlines what has been shown in international research on policy practice engagement as well

Conclusion: social work and the making of social policy – lessons learned

Table 14.1: Social work influencing the making of social policy: summary of furthering and inhibiting factors identified in the book's case studies

Furthering factors	Inhibiting factors
Problem (re)definition and agenda setting	
• Policy issues are concerned where social work's involvement is perceived as legitimate, and where the claims for expertise appear particularly credible • Critical theories are taught in social work education • Social workers hold decisive political office positions* • Social workers are involved in social policy evaluation • Political windows of opportunities for agenda setting appear	• Individualising tendencies in social work leading to a problem focus on individuals, families and private issues • Unfavourable working conditions for professional social work under conditions of austerity* • Structural issues are not regarded as part of the social worker's job*
Policy formulation and decision making	
• Outstanding individual actors as political entrepreneurs* • Support by academic research, research-based political action (also as part of social work education)* • Political opportunity structures to pursue collective policy practice • Network building and cross-sectional alliances with other societal interests*	• Unfavourable working conditions for social work academics do not leave room for political engagement
Policy implementation according to state-intended reform aims	
• Organisations that provide social workers with the appropriate conditions, qualifications, resources and support • Room for social workers to act due to intentional vagueness of policies	• Insufficient training and qualification of social workers • Organisational and cultural barriers in the form of heavy workloads of the social workers • Lack of strong leadership of superiors, inadequate supervision and support • Increasing bureaucratic obligations • An organisational culture that seeks opportunities to take shortcuts in processes • Absent dialogue between political leaders and relevant social work actors
Opposition against and/or re-interpretation of state-intended policy implementation ('discretion')	
• Conditions of crisis and austerity* • Institutional layering and pillarisation of organisational structures and financial mechanisms • New public management approaches/ efficiency targets at the organisational level of the employer • Discretion as reflection of political and managerial strategies to deflect responsibility (and the risk of blame) from policymakers and managers to non-political experts • Professional norms, code of ethics* • Willingness of social workers to take an active role and to protect the dignity of both clients and themselves*	• Professionals feeling that they must follow policies and procedures because they should respect the legitimacy of government policy

* Potentially relevant across several stages of the policy cycle

Source: Own compilation based on the case studies of this book.

(Weiss-Gal & Gal, 2014): it seems to be the interplay of (favourable or unfavourable) structural conditions and political opportunities at the macro level with organisational and cultural characteristics of the social workers' workplaces at the meso level with individual agency at the micro level that enables social work(ers) to take political action along the policy cycle.

Clearly, the vision of the compassionate and emphatic social worker concentrating on their client's well-being is still alive, whereas social work itself is confronted by rapidly changing political and social conditions and will continuously have to face the challenge of influencing social policy in order to contribute to the development of society. As the contributions to the book show, we can find many approaches and good examples of social work as political action – but there is also still room for more political practice and systematic (comparative) research in this field.

Notes

[1] www.ifsw.org/what-is-social-work/global-definition-of-social-work/; see also Chapter 1.
[2] www.iassw-aiets.org/2018/09/06/dgsa-position-paper-appeal-for-global-solidarity-and-the-right-to-asylum_july2018/

References

Elmore, R. F. (1982) 'Backward mapping: implementation research and policy decisions', in W. Williams (ed) *Studying Implementation: Methodological and Administrative Issues*, Chatham: Chatham House Publishers, pp 18–35.

Majone, G. and Wildavsky, A. (1978) 'Implementation as evolution', in H. Freeman (ed) *Policy Studies Review Annual 1978*, Beverly Hills: Sage, pp 103–17.

Kingdon, J. W. (1984) *Agendas, Alternatives and Public Policies*, Boston: Little, Brown.

Lipsky, M. (1980) *Street-level Bureaucracy: Dilemmas of the Individual in Public Services*, New York: Sage.

Weiss-Gal, I. and Gal, J. (2014) 'An international perspective on policy practice', in J. Gal and I. Weiss-Gal (eds) *Social Workers Affecting Social Policy: An International Perspective on Policy Practice*, Bristol: Policy Press, pp 183–209.

Index

Note: Page numbers for figures and tables appear in italics.

A

Abbott, E. 80, 81, 82, 84
Abbott, G. *78*, 81
abuse 42, 47
academics, social work 5, 8, 27, 32, 89, 90–102, 123, 125, 220–1, 223, *227*
accountability 192, 213
actions/campaigning 126–7
activation paradigm 6, 205
activation policy 185–6, 190, 191, 192, 193, 194, 195, 226
activism 24–6, 31, 34
Addams, J. 71, 72, 76, 80
ADGSS (Association of Directors and Managers of Social Services)/Spain 114
advocacy 3, 10, 31, 32, 37, 48, 49, 79, 94, 226
advocacy coalition framework (ACF) 10, 83
agenda setting *4*, 5, 8, 30, 83, 213, 217, 219, 222, *227*
agent/principal perspective 144–6
AGS (Arbeitgeber-Service)/Germany 207
Alfandari, R. 221–2, 224–5
alliance building 125–6
Alliance for Counselling and Psychotherapy 131
Alliance for the Defence of the Public System of Social Services 112
anti-racist organisations 126
assistenti sociali 109
Association of Neighborhood Workers 77
Association of Professional Social Work (US) 82

austerity 28, 30, 109, 112, 113, 116, 128, 132
authority, democratic 144–6
autonomy 6, 147–9, 150

B

BA (German Federal Employment Agency) 201–2, 205–6
Bailey, R. 25
BASW (British Association of Social Workers) 24, 25, 26, 28, 30–1, 113, 126
  codes of ethics 147, 148
BASW code 147, 148
Beck, U. 196
Behrend, O. 205
Bevir, M. 145
Bode, I. 203
Bommes, M. 202–3
Booth, C. 74
'Boot Out Austerity' campaign 28
Boston School for Social Workers 80
BPS (British Psychological Society) 131
Brake, M. 25
Branco, F. 74
Braverman, H. 124
Breckinridge, S. 80, 81, 82
Britain 21–34, 121–32, 139–51

C

campaigning/actions 126–7
Capano, G. 106
Care Act (UK) 23
CAS (*Carta Acquisti Sperimentale*) 54, 57, 58–61, 65
Case Con (campaigning group) 24
Case Con (magazine) 24–5
CAS of PA (Children's Aid Society of Pennsylvania) 77

CGTS (*Consejo General del Trabajo Social*) 109, 112–14, 115, 222
charity 177, 178
Charter for Mental Health 127, 128–9, 131
child labour 72, 75, 77
child protection 155–66
children, and subjugation and oppression 38
Children Act (England and Wales) 23
Children's Bureau (US) 72, 76, 78, 80, 83, 220
children's services 30, 32
child trafficking 41–2
circle of social reform 74–5
civil society coalitions 94
CNOAS (*Consiglio Nazionale Ordine Assistenti Sociali*) 109, 110–12, 115, 222
'Code of Ethics for Social Work' (BASW) 147, 148
codes of ethics 147–9, 150, 224
co-determination 3
coercive conditionality 130
collective agenda setting 219
    see also agenda setting
collective policy practice 106–17
'Commercial Sexual Abuse of a Minor' charge 47, 49
commitments, professional 148–9
community ties 175
conditionality 60–1, 63, 187, 191
Connecticut 37, 42–9
Connor, S. 1–2
conversation technique 208
Cook, K. 22
Coordination Round Table 61, 62–3
Cramer, M. 204–5, 212
Crane, Senator W. M. 78
'creaming' 193–4
Critical and Radical Social Work 126
critical consciousness-raising 39–40
critical consciousness theory 38, 40–1, 48, 49, 219
CSCP (Chicago School of Civics and Philanthropy) 80, 81
Cummins, I. 28

D
Davies, M. 31–2
DCF (Department of Children and Families)/Connecticut 43, 45, 48
decision making 220–3
democratic authority 144–6
Descriptive Map of London Poverty (Booth) 74
desocialisation 41
Devine, E. T. 77
DGSA (German Association for Social Work) 219
discretion 12, 124, 139, 141–2, 150–1, 170, 171, 186, 187, 192, 193, 202, 211, 213, 222, 223, 225, 226, *227*
domestic minor sex trafficking (DMST) 37, 38, 40, 42–9
Dominelli, L. 27
'double mandate' 12
Drakeford, M. 22–3
DWP (Department for Work and Pensions)/UK 130, 131

E
EASSW (European Association of Schools of Social Work) 5
Eberwein, W. 203–4, 205, 206, 207, 212
'economic efficiency' 122
economisation 7
education, social work 80–2
empowerment 3, 40, 110, 116, 186
ethics 139, 142–4, 145, 146–7, 149, 151, 224
European Social Fund 193
Evans, T. 151, 223–4
exclusion 6, 38, 56, 92, 109, 181

F
facilitation 90, 96–7
familialism/familism 170, 181–2
family assistants 189–90
family support 175

Index

Ferencz, N. 126
Foot, P. 142
formal-institutional activities 92–3
Foro Servicios Sociales de Madrid 114
Freire, P. 40
Friedson, E. 147–8

G

Gal, J. 2–3, 108, 116
Gardner, J. J. 78
German Federal Employment Agency 201–2, 205–6
Germany 201–14, 226
Gilson, L. 12
Glasgow rent strikes 123
Global Social Work conferences 126
Gottwald, M. 226
grassroots campaigning/actions 126–7
Grounded Theory 56

H

Haidt, J. 143
Harris, J. 151, 189
Hartz reforms (Germany) 201, 205, 213
Hine, L. 78
Horton, J. 144
housing 32, 74, 92, 171, 173, 174, 178
Howlett, M. 106
Hull-House Maps and Papers (Sklar) 74
human rights 24, 25, 41, 139, 146, 148
human trafficking 41, 42–9

I

ICSW (International Council on Social Welfare) 5
IFSW (International Federation of Social Workers) 5, 113, 124
IMSSSA (Israel Ministry of Social Services and Social Affairs) 157
inequality 22, 26–7, 92, 124, 179, 180
informal economy 177
INPS (National Institute for Social Security)/Italy 55

institutionalised political exchange (PE) 106–7, 108, 115, 116
Israel 89–102, 155, 156–66, 221, 224, 225
Italy 53–66, 109–12, 115, 116, 219, 222

J

Jansson, B. S. 2
Jenkins-Smith, H. 83
job coaches in GP practices 130, 131
job placement officers 201, 202, 203–5, 207–14, 226
Jordan, B. 22–3
Juvenile Court (US) 72

K

Kadish, M. 150
Kadish, S. 150
Kaźmierczak, T. 195–6
Kelley, F. 77, 79
Kingdon, J. W. 8
Knill, C. 84

L

Labour Party 131
Lathrop, J. 78, 80, 81
Lavalette, M. 106
layering 187–93, 225
left-wing politics 125
legitimacy 144–7, 149
Leighninger, L. 2
Lengermann, P. 73
Lipsky, M. 12, 33, 83–4, 124, 225
Ludwig-Mayerhofer, W. 205

M

MacLean, V. M. 74, 81
management by objectives 201
managerialisation/managerialism 127, 188, 189
'Manifesto for Welfare' 111
manufactured uncertainties 196

Marea Naranja 112–13, 115, 116
marketisation 7, 127, 128, 129
Mathews, G. 10
McLeod, E. 27
mental health policy 127–9, 130–1, 132
mental health service cuts 126
Mercier, H. 143
MHAA (Mental Health Activist Alliance) 131
MHRN (Mental Health Resistance Network) 130, 131
Milne et al 33–4
MLSP (Ministry of Labour and Social Policies)/Italy 55
model of external mobilisation 83
modern-day slavery 41
Molina, O. 107
Montaigne, M. 149
moral responsibilities 148, 150
Moreau, M. 7–8, 39
Morris et al 28
motivation 89, 96, 97, 100, 102
Mullaly, R. 39
Muncy, R. 76, 77, 81, 82
Munro, E. 155, 158
Murphy, E. G. 77

N

national associations of social work 222
   see also BASW (British Association of Social Workers)
NCCC (National Conference of Charities and Corrections)/US 77
NCLC (National Child Labor Committee)/US 77, 78, 79
neglect 42, 47
neocorporatism 106–7, 221
neo-corporatist systems 9, 10
neoliberalism 106, 124, 140
network/networking 10, 25, 31, 56, 58, 64, 76, 79, 83, 108, 169, 181, 218–19, 220, 227
   CGTS 112, 222
   policy 107, 221
   see also SWAN (Social Work Action Network)
New Labour 140
New Public Management 124, 201
New Right reforms 140
New York Child Labor Committee 77
NGOs (non-governmental organisations) 169–70
NHS (National Health Service)/UK 128
Niebrugge, G. 73
Norris, A. 25
Northwood, L. K. 10
NYSPCC (New York Society for the Prevention of Cruelty to Children) 77

O

older people 33–4
opportunity 90, 97, 98–9, 102
oppression 22, 27, 31, 38, 39, 40, 43, 47, 124, 149
orders
   following 144–7
   not following 147–9
outside initiative model 83
'outside working hours' 29–30

P

Parker, M. 10
'Patronizing a Prostitute' 46, 47, 48
Pennsylvania Child Labour Committee 72
performative justice 6
Philadelphia Training School for Social Work 80–1
Pittman-Munke, P. 75
Pizzorno, A. 107
placement officers 201, 202, 203–5, 207–14, 226
Planning, Intervention and Evaluation Committees (PIECs) 156, 157, 160, 161–2, 163, 164, 165
pluralist systems 9–10

Poland 185–97
Poławski, P. 225
police
    and DCF 45
    and social workers 48
policy cycle 3, *4*, 5, 7, 39, 41, 106, 139, 155, 217, 219, 220, 226, 228
policy formulation 89–102, 220–3
policy network 10, 107, 221
policy-oriented practice 31–3, 71–3
Policy Practice Engagement (PPE)
    conceptual framework 9, 89–90
policy proposals 8
policy window 8–9
Political Action Committees (PAC) 10
political actor 2, 3, 5, 105, 217, 220
political exchange (PE), institutionalised 106–7, 108, 115, 116
political legitimacy 144, 145, 149
political responsibility 105–6, 115
Popple, P. R. 2
poverty 22, 27, 28, 29, 30, 72, 92, 124, 186, 195, 196, 218, 225
    Italy 53, 54, 56, 57, 58, 61, 65, 109, 219
    Spain 109, 169, 170, 171, 173, 180, 181–2
'poverty paradox' 28, 29
principal/agent perspective 144–6
privatisation 7
professional autonomy 147–9, 150
Professional Capabilities Framework for Social Workers 24
professional qualifications 66, 159, 225
Progressive Era 71, 81
prostitution 44, 45, 46
psychocompulsion 130, 131, 132
public employment service (PES) 201, 202, 204, 213
public policy training 80–2

Q

qualifications 66, 159, 225

R

radical social work 24
Reason, J. 166
recourse roles 150
recovery 127
refugee support work 126, 127
REI (*Reddito di Inclusione*) 54
rent strikes, Glasgow 123
research
    and policy involvement 95, 100, 102
    and social reform 73–4
research-based political action 220
responsibilities, moral 148, 150
Rhodes, M. 107
Rhodes, R. 145
Richmond, M. 71, 72–3, 74–6, 77, 79, 83
risk analysis 188
risk management 195, 197
Robbins, R. 22
Roosevelt, President T. 77, *78*

S

Sabatier, P. A. 83
Sanchez, C. S. 224–5
Saraceno, C. 171
Saville, J. 122
Scherr, A. 202–3
Schmitter, P. C. 107
School of Social Service Administration 81
self-determination paradigm 6
self-responsibility paradigm 6
Selznick, P. 213–14
sex trafficking 37–8, 39, 41–9, 219
sexual exploitation 219
SIA (*Sostegno per l'Inclusione Attiva*) 54, 57, 58, 61–4
Simpson, G. 1–2, 29, 30
'sites of engagement' 29–31
Sklar, K. K. 74
slavery, modern-day 41
Smart, J. 143
Smith, R. 217–18
social action 92, 93–4, 97, 102
social advocacy 3

social assistance
  Poland 186–7, 188–9, 190, 193, 196
  Spain 169, 170, 171, 172, 173–82
social contracts 187, 193–5
social impact 97, 99
social justice 27, 33, 105, 107, 148
  Israel 97–8, 100, 102
  southern Europe 115, 116
social movements 107–8, 115, 116, 121, 122, 123–32
social protection 170, 224
social reform 71, 72–84
'Social Science and Arts Training for Philanthropic and Social Work' course 80
social security 92
social services 11, 43, 53, 105, 223
  Britain 140, 142
  Israel 160, 163, 164
  Italy 56, 57, 58, 59, 61, 62, 64, 65
  personal 92
  Spain 114, 171, 173, 174, 178
social services departments (SSDs) 156, 157, 161, 163
Social Welfare and Professional Education (Edith Abbott) 82, 84
social work academics 5, 8, 27, 32, 89, 90–102, 123, 125, 220–1, 223, 227
social work education 23, 25, 48, 80–2, 219
social workers 44, 47, 48, 58–61, 62, 65, 124, 220
  collective policy practice 106–17
  Germany 202–4
  Israel 159–61, 164–5, 166
  Italy 115
  Poland 188–9, 190–2, 194–7
  as policy implementers 223–8
  and policy practice engagement 89–90
  and political responsibility 105–6
  and practitioner discretion 141
  Spain 113–14, 115, 116, 170, 171–5, 176–80, 181–2
'Social Workers and Service Users Against Austerity' 32, 126

'Social Work Manifesto' 123, 124, 125, 126
Society to Protect Children from Cruelty (US) 72
solidarity 6
Sondermann, A. 205
Sowa, F. 226
Spain 109–10, 112–14, 115, 116, 169–82, 222, 224–5
Spanish National Law on the 'rationalisation and sustainability of local administration' 113
Sperber, D. 143
Stand Up to Racism 126
State Committee for the War Against Poverty in Israel 102
St Louis School of Philanthropy 80–1
Streeck, W. 107, 187
structural social work theory 38, 39–40, 42, 219
'Study of nine hundred and eighty-five widows known to certain Charity Organization Societies in 1910' 74
subjugation 38
SWAN (Social Work Action Network) 11, 24, 25, 31, 113, 121, 123–32
systems approach 157–8, 164

T

Taft, W. H. *78*
target management 211–12
Tarragona 171–2, 173
Tarrow, S. 107
Taylor, G. 80, 81
teaching and policy involvement 95–6, 100, 102
Thatcher, M. 140
Thelen, K. 187
Tholen, J. 203–4, 206, 207, 212
tools package 156–7, 160, 161
Tosun, J. 84
trabajadores sociales 109
trade unions 126, 129
trafficking 37–8, 39, 41–9, 219

Trafficking in Persons (TIP) Council 44, 219
Trafficking Victims Assistance Program (TVAP) 42
training programmes 80–2
Trattner, W. 81
trust 192, 193, 197
Tunstill, J. 32–3
'Twenty-one Years of University Education for the Social Services, 1920–41' (Edith Abbott) 81
Twenty Years at Hull-House (Addams) 74

U
UCU (University and College Union) 126
UK (United Kingdom) 21–34, 121–32, 139–51
unemployment 203
'unemployment benefit I' (Germany) 201
'unemployment benefit II' (Germany) 201
unemployment benefits 205
unemployment insurance 202
Unison 126
Unite 126, 129
Unite Against Fascism 126
United States (US) 38–9, 40, 41–9, 72–84
US State Department 42

W
Wald, L. 77, 79
Weiss-Gal, I. 2–3, 9, 108, 116
welfare policy 33, 116, 121, 122–3, 130
welfare reform 2, 123, 129–32
welfare regimes 122
welfare state 1, 2, 6, 7, 11, 12, 109, 185, 217, 223, 225
welfare-to-work 131
What Is Social Case Work? (Richmond) 73
White House Conference on the Care of Dependent Children 78
Wife Desertion Law (US) 72
Wildavsky, A. 61–2
Wilks, T. 31–2
Williams, Bernard 143, 146–7, 149
Williams, J. E. 74, 81
Willow, C. 32–3
Wolf, S. 142–3, 148
women
  and DMST 42
  groups for 78
  and subjugation and oppression 38, 43
  and systemic disadvantages 27
  threatened and judged by social workers 21–2
  welfare of 72
Work Capability Assessment (WCA) 130